M U

STANG

AN AMERICAN CLASSIC

YESTERDAY • TODAY • TOMORROW

The Ford Oval and nameplates are registered trademarks owned and licensed by Ford Motor Company.

Published by Universe Publishing
A Division of Rizzoli International Publications, Inc.
300 Park Avenue South
New York, NY 10010
www.rizzoliusa.com

Design: Lori S. Malkin
Text: Mike Mueller
Project Editor: Melissa P. Veronesi
Assistant Editor: Candice Fehrman

All photography and artwork are the property of and copyright © 2009 Ford Motor Company unless otherwise identified.

2009 2010 2011 2012 / 10 9 8
 7 6 5 4 3 2 1

Printed in China

ISBN-13: 978-0-7893-1885-5

Library of Congress Catalog Control Number: 2009901018

www.ford.com

CONTENTS

No doubt most of us wish we could look half as good as we did when we were younger. In April 2009, Ford's wildly popular Mustang turned 45. Forty-five! Who would have thought? Certainly not Lee Iacocca, the main man behind this machine. Better ideas in the automotive realm simply weren't capable of such "long legs" when Ford Division's newly appointed general manager first envisioned his little "youth car" early in 1961, although at the time, Chevrolet's two-seat Corvette, then only eight years old, was just beginning to stretch its lower appendages on the way to its own impressive longevity standard. The Corvette legacy now stands 56 years young, meaning these fantastic plastic flights of fancy have finally grown older than many of their owners.

A BREED APART

A case of apples versus oranges? Certainly. General Motors presently keeps its dream alive by building about 30,000 narrowly focused, niche-market Corvettes every year. As the Mustang's 45th

PAGES 18–19: Ford's latest, greatest Mustang reminds many witnesses in 2009 of classic models of yore, just as design chief J Mays planned. The horse logo in the grille has been a staple since 1994.

ABOVE: Born in April 1964, the first Mustang was a mid-year model—hence the "1964-1/2" tag long recognized by the pony car faithful. Ford originally preferred the "1965" reference for all original models built in 1964 and 1965.

birthday neared, the all-time count for Mustangs was roughly 9 million, meaning Dearborn's annual production average amounts to between six and seven times Chevrolet's. In fact, Ford sold more than 600,000 Mustangs in 1966 alone, a zenith that simply will never be reached again—by any other car, from any other company.

Timing, of course, represented one major key to the original Mustang's early outrageous success. A youth car wouldn't have stood a chance had a youth market not been present to support it, and we can thank all those "Baby Boomers" for coming of age just in time, just as Iacocca predicted. Apparently unlike other Detroit execs, he had eyes and he could see that much of the U.S. population would be "getting younger" after 1960. He set out to build the perfect car for the times, a machine that appealed to both young buyers as well as those young at heart.

Few witnesses—young, old, or otherwise—have forgotten what the original Mustang meant to the marketplace when it burst onto the scene on April 17, 1964. No previous new model had inspired so much anticipation, nor had buyers ever flocked into dealerships in such numbers— as many as 4 million of them during that first weekend alone. Record sales predictably followed. More Mustangs found homes during those first 12 months on the road than any newly introduced automotive sensation before. And Iacocca's little baby also reached the 1 million total production plateau faster than any American car ever.

Mass appeal plainly represented the Mustang's forte from the get-go, just as Iacocca had planned. Hands down, no automobile in Detroit history had ever offered so much to so many for so little—roughly $2,300 in basic form. It was a small car, but not too small; it was affordable, but it also looked like a million bucks; and it was economical and practical, but it also was sporty and fashionable. Even with a standard, cost-conscious six-cylinder leading the way, the car's clean, crisp looks, working in concert with a standard bucket seat interior (with a standard floor shifter), at least helped make a driver feel like he was traveling in fast company even if he actually wasn't.

Or she. Iacocca's team enthusiastically targeted young women (to unprecedented degrees) along with their male counterparts, making the first Mustang as gender-neutral as anything seen before on four wheels. In 1964, Ford's milestone model exemplified the phrase "many different cars for many different drivers"— male or female. And, at the same time, it also defined a new breed of American automobile—the "pony car"—a type still recognized today by its trademark long-hood/short-deck profile but also widely known for its affordable sportiness.

Funny thing, though: many historians continually overlook the fact that Chrysler Corporation actually beat Ford to the punch in 1964. Nearly two weeks before *Time, Newsweek*, and the rest started stumbling all over themselves to get the scoop of the century, Plymouth's sporty, compact Barracuda had debuted with its long hood, short rear deck, and tidy price tag, only to find itself quickly lost in the giant shadow cast by Dearborn's magazine cover model.

Ford teased industry watchers in 1963 with its Mustang II concept car, basically a customized pilot model dressed up with a chopped windshield and special nose and tail treatments. Here the Mustang II struts its stuff at the 1964 Detroit Auto Show.

Like the first Mustang, the first Barracuda offered a decent dose of sporty imagery (bucket seats were standard) at a fair price, about $2,350. But unlike the Mustang, Plymouth's rival didn't feature a totally fresh look. Its glassy "fastback" form, though considered truly great in many minds, still couldn't quite mask the fact that the 1964 Barracuda represented little more than a mundane Valiant in disguise. Forget the fact that the original Mustang was basically a yeoman Falcon beneath its beautiful skin. But it was that carefully fashioned façade that helped set the two newborn rivals apart—by many, many miles.

While Ford was selling more than 400,000 fresh-faced Mustangs during that first year, Plymouth was rolling out a little more than 23,000 made-over Barracudas, and those highly skewed numbers on their own helped convince industry-watchers to give credit where it wasn't necessarily due. By the time additional rivals began appearing in 1967, curbside kibitzers had formulated a well-recognized name for this breed—and no, it wasn't "predator-fish car." Regardless of marque, be it Camaro, Firebird, Cougar, Javelin, 'Cuda, or Challenger, they're still all known as pony cars.

The Mustang's surviving rivals, Camaro and Firebird, retired in 2002, leaving only Detroit's pony car progenitor to keep the story alive until Dodge revived its Challenger six years later. Looking a lot like its ancestors built from 1970 to 1974, the 2008 Challenger SRT8 certainly qualified as a time machine, but that design approach represented nothing new around Detroit. This time it was Chrysler's turn to clearly follow in Ford's tire tracks. Introduced to the press in January 2004, the latest-generation Mustang brought back many memories, too, just as Ford Motor Company Design vice-president J Mays planned.

"We weren't just redesigning a car, we were adding another chapter to an epic," said Mays about the 2005 Mustang. Talk about having your cake and eating it, too. So much of that redesign harked back to epic models of the past, yet overall impressions, inside and out, were as cool as it gets these days. Aging baby boomers experienced a serious blast from their pasts, while today's youthful buyers found themselves attracted to a hip machine that just couldn't be beaten, certainly at the price, as far as looks and performance are concerned.

"Mustang attracts two kinds of drivers—those under 30 and those over 30," added Mays. "America's most popular nameplate transcends demographics and socioeconomic trends because Mustang is really more than a car. It's an icon that's been woven into the fabric of America for 40 years running."

Four decades before, Mustang had hit the ground running like nothing seen before due in part to an unprecedented publicity push that in turn translated into an unprecedented media

The 1971 Boss 351 (left) was one of the first-generation (1964–1973) Mustang's highest-flying muscle cars. The cost-conscious, compact 1974 Mustang II (middle) brought the breed back down to earth. The second-generation Mustang II was superseded by the Fox-chassis model in 1979. Built from 1984 to 1986, the Euro-style SVO Mustang (right) represented one of the prime Fox highlights.

response. Headlines transcended the automotive press to degrees never imagined, even by Dearborn's hard-charging marketing men. The coincidental *Time/Newsweek* covers would've made real news if not for all the other mainstream publications that at the same time couldn't resist paying homage to Lee Iacocca and his little pony.

But even Ford's runaway success couldn't keep up such a dizzying pace forever. Sales first started falling off after that pinnacle in 1966, thanks primarily to increased competition supplied mostly by Chevrolet's new-for-1967 Camaro. Helping cool things further were purists' distaste for an upsizing trend that would continue in Mustang ranks for six years. First came a bigger, heavier, more expensive pony car platform in 1967, followed by a truly large, even costlier makeover in 1971.

Iacocca tried turning back the clock in 1974 with his Mustang II, a markedly compact vehicle that was, in admen's terms, "the right car at the right time." Based on Ford's diminutive Pinto platform, this second-generation pony immediately soared in popularity to 1964-like standards then quickly fell as customers became disenchanted with its cramped quarters and wimpy performance.

A second next-generation pony car appeared for 1979 based on Dearborn's newly designed Fox chassis, a slightly larger platform topped off by Jack Telnack's European-inspired, aerodynamic shell. Performance began percolating again during the Fox-chassis run, which didn't end until 1993. A proud legacy within a proud legacy also began to evolve as the Mustang's 5.0-liter High Output (HO) V8 continually gained extra muscle to soon become one of Detroit's best performance buys.

Next to nothing could stop the HO V8, at least not until Ford redid its pony car again for 1994. The venerable 5.0-liter pushrod motor initially carried over from the Fox-chassis era into the "SN95" years, but then was superseded in 1996 by the much improved 4.6-liter "modular" V8 with its single-overhead-cam (SOHC) heads. An even hotter version of this engine, fitted with dual overhead cams (DOHC) and four valves per cylinder, was created for the Special Vehicle Team's Cobra, which had debuted in 1993. Thus armed, the 4.6-liter dual-overhead-cam Cobra surpassed 300 horsepower in 1996, and was up to nearly 400 horses in 2003 when SVT marked its 10-year anniversary.

That same year was Ford Motor Company's 100th anniversary, and the Mustang's own 40th birthday followed in 2004. Fortunately those little anniversary badges weren't the only presents unwrapped by party-goers during the Mustang's celebration. Unveiling the latest,

There was no mistaking the Mustang heritage when Ford introduced its fifth-generation pony car in 2005. Tri-bar taillights in back served as further reminders of fondly remembered forerunners.

There was no mistaking the Mustang heritage when Ford introduced its fifth-generation pony car in 2005. Tri-bar taillights in back served as further reminders of fondly remembered forerunners.

greatest pony car that January was the real icing on the cake. "New" was a serious understatement in the 2005 Mustang's case.

Four years later, Ford's long-running pony car now stands poised to celebrate its 45th birthday. Another restyle (for 2010) is waiting in the wings as we speak, and once again there will be no mistaking that this new Mustang will still be a Mustang. Without a doubt, no other American car carries around so many memories, so much tradition, because so many Americans have been allowed the chance to take one for a ride. As much as collectors have put Ford's pony car up on a pedestal, the fact remains that Mustangs have always been fully practical daily transports for the masses, available to hundreds of thousands instead of a select niche. Finding someone over 40 who has never encountered one is not an easy task; locating a driver who has always wanted one is a piece of cake.

And can you name an American automobile more memorable? Even people who don't know anything about cars will recognize a pony car when they see one. Baseball, apple pie, and Mustang—it doesn't get more patriotic, no matter what Chevrolet promotional people tried to tell us a couple decades back. Turn on the tube, rent a flick, and odds are you'll catch a glimpse of this car, be it Ford's latest or one of those coveted vintage examples. Maybe The Beach Boys never sang about a Mustang, but that was their loss. It's a fair bet that "I Get Around" probably played on more Mustang radios than any others during the 1960s.

A half century later the tune hasn't changed. There may be a lot of upheaval going on in Detroit these days, but at least one constant remains. We'll be wishing Mustang a happy 50th soon.

Developing the Mustang, 1961–1964

ind a Webster's Dictionary, turn to the "F" pages, and locate "failure." Odds are you'll see a picture of an Edsel, the ill-fated automobile some Ford people still regret building. The butt of countless cracks and jibes for decades to follow, Edsel debuted in 1958, then was unceremoniously cancelled two years later after sales levels never even neared expectations. But don't be fooled by revisionist history, casual or otherwise. Despite all those comedic claims, the Edsel debacle was more a matter of bad timing than bad car. Ford simply tried to force too much machine on a recession-racked market at a time when less surely would've resulted in more.

Fortunately the little Falcon showed up in 1960 to save the day, in the process transforming Dearborn's jesters into kings

RIDE TO MARKET

overnight. This popular compact was no joke, though Ford folks were soon laughing all the way to the bank after Falcon established a new industry record for first-year sales. Flush with

PAGES 24–25: Sketched in September 1961, this concept demonstrated what a Falcon-based sports car might look like. Using the compact Falcon platform as a base for the upcoming Mustang was Lee Iacocca's main plan all along.

ABOVE: Early design ideas in styling chief Gene Bordinat's studio, depicted here in July 1961, included various two-seaters that followed in the 1955–1957 Thunderbird's tire tracks.

BOTTOM RIGHT: One of many Mustang forerunners, the four-place Allegro was initially created in response to Chevrolet's sporty Corvair Monza.

BELOW: The Mustang I's two bucket seats were fixed in place—it was the pedals that adjusted fore and aft to account for a driver's height.

BOTTOM LEFT: A true roadster, the two-seat Mustang I concept car debuted in 1962, convincing some witnesses that Ford indeed planned to introduce a real sports car.

such success, and apparently feeling confident as hell, newly appointed Ford Division President Robert McNamara even opted to try out a smaller compact on the American market—the German-built Cardinal—a plan that surely would have taken his company down another wrong road had it been executed.

McNamara was by no means responsible for Ford's fumbling in 1958, when he was division general manager, but here he was a few years later on the verge of "out-Edseling" the Edsel. Or so thought Lee Iacocca, who had replaced McNamara in Ford's general manager office in November 1960. One of Iacocca's first tasks as general manager involved flying to Germany to oversee production of the Cardinal, then scheduling it for U.S. debut in the fall of 1962. But "underwhelmed" was his immediate response after setting eyes on the tiny vehicle that Ford had already spent $35 million developing.

"It was a fine car for the European market, with its V-4 engine and front-wheel drive," concluded Iacocca later in his autobiography. "But in the United Sates there was no way it could have sold the 300,000 units we were counting on." In his mind, the Cardinal was too small, even too ugly. Additionally, it didn't have a trunk, and its main merit—excellent fuel economy—at the moment represented no big deal from a Yankee perspective. "As usual, McNamara was ahead of his time—ten years to be exact," continued Iacocca. "A decade later, after the OPEC crisis, the Cardinal would have been a world-beater."

Back in Dearborn, Iacocca told Henry Ford II he had a real loser on his hands. "To bring out another lemon so soon after the Edsel would bring this company to its knees," he explained. He suggested they forget about that 35 million, cut their losses, and get out of the Cardinal deal while they still could. Not all his bosses agreed, but Henry II did, and his opinion mattered most. A Volkswagen-beater from Ford would have to wait, leaving Chevrolet's air-cooled, rear-engined Corvair, introduced alongside the Falcon for 1960, to carry on that fight.

While pitching his plea to Dearborn's top brass, Iacocca also hinted at the direction he felt the company's next big seller should take. "We simply can't afford a new model that won't appeal to younger buyers," he said. Along with eyes, Iacocca had enough fingers and toes to help him determine a new market trend was just then taking shape. You do the math: 1945 plus 16 equals

MAN WITH A PLAN: LEE IACOCCA

Look up "mover and shaker" in the dictionary and you'll likely find a photo of Lido Anthony Iacocca, arguably one of the most recognized names in Detroit annals. A major player at both Ford and Chrysler during his illustrious career, "Lee" Iacocca was born October 15, 1924, in Allentown, Pennsylvania, to Italian immigrants who ran a local restaurant. He got his first taste of business experience while operating a hot dog stand as a youngster, and later went on to Lehigh University in nearby Bethlehem where he earned an industrial engineering degree. Then, a Wallace Memorial Fellowship allowed him to do post-graduate studies at Princeton.

Iacocca went to work for Ford, first as a student engineer, in August 1946. But he quickly lost interest in nuts and bolts and negotiated his way into a sales management position. By 1949 he was a zone manager in Wilkes-Barre, Pennsylvania, working closely with 18 dealerships. Seven years later he made a major name for himself after instituting his nationally recognized "56 for 56" plan, which enticed customers behind the wheel of a new 1956 Ford for 20 percent down, $56 a month over a three-year span. This idea not only vaulted sales in his district, it also helped send him soaring up the executive ranks in Dearborn. He was only 36 when he ascended to the Ford Division general manager's chair in November 1960, and the Ford Division presidency followed on his 40th birthday four years later.

The Mustang was, of course, up and rolling big-time by then, as was the man behind the history-making machine himself. By the mid-1960s he was sure he was next in line to take over the president's office at Ford Motor Company once Henry Ford II finally moved out to concentrate on other affairs. But Henry Ford's grandson shocked everyone, inside his firm and out, by handing the job to former General Motors Executive Vice President Semon "Bunkie" Knudsen in February 1968.

"Henry [II] was a great GM admirer," explained Iacocca in his 1984 autobiography. "For him, Knudsen was a gift from heaven. Perhaps he believed Knudsen had all that famous GM wisdom locked in his genes. In any event, he wasted no time in making his approach. A week later, they had a deal. Knudsen would take over immediately as president at an annual salary of $600,000—the same as Henry's."

According to Iacocca, Henry II went out of his way to assure him that Knudsen's hiring did not mean that the Mustang's prime mover had nowhere left to go at Ford. But Iacocca nonetheless still considered retirement for a few weeks after the big announcement was made. He changed his mind, however, deciding instead to stick around and watch events unfold. "I was counting on the prospect that Bunkie would not work out and my turn would come sooner rather than later," he continued.

Iacocca was right. Knudsen proceeded to rapidly upset more than one apple cart in Dearborn, and following countless clashes he was fired by Henry Ford II just 19 months after his headline-inspiring hiring. Henry II didn't technically replace Bunkie, but he did immediately promote Iacocca in September 1969 to run the show as part of an executive triumvirate with Robert Stevenson and Robert Hampson. The Mustang's proud father was officially made corporate president in December 1970.

Unfortunately Lee Iacocca didn't get along with Henry Ford II any better than Bunkie Knudsen. Like Knudsen, Iacocca apparently grew too big for his britches, at least in Henry II's not-so-humble opinion, and he too got the boot in June 1978. Iacocca was fired after 32 years at Ford, in Henry II's words, "for insubordination." Privately Henry admitted he simply came to dislike Iacocca's aggressive marketing genius.

Iacocca didn't remain out of work for long. He joined Chrysler Corporation in November 1978 and proceeded to save the day for a Detroit mainstay then on the verge of a major downfall. In 1979 he engineered a federally backed financial bailout to keep the Big Three roll call at three. Also helping revive Chrysler's fortunes were two new trendsetting minivans, Dodge's Caravan and Plymouth's Voyager, both introduced in 1984. It was no coincidence that these two "garagable" utility vehicles looked a lot like a stillborn concept, called Carousel, developed at Ford during the early 1970s. Clearly Iacocca left with more than just his Rolodex after packing up his office in Dearborn.

While at Chrysler, Iacocca also was credited with acquiring American Motors in 1987, a move that brought the profitable Jeep Division into his realm. He remained Chrysler Corporation chairman until retiring at year's end in 1992. Three years later he played a supporting role in billionaire Kirk Kerkorian's attempted hostile takeover of Chrysler. After Kerkorian's plot failed, Iacocca was put under a gag order preventing him from discussing Chrysler affairs in public for five years. He then became a Chrysler spokesperson on television in the summer of 2005. "If you can find a better car, buy it," went his pitch, echoing the trademark line he had first uttered commercially back in the 1980s.

Lee Iacocca became Ford division general manager in November 1960 and almost immediately began work on the car of his dreams, the Mustang.

TWO-SEAT TREASURE

With its long hood and really short rear deck, Dearborn's original pony car reminded more than one witness in 1964 of a modern classic released by Ford about 10 years before: the unforgettable two-seat Thunderbird. Still recognized fondly even by people who know nothing about cars, the 1955–1957 T-bird itself was inspired by another memorable two-seater, the Corvette, introduced by Chevrolet in January 1953 during General Motors' Motorama auto show in New York. Decision-makers in Dearborn weren't about to stand by and let Chevy's fantastic plastic playtoy go unchallenged, so the word went down about a month later to get right to work on a Ford counterpart.

Chief engineer William Burnett directed mechanical development, while William Boyer handled the bulk of the styling chores under the watchful eye of legendary designer Frank Hershey. A wooden mockup was prepared for public review by early 1954, and more than one witness quickly recognized how much that model looked like a scaled-down version of the existing full-size Ford. Reportedly, the rapid fire design process began with Burnett's engineers simply cutting a standard sedan apart, then welding it back together on a shortened 102-inch wheelbase.

Some press critics, on the other hand, instantly noticed that Ford had done Chevrolet one better. "Perhaps the outstanding feature of the new Thunderbird is the clever wedding of sports car functionalism with American standards of comfort," wrote Don MacDonald in the April 1954 edition of *Motor Trend*. Unlike the Corvette, the original Thunderbird would have roll-up windows, a removable hardtop, and standard V8 power. All Corvettes built in 1953 and 1954 featured Chevy's old, reliable "Stovebolt" six-cylinder, and all were true Euro-style roadsters with flimsy convertible tops, clumsy side curtains, and no exterior door handles. A V8-powered Corvette didn't arrive until 1955; conventional door releases, roll-up side glass, and an optional lift-off hardtop followed in 1956.

MacDonald also explained that Ford General Manager Lewis Crusoe insisted on an all-steel body, as opposed to the fiberglass shell used by the Corvette. Crusoe's idea not only involved building more automobile compared to Chevrolet's relatively uncivilized sports car, but also involved building more automobiles, period. Sticking with traditional steel kept manufacturing difficulties down, which in turn translated into high production speeds.

Comparing notes again, Chevrolet's St. Louis plant rolled out 3,640 glass-bodied two-seaters in 1954, most of which were still sitting unsold in Missouri at year's end due partly to the fact that their comparatively crude nature didn't sit well with American sensibilities. Ford dealers, meanwhile, accepted more than 3,500 orders within 10 days of the 1955 Thunderbird's public introduction in October 1954. Dearborn's initial plan called for building 10,000 T-birds that first year. The final tally was 16,155. Following

a slight sales dip in 1956, the production count for the last—and in most minds the greatest—two-seat Thunderbird jumped up to 21,380 in 1957.

According to a 1992 *USA Today* poll, the 1957 Thunderbird then ranked as "America's Favorite Classic Car." In its heyday 35 years prior, it easily represented the best of both worlds in that it looked like a sports car; it was small, light, and fast, yet it also impressed drivers with its luxurious prestige. At the same time it was far more comfortable and offered a much smoother ride than the machine Chevrolet later started calling "America's only sports car."

Ford preferred the "personal luxury" label for its original Thunderbird, but that didn't deter continued comparisons with the sporting genre. "To the purist the Thunderbird has far too much luxury to qualify as a sports car, but even that group will find much of interest in the specification of this car," claimed a *Road & Track* review. "Although Ford is the first to deny it, they have a sports car in the Thunderbird, and it's a good one," added *Motor Trend*'s Walt Woron.

Some purists still insist Ford stopped building Thunderbirds after 1957. Though a disappointment to those who preferred their personal luxury in a more intimate form, the enlarged, four-place "Squarebird" of 1958 ensured Thunderbird drivers of a ride into a new decade. Ford Division chief Robert McNamara's decision to widen the Thunderbird's scope by enlarging its parameters was a wise move. With family men now able to partake in a little Thunderbird prestige, T-bird sales jumped a whopping 76 percent in 1958—this in a recession-racked year that featured only one other American car laying claim to a sales increase. Production then topped 90,000 in 1960, a model-line high that remained unsurpassed until 1977.

That line reached the end of the road in September 1997 after the last Thunderbird rolled out of Ford's plant in Lorain, Ohio. "Last with a back seat" was more to the truth. In January 1999, design executive J Mays unveiled an all-new T-bird at Detroit's North American International Auto Show, and show-goers couldn't help but once again see resemblances to a true classic. Mays' nostalgic two-seater then became a production reality in 2002, proving that at least some things old can be new again, to the delight of those who never have forgotten the original.

Many Ford fans have never forgiven their favorite car-maker for making the 1957 Thunderbird (right) the last of the two-seat variety. Dearborn officials then brought back a two-seat T-bird (left) in 2002.

what? An army of young buyers just reaching legal driving age as the '60s dawned, that's what. With so many lonely soldiers returning home after World War II ended, these "Baby Boomers" would be growing up into potential customers soon—why not be ready for them with a truly new automobile they'd want to eat up with both a fork and spoon? "Whereas the Edsel had been a car in search of a market it never found, here was a market in search of a car," said Iacocca.

So along came his baby, the perfect car for what many Americans still feel was the perfect time to be alive. Even today, a half century after its conception, mention Ford's still-popular pony and only one name comes to mind: a moniker that, as *Time* magazine explained in 1964, "rhymes with 'try-a-Coke-ah.'" "I'm generally seen as the father of the Mustang," said the man behind this history-making machine, "although, as with any success, there were plenty of people willing to take credit."

Not long after his promotion to general manager, Iacocca called together a group of creative minds to help him grow his seed. Included were product planners Donald Frey, Hal Sperlich, and Donald Peterson. Marketing man Bob Eggert and public relations manager Walter Murphy were present, too. This team met regularly for 14 weeks at Dearborn's Fairlane Inn and thus became known as the "Fairlane Committee."

Various ideas quickly formulated during those motel meetings, some inspired by letters customers still sent demanding that Ford bring back a two-seat Thunderbird. Introduced in 1955, the T-bird was an instant hit that Dearborn couldn't build fast enough at first, but its limited scope doomed it even before the dust settled that year. Ford officials quickly recognized that there was no future in selling about 15,000 sporty convertibles a year, so they decided to add a backseat and expand the Thunderbird in 1958 to attract more buyers. Purist protests were quickly drowned out that year by the proverbial cash register's "cha-ching" as sales soared.

Iacocca wanted his new car to possess a sporty flair but he wasn't about to fall into the same trap the original Thunderbird encountered. The Fairlane Committee instead looked outside the company, to Chevrolet, for inspiration. "It started with a few guys sitting around," remembered Donald Frey. "We started watching registrations of the Corvair, which was a dog. I guess in desperation they put bucket seats in the thing, called it the Monza, and it started to sell. We got the idea that there must be something to it. And that's how it all started—watching Monzas."

Initial parameters for Ford's response to the Corvair Monza involved a similar sporty image based on a body that, like the original Thunderbird, featured a long hood and short rear deck. It was to be a small car, but not too small; initial maximum length was pegged at 180 inches, weight at about 2,500 pounds. The planned price was no more than a buck a pound. Lastly, per Iacocca's specific demand, it would have room for four. Sporty cars didn't have to be limited to two seats, and he would prove this fact at all costs. Putting ideas down on paper began in earnest late in 1961.

A target date for "Job One," Ford's term for the very first regular-production example of a given new model, was inked first. "The New York World's Fair was scheduled to open in April 1964, which sounded to us like the ideal place to launch our new car," said Iacocca. "Although

Ford's two-seat Thunderbird was unveiled in 1955 as a response to Chevrolet's Corvette. The original two-seat model was built for three years only. This 1957 model is powered by an optional supercharged V8.

Chevrolet's 1960 Corvair Monza (top) came standard with bucket seats, inspiring Ford designers to consider a similar sporty tack for their upcoming new model. One conceptual response, the Avanti (above), was mocked up by March 1962.

new models are traditionally introduced in the fall, we had in mind a product so exciting and so different that we would dare to bring it out in the middle of the season. Only the World's Fair had enough scale and drama for the car of our dreams."

According to Iacocca, Ford stylists sculpted 18 different clay models during the first seven months of 1962, none of which lit his fire. During the summer of 1961, Gene Bordinat's Advanced Styling studio also had created various conceptual sketches of the two-seaters T-bird fanatics were clamoring for, as more than one mind at Ford apparently still believed the company could build a lighter, lower-priced 1955–1957 Thunderbird. Iacocca himself even gave Bordinat the thumbs up for a full-fledged prototype based on a Euro-style two-seat roadster platform. But showing off this mid-engine wonder named Mustang in October 1962 proved to be nothing more than a publicity stunt, a ploy to prime the pump, to let the public know that Ford would be rolling out a sporty new model soon.

Ford styling head Gene Bordinat (middle) was especially fond of the two-seat Mustang I concept vehicle. To the left of Bordinat is engineering vice president Herb Misch; seated in the Mustang I is chassis engineer Roy Lunn, the main man behind the car's design and development.

The initial in-house code for Lee Iacocca's pony car project was "T-5," a tag Ford later had to use for models exported to Germany because another company there already owned the rights to the Mustang name.

TOPLESS TEASE

The journalistic grapevine was ripe with speculation leading up to the Mustang's earth-shaking introduction in the spring of 1964. Ford people, of course, hadn't helped matters much by prominently promoting the two-seat Mustang I in 1962, inspiring *Motor Trend* to report late in 1963 of "rumors that Ford will produce a sports car to compete with the Corvette." Other small, sporty design experiments only fanned prognosticative flames further.

Thoughts of a lighter, lower priced take on Ford's original two-seat Thunderbird theme remained in consideration around Gene Bordinat's styling studios throughout early Mustang development stages, then one particular clay model, enthusiastically endorsed by veteran racer Dan Gurney, was morphed into a running prototype in May 1962. A design team headed by John Najjar and Jim Sipple

front; yeoman drums brought up the rear. Inside, both the foot pedals and steering wheel could be adjusted to fit the driver, this because the leather-covered aluminum bucket seats were fixed in place.

Ford's first Mustang made its public debut in October 1962 on the road course at Watkins Glen in New York, where Dan Gurney reached 120 mph behind its adjustable wheel. *Car and Driver* called it "the first true sports car to come out of Dearborn," and Barrie Gill of the *London Daily Herald* claimed it was "one of the most exciting cars I have ever ridden in."

Other sports car purists also piped up about the prospects of Ford fulfilling their dreams, so Gene Bordinat just had to create another prototype in 1963. This one was an entirely different animal, a vehicle that was meant to serve as a link between Bordinat's two-seat dream car and the regular-production reality already scheduled for release into the wild the following year. Named Mustang II to keep the legacy alive, this second showboat was more or less a

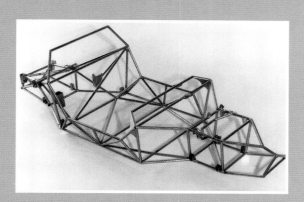  

had drawn up plans for this innovative mid-engine machine, and it was Najjar who reportedly named the thing after North American Aviation's P-51 fighter plane of World War II fame. Known initially as simply "Mustang," this petite plaything later evolved into the Mustang I after the Mustang II showcar showed up in 1963.

Bordinat made Bob Maguire and Damon Woods chief stylists of this project early in 1962, with Maguire overseeing the exterior, Woods the interior. Roy Lunn, the chassis engineer who later was responsible for Ford's world-record-beating GT-40 race car, was assigned the task of fashioning the aluminum-bodied Mustang I's foundation, which consisted of a tubular-steel "birdcage" space-frame complete with roll bar.

Power came from a V4 engine borrowed from Ford of Germany's Taunus front-wheel drive compact. This European 1500cc V4 was bulked up from its standard 89 horsepower to 109 by increasing compression to 11:1 and adding dual Weber carburetors and a more aggressive cam. Bolted up behind a hydraulic clutch was a four-speed transaxle, also copped from Taunus parts bins. The shifter worked via cables.

Control arms at the space-frame's corners also were tubular steel and were suspended by coil-over shocks. Wheels were cast magnesium units measuring 13x5 inches. Disc brakes went up

pre-production pilot model customized with special nose and tail treatments and a chopped roof. Like the Mustang I, it also was done in white paint accented with blue racing stripes.

In Lee Iacocca's words, showing off the Mustang II at "The Glen" in October 1963 was part of "a pre-test of likely customer responses to styling and mechanical innovations we may be considering for future production models." But according to some in the automotive press, the Mustang II failed this test. *Motor Trend* staffers especially felt this car didn't make the grade. "Ford's Mustang II may herald the general lines of that division's upcoming sports car, but it likely isn't an actual prototype," announced a January 1964 *Motor Trend* report. "It resembles the original Mustang not at all. It's rather a shame that the Mustang name had to be diluted this way."

Within six months all such complaints were drowned out by the roar of a veritable stampede as buyers flocked madly into Ford dealerships from coast to coast to lasso one of Iacocca's little ponies for themselves.

Introduced in October 1962, the Mustang I featured a tubular steel space-frame (left), independent rear suspension (middle), and a 109-horsepower four-cylinder engine (right).

Among many names considered early on during Mustang development was "Cougar," demonstrated here in logo form. The "Sign of the Cat" later was used in 1967 by Mercury for its new pony car.

When the Mustang debuted in April 1964 it was offered in two forms, a notchback coupe and a convertible. A third body style, a sleek fastback, shown here mocked up in May 1963, appeared in the fall of 1964.

Pontiac people weren't the only ones who considered copying Ferrari's famed badge. Dearborn's better idea guys had given up on this notion by the time Pontiac's GTO appeared in the fall of 1963.

Up until the summer of 1962, the only mockup Iacocca had seen that came close to his four-seat ideal was Bordinat's attractive "Allegro," an intriguing concept but not exactly what he had in mind. With that World's Fair deadline looming, he decided to stage a competition among Ford Motor Company design teams. On July 27, 1962, Bordinat kicked this contest off, inviting three players: Advanced Studio, Ford Studio, and Lincoln-Mercury Studio. Seven models were presented to division management on August 16, and, according to Iacocca, the initial favorite was a Ford Studio design named "Stiletto." Projected costs for the Stiletto were prohibitively high, however, and it was stamped out right there.

Bordinat preferred another design named "Cougar," the work of Dave Ash, Joe Oros' assistant in the Ford Studio. Reportedly Oros had left Ash in charge during the competition because he had to leave town. His assistant created the winning design, but history commonly gives Oros the bulk of the credit. At least Ash knew that his idea rolled right into production with only minor revisions. Talk about hitting the nail on the head.

Of course the same couldn't be said about Ash's name, one of many proposed during the development process. Before Cougar there was simply the project code, "T-5," a tag Ford was later forced to use for exports sent to West Germany due to a trademark conflict there. "Special Falcon" was seen early during initial planning stages, and Henry Ford II suggested "T-bird II," to no avail.

At one product strategy meeting, the choices were narrowed down to four: Monte Carlo, Monaco, Cougar, and Torino. Torino was initially considered then nixed. Iacocca then contacted John Conley, of J. Walter Thompson, Ford's advertising agency, because of his recognized prowess naming cars. Conley was asked to come up with a collection of suitable animal names, and six of these made the final cut: Bronco, Puma, Cheetah, Colt, Cougar (yet again), and Mustang. Already used for Bordinat's two-seat "prototype," "Mustang" was the one Iacocca and the other execs liked the best. Still not dead, Cougar later graced Mercury's first pony car, introduced in 1967.

When designers traded the stylized Cougar seen in the grille of Ash's 1962 model with a running horse, many thought they had made a mistake. While the cat faced right, the Mustang was galloping to the left, opposite of the clockwise course taken by all racehorses on all American racetracks. "My answer to that has always been that the Mustang is a wild horse, not a domesticated racer," said Iacocca. "And no matter which way it was running, I felt increasingly sure that it was headed in the right direction."

That name game was still undecided when Iacocca went before Henry Ford II for final approval in September 1962. Even with the Falcon's success so fresh, he knew the ivory tower execs would be leery of such an unproven ideal considering what had happened with the Edsel four years before. He also knew purse strings would be tight due to the $250 million already set aside to retool the Ford Division lineup for 1965. Then there were the Ford officials who were concerned about the bite Iacocca's little "youth car" would take out of Falcon sales. Still others doubted that his youth market would materialize.

As it was, it was the Falcon's proven presence that allowed Iacocca to make what he called the toughest selling job of his career. Henry Ford II liked what he saw, especially after he learned he wasn't being asked to spend the $300 to $400 million typically required in those days to get a brand new model into production. Iacocca proposed using as many existing Falcon components as possible beneath the sporty skin of his pet project, saving a small fortune in tooling costs in the process. In the end, he spent only $75 million getting the first Mustang up and running—veritable peanuts.

Yet as much as the Falcon foundation idea looked like the only way to get the job done, some at Ford didn't believe the plan would work out as envisioned. According to Iacocca, product

The partially constructed Mustang II showcar appears here in September 1963. Notice the chopped top and customized rear fascia.

planner Dick Place claimed that "making a sporty car out of a Falcon was like putting falsies on Grandma." Frey and Sperlich, however, determined the idea would work fine after experimenting with various models, but only if the exterior was completely original. "We could keep the platform and engine from the Falcon," said Iacocca, "but the car needed a whole new skin and greenhouse—the windshield, side glass, and backlight."

    In the end, the new Mustang relied on modified suspension and steering components borrowed from the Falcon. Much of the basic unit-body substructure, that is the floorpan and cowl, carried over as well, as did all of its powertrain choices. Dimensions differed here and there with the most noticeable change involving the Mustang's height. The pony car's Falcon-based floorpan was dropped down around the engine/transmission to bring both the passengers and the

A dashboard proposal is shown here in November 1962 for the developing model that was still deemed a "Special Falcon." A Falcon-based dash was used inside Ford's first Mustang.

roof closer to the ground. Cowl height in turn was cut, and this lowering proved to be just what the doctor ordered as far as imparting sporty impressions were concerned—just as Iacocca ordered, too. Also, Iacocca's original 180-inch length gained about 1.5 inches, this after Henry Ford II demanded an extra inch of rear seat room be added.

All those borrowed components and structures may have made Iacocca's plan work, but they also invited more than a few slings and arrows. General Motors design executive Bill Mitchell called the Mustang "a Hamtramck Falcon." For those wondering, the premise behind Mitchell's dated, off-color crack involved the widely known fact that the population of Hamtramck, a Detroit suburb, is largely of Polish descent. Then all the rage in America, and still garnering guffaws well into the 1970s, the bad, old "Pollack joke" has fortunately since gone the way of Playboy Clubs, cigarette commercials, and cyclamate-sweetened soft drinks.

Casual history too has since commonly referred to the original Mustang as a Falcon beneath the skin, causing at least one of the car's original designers to speak out in response. "The Mustang had a lot of Falcon parts in it," said Gail Halderman, "but it was not a glorified Falcon as many believe."

The Mustang that Bill Mitchell referred to was, in fact, a showcar built in 1963 as part of yet another publicity push. After drawing considerable attention with his mid-engined Mustang roadster at Watkins Glen in 1962, Gene Bordinat returned to the New York race track again the following year with a second "idea car," this one named Mustang II. This time around the ploy involved a little bit of trickery borrowed from GM, which more than once before had customized an upcoming regular-production model and passed it off as a predictive concept car. It then appeared as if a futuristic dream machine rolled right off an auto show stage into reality, when the reverse progression was actually the truth.

The 1963 Mustang II was simply a customized pilot car, a gussied-up precursor to the regular-production mass-market marvel Americans would be buying up by the boatload one year later. On March 29, 1964—571 days after Iacocca, Bordinat, and the rest gave the Oros/Ash Cougar their full support—Job One, Ford's first Mustang, rolled off the Dearborn assembly line. So many cars followed in record-setting fashion that Iacocca decided a few weeks later to push for a second assembly line, this one in San Jose, California.

Clearly Iacocca was right; it was possible to create a new breed of automobile without breaking the bank, and yes, a major market obviously did exist in 1964 for an affordable, sporty "youth car." Jealous GM designers could be as politically incorrect as they liked, and fellow Ford execs could throw stones, too, but none of that mattered after Mustangs started hitting the streets by the hundreds of thousands. "The bean counters went back into the bunkers muttering that there was evidently more than one way to build a car," said the man with the proven plan in 1984. "It was the styling that did it, which was something they hadn't counted on. But they weren't shy when it came time to count the money." According to Iacocca, the Mustang rang up $1.1 billion in net profits during its first two years on the road.

He was plainly correct, too, about his little pony running in the right direction.

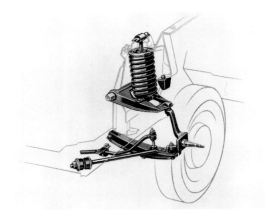

Conventional unequal-length A-arms made up the new Mustang's front suspension, but completely atypical was the coil spring's location—above the upper A-frame instead of positioned between the two arms.

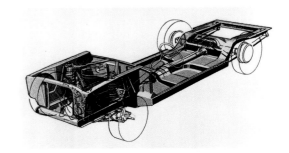

The original Mustang's unit-body foundation was taken right out from under Ford's Falcon, a popular compact introduced for 1960. A sheet-steel "housing" up front, among other things, served as an upper mounting location for the springs and shock absorbers.

Parallel leaf springs brought up the 1964-1/2 Mustang's tail. Drum brakes were standard at all four corners; front discs were optional.

Gene Bordinat loved the two-seat idea, and his studios were still concocting clay models of just such a Mustang as late as the spring of 1964.

Like the Mustang I two-seater, the Mustang II concept car was unveiled to the press at the Watkins Glen road course in New York in October 1963.

The 1964-1/2 Mustang convertible's base price was $2,557.56, compared to $2,320.96 for its coupe running mate. Forty-five years ago, the optional 14-inch wire wheelcovers appearing here cost $44.83.

CHAPTER ONE

The Original Pony Car, 1964–1966

The Mustang didn't even constitute a glint in Lee Iacocca's eye when his company's first sensational small car began making its own brand of history. First shown off to the press in July 1959, the 1960 Falcon proved to be just what customers were looking for, at least then. Massive first-year sales totaled 417,174, by far a Detroit record for an all-new model right out of the box.

Such unprecedented prosperity certainly represented nothing to shake a stick at, yet some at Ford still wondered what might've developed had the Falcon not been such a ho-hum machine. Most curious, of course, was Ford's newly appointed, 36-year-old general manager. Like the division's former general manager, Robert

OUT OF THE CHUTE

McNamara, Lee Iacocca also favored the compact ideal, only he was looking for something hotter as the 1960s started cooking. In his not-so-humble opinion, McNamara was just too damned conservative. "He was a good businessman, but he had the mentality of a consumerist," said Iacocca later in his autobiography. "He believed strongly in the idea of a utilitarian car, whose purpose was simply to meet people's basic needs."

According to Iacocca, McNamara more or less played it safe with the Falcon. "[He] was the quintessential bean counter," continued the man behind the Mustang. "At their best, bean counters [have] impressive analytical skills, [but] by their very nature tend to be defensive, conservative and pessimistic. On the other side are the guys in sales and marketing—aggressive, speculative and optimistic. In any company, you need both sides, because natural tension between the two creates its own system of checks and balances. If the bean counters are too weak, the company will spend itself into bankruptcy. But if they're too strong, the company won't meet the market or stay competitive."

Part of Ford's plan to stay competitive—once McNamara moved on from Dearborn, Michigan, to Washington, D.C., to serve in newly elected President John F. Kennedy's cabinet in 1960—involved a revitalized interest in horsepower, an automotive aspect Dearborn officials had cooled on in 1957. That year McNamara and crew agreed to the Automobile Manufacturers Association's "ban" on both factory-supported racing and the general promotion of performance. While Ford dropped all such projects like fresh-out-of-the-oven potatoes per the AMA mandate, Chrysler and, to a far greater degree, General Motors kept on building racing machines, for both the track and the street, albeit in a much quieter fashion. But after eating dust for a couple years, Dearborn engineers starting toying with hot parts again in 1960. Henry Ford II issued a statement two years later claiming that the AMA "resolution has come to have neither purpose nor effect." "Accordingly," he continued, "we have notified [the AMA] that we feel we can better establish our own standards of conduct with respect to the manner in which the performance of our vehicles is to be promoted and advertised."

Racing legend Carroll Shelby began building Ford-powered sports/racing cars in 1962, first using Britain's A.C. Ace as a base for his venomous Cobra, shown here leading another Shelby product—a Daytona coupe—on the Goodwood road course in England in August 1964. Shelby's famed GT 350 Mustang went into production two months later.

Iacocca took it from there, announcing an exciting new promotional campaign to the press in April 1963. "We at Ford believe in performance, because the search for performance, 'Total Performance,' made the automobile the wonderfully efficient, pleasurable machine it is today—and will make it better tomorrow," he concluded. Translated, he recognized that speed sells—speed on race tracks around the world, that is. Back on the streets here at home during the '60s, "Total Performance" represented only words. Mainstream Blue-Oval vehicles didn't come close to out-performing comparable rivals until 1968 and 1969. But it was another story entirely in competition circles worldwide as Henry II's multi-million-dollar motorsports program kept busy during the decade, demonstrating what "Powered By Ford" truly meant.

"We will stay in open competition as long as we feel it contributes to better automobiles for the public," explained Iacocca in 1964. "It's estimated that 43 million people a year now go to motorsport events. We may be old-fashioned, but with that many people in the stands, we figure it's a pretty good place to show how well our products can perform in direct competition with the products of other manufacturers." Did racing actually help improve the Better Idea breed, or did it simply help improve sales? You be the judge.

Whatever the case, both Iacocca and his big boss would be changing their tunes soon enough, and Ford's massive motorsports teams would be disbanded by the end of 1970. But, at the time in 1964, playing with race cars represented the best way to make it big in Detroit. As long as Henry II's beloved competition projects served Ford's marketing goals, Iacocca was all for them. But as far as street-going muscle cars were concerned, he was never a big fan. Iacocca couldn't have cared less about installing ungodly amounts of horsepower into a few regular production models here and there. What he wanted from the beginning was, in his words, "a good-looking little youth car"—a practical machine available to the masses that on

one hand was affordable, on the other sporty-looking. Work on his "youth car" began in earnest in 1961.

Three years later, on Friday morning, April 17, 1964, Ford dealers welcomed customers to become the first on their blocks to own one of Iacocca's mass-market marvels, in the process kicking off a feeding frenzy the likes of which Detroit had never known before, nor, undoubtedly, will ever see again. The initial plan, instituted as production began on March 9, was to build a minimum of 8,160 pony cars by April 17 to guarantee that every dealer in America had at least one serving as the centerpiece in his showroom once official sales started. Yeah, right.

Estimates claimed as many as 4 million people pushed their way into Ford dealerships that weekend alone. Some dealers were forced to lock their doors and call police when the rush grew too great. Reportedly, a dealer in Pittsburgh put a Mustang up on a wash rack, then couldn't bring it back down due to the crush of gawkers assembled. While some in those crowds were simply curious, most were ready, willing, and able to buy that first day. The few Mustangs on hand were snapped up immediately and another 22,000 orders were placed on April 17 alone.

Waiting two months or more for delivery was common, a painful reality that helped move some potential buyers to extremes to get their hands on one of those early showroom models. As many as 15 customers laid claim to a dealership's last Mustang in Garland, Texas, convincing management to auction off the car to the highest bidder. The winner insisted on spending the night behind the wheel to guarantee the car wouldn't be sold to someone else before his check cleared the bank the following day.

Limited availability represented the only loud complaint heard when Ford's first pony car burst onto the scene. A famous telegram sent to Henry Ford II perhaps said it best: "Henry Ford, I do declare; You have your Grandpa Henry's flair; He put a Ford in every home; You put a Mustang there; Congratulations; The wait out here is somewhat sickly; Could you fix me up more quickly?"

Other interested parties expressed desires to own a Mustang against all odds. "I'm not much on cars, and I haven't been since most cars got pregnant," began a Brooklyn man's letter,

Ford's new Mustang was available with either a six-cylinder or V8 (shown here—notice the fender badge just behind the headlight) in 1964. Two V8s were offered early on; one at 260 cubic inches, the other at 289.

Of the 559,451 1964–1965 Mustangs built, 73,112 were convertibles. Power operation for the soft top was a $52.95 option.

HISTORY MAKER

About two weeks before the Mustang's big public debut in April 1964, Captain Stanley Tucker, an airline pilot from St. Johns, Newfoundland, was out for a ride around his hometown when he came upon a considerable crowd gathering outside a local dealership, George Parsons Ford. Attracting all this attention was a Wimbledon White Mustang convertible, a sensational machine like nothing Newfoundlanders had ever seen before. This fresh-off-the-line convertible had been sent on a tour of Canada as a promotional tool to invite America's northern neighbors to rush to their nearest Ford dealer and take home their own brand-new pony cars.

Captain Tucker decided to do just that as soon as he set his eyes on the white droptop at Parsons Ford. He immediately corralled a salesman, signed on the dotted line, then drove away with his coveted convertible the next morning. In the process he not only made himself the first Canadian to buy a new Mustang, but he also became the owner of the very first of the breed.

Apparently no one at Parsons Ford received the memo: they weren't supposed to sell that white convertible because it was serial number 100001, a historic pony car that Ford Motor Company officials had planned to enshrine in the Henry Ford Museum, right next to the Mustang I prototype, following its promotional tour north of the border. Not at all happy about this mistake, officials back in Dearborn were quick to try to correct it. But attempts to buy the car back from the 33-year-old pilot proved unsuccessful. Tucker was no dummy. Besides, he enjoyed the notoriety.

"For a long time, I was the only Mustanger in Newfoundland," he told *Mustang Monthly* nearly 20 years later. "It was quite an experience. Many times, motorists would force me to the side of the road to ask me about the car—what it was, who made it, how did I like it, and how much did it cost. The car has been a real joy to own and drive. Getting into it is something like slipping into a cockpit, and I feel as much a part of the machine as I do when I'm flying."

Tucker's joy lasted two years and 10,000 miles, after which time he found Ford people ratcheting up efforts to get their piece of history back. Their latest offer involved a trade: in exchange for serial number 100001, he'd get a new 1966 Mustang built to his exacting specifications. But that wasn't all. At the time Ford was preparing to celebrate the production of its 1 millionth Mustang, and someone in Dearborn determined it would be a great idea to trade the 1,000,001th Mustang for number 1.

Tucker agreed, returning his 1964-1/2 convertible to George Parsons Ford in early 1966. "What the heck, there was a new car in the deal," he continued in 1986. "But it was actually foolish on my behalf when I think about it today." Maybe so, but it wasn't like he got stiffed. When presented with an order sheet he simply marked a big X across the entire page. Save for the 271-horsepower 289 High Performance V8 (he opted for the 225-horse 289), the Silver Frost 1966 convertible Tucker ordered ended up carrying nearly every major option offered that year. Then there was the little matter of picking up his fully loaded prize.

On February 23, 1966, less than two years after Tucker's number one Mustang rolled off the Dearborn line, Ford's 1 millionth pony car did the same. Tucker then joined Lee Iacocca, Donald Frey, and Gene Bordinat on March 2 to pose for publicity photos at the end of the assembly line with Mustang number 1,000,000, a white 1966 convertible. Following that photo op, Tucker was invited to tour the country with his former car, serial number 100001, but he declined.

So it was that Ford's first Mustang finally found its way, as originally planned, into the Henry Ford Museum. As for the millionth model, it slipped into the dealer network and obscurity. Number 1,000,001 stayed in Tucker's hands for five years until it was sold, rusted and tired, to a St. John's mechanic. And though he never rode another pony after he let his 1966 convertible go in 1971, Stanley Tucker is still remembered as the "original Mustanger."

....

Airline pilot Stanley Tucker bought the first Mustang to roll off Ford's Dearborn assembly line from a Canadian dealer in April 1964.

which Iacocca opened four days after his brand new baby went on sale. "Furthermore, New York is no place to have a car. Pet owners urge their dogs to urinate on the wheels. Slum kids steal the hubcaps. Cops give parking tickets. Pigeons roost on the car, and worse. Streets are always torn up. Buses crush you, taxis bump you, and inside parking requires a second mortgage on the house. Gas costs 30 percent more [here] than anyplace else. The insurance rates are incredible. The garment district is impassable, the Wall Street area impregnable, going to New Jersey impossible. So as soon as I can raise the nut, I'm buying a Mustang."

Ford's earliest forecasts, dating back to the initial project approval, predicted first-year sales of 75,000, but Iacocca knew better. By April 17, 1964, he was reasonably sure he could sell at least 200,000 Mustangs that first year, though not without opening a second assembly line at Ford's San Jose plant in California. Although annual capacity increased to 360,000 after the West Coast line began operation, even that wasn't enough to handle runaway demand. An expensive risk, a third Mustang plant opened for business soon afterward in Metuchen, New Jersey.

Meanwhile, the battle cry around Dearborn had become "417 by 4–17." Iacocca's latest goal involved breaking the Falcon's record by selling more than 417,000 Mustangs by April 17, 1965. No problem. Just before the close of the business day on April 16, 1965, a California man bought a red convertible, making him the original Mustang's 418,812th customer. In one year's time, Mustang sales had surpassed the 1960 Falcon's historic total by 1,638 cars.

Later, in 1966, the Mustang broke another record formerly held by the Falcon. Just before noon on Wednesday, February 23, Ford's one millionth pony car rolled off the Dearborn assembly line, making Mustang the all-time fastest to reach seven digits. Clearly Iacocca had redefined "success." Someone he knew even saw a sign hung in a bakery window in 1964 claiming, "Our hotcakes are selling like Mustangs."

Of that initial record-breaking tally, 121,538 were so-called "1964-1/2" models, an unofficial reference resulting from the original Mustang's extended production run, which began unconventionally midway in 1964 and ended traditionally in August the following year. Most sources 45 years ago, including Ford, preferred not to break up the pony cars assembled during those 18 months. All examples built prior to the start of 1966 Mustang production in September 1965 were simply labeled 1965 models. But, as enthusiasts soon discovered, various running changes did differentiate the Mustangs manufactured before August 1964 from those created afterwards, thus making it relatively easy to discriminate—hence the existence today of both 1964-1/2 and 1965 categories. Though most of the changes were minor, one stands out as the most recognizable clue separating one model from the other: all 1964-1/2 Mustang engines used generators, all 1965s used alternators.

Prior to breaking those records, Ford also embarked on an equally unprecedented promotional campaign to help prime the pump. Outsiders actually got their first look at Iacocca's "youth

Lee Iacocca (left) stands proudly with righthand man Donald Frey beside Detroit's first pony car. Notice the license plate—Iacocca intended to sell 417,000 Mustangs by April 17, 1965, breaking the industry's record for new model first-year sales.

Frey (left) and Iacocca pose again, this time with the car that owned Detroit's first-year sales record before the new Mustang broke it. Introduced in 1960 to go toe-to-toe with Chevrolet's Corvair, Ford's first Falcon (left) was an instant success with sales of about 417,000.

car" in the fall of 1963 when he invited some of the nation's most prominent journalists to Dearborn for a confidential briefing on what the public would see some six months later. All the top magazines were represented: *Time* and *Newsweek*, *LIFE* and *Look*, *Esquire* and *Sports Illustrated*, to name just a few. Press people experienced a long day's worth of slide shows and speeches, and that was just the start.

What came during the following months represented Detroit's most extensive, most effective public relations push ever. Major Mustang press kits were shipped to about 11,000 newspapers and magazines, and foreign language versions were even sent overseas. Ford dealers in 13 top markets got their own presentations, as did about 200 of radio's most popular disc jockeys just weeks before sales started in April 1964.

As planned from the beginning, the Mustang's official, full-force press introduction was held four days prior to the on-sale date, on Monday, April 13, at the New York World's Fair. More than 125 representatives from all forms of media showed up from the United States, Canada, and Puerto Rico. Iacocca spoke about the youth-oriented market, then the gathered throng was allowed an up-close look at the most anticipated automobile since Henry Ford replaced the Model T with the Model A in 1928. Later that day, about 100 media people set out in a caravan of 70 Mustangs on a 750-mile rally from New York to Detroit. Along with impressing the media, this drive also allowed countless innocent bystanders their first chances to gawk, and more importantly, to tell everyone they knew about what they'd just seen.

An unprecedented broadcast barrage began on Thursday evening, April 16, with a remarkable domination of television commercial time occurring on *all* three networks (imagine that!) during the coveted 9:30 to 10 p.m. time slot. Conservative estimates claimed the new Mustang made its way into 29 million U.S. households that Thursday evening. Millions more got the chance to read all about it over the following week, thanks to a print ad push that included full-page advertisements in at least 24 national magazines and more than 2,500 major newspapers. Feature stories soon showed up in magazines of all kinds, from *Business Week* to *Sports Illustrated*, *LIFE* to *Look*, *Popular Science* to *Playboy*.

Let's not forget those coinciding cover stories in *Time* and *Newsweek*, a publicity coup credited to public relations whiz Walter Murphy. Of the new Mustang, the latter magazine reported that "Ford is spending more than $10 million to imbed it in the national consciousness like a gumdrop in a four-year-old's cheek." That investment, according to Iacocca, was more than worth it; he claimed the *Time/Newsweek* coverage alone helped sales soar by at least an extra 100,000. Talk about "power of the pen."

The absence of any engine identification badge on the fender (just ahead of the front wheel) of this Arcadian Blue 1966 2+2 means it's equipped with the base six-cylinder, a 200-cubic-inch mill rated at 120 horsepower.

Introduced just in time for Christmas in 1964, the Midget Mustang pedal car, priced at $12.95, was supplied by the American Machine and Foundry Company (AMF) and marketed through Ford dealerships.

A third model, the sexy 2+2 fastback, joined the original Mustang coupe and convertible in September 1964. Base price for the 2+2 was $2,533.19.

Beneath the 2+2's sweeping roof was a backseat that folded down for increased cargo stowage. The panel behind that seat also opened up, extending the cargo floor into the trunk area. The louvers in the C-pillars were functional; they helped ventilate the interior.

Helping spread the word even further was a seemingly endless stream of independent companies that all "borrowed" the Mustang name, with explicit permission, to help hawk everything from earrings to key chains, sunglasses to boots, hats to cuff links. Young Americans were especially targeted; one retail chain even renamed its youth-oriented clothing department the "Mustang Shop." In California, the term "Mustang Generation" was coined to describe the youthful, single set, and a *Wall Street Journal* front-page headline used this term atop a report on advertising targeted at the 20–34 age group.

Apparently Dearborn's merry marketeers felt the targeting shouldn't stop, on the bottom end, with 20-year-olds. Nor licensed drivers, for that matter. Correctly predicting that children would soon grow into young adults, Ford's best and brightest opted to enter into the toy business as well in 1964. The first 50,000 customers who responded to Ford's Order Holding Program that year not only got a shot at the real thing, but also received a 1/25-scale plastic Mustang model supplied by AMT. Dealers stocked a Philco-Ford transistor radio (hidden in another 1/25-scale Mustang replica) and a 1/12-scale battery-powered Mustang, made by Cox. Many other Mustang toys and models were produced and sold through a wide variety of after-market sources including Matchbox®, Tomy Toys, and Shredded Wheat breakfast cereal. Perhaps the most memorable pitch aimed at the truly youthful market was AMF's Mustang pedal car, introduced just in time for Christmas 1964.

Back in the grown-up world, the full-sized Mustang also gained priceless publicity in May 1964 while pacing the field prior to the start of that year's Indianapolis 500. Ford's first pony car was honored too with the coveted Industrial Designers' Institute Award. Even more prestigious, at least in Henry Ford II's opinion, was the Tiffany Gold Medal Award bestowed upon the Mustang "for excellence in American design." It was the first time that Walter Hoving's Tiffany & Company had extended this honor to an automobile, though it might be pointed out that Ford people in truth solicited the award from Tiffany.

MINI MUSTANGS

Licensed drivers weren't the only ones to jump on Dearborn's runaway pony car bandwagon in 1964. Late that year, just in time for Christmas, Ford also released another mass-market marvel, this one targeted at truly youthful buyers. Manufactured by the American Machine and Foundry Company (AMF) of Olney, Illinois, and sold through Ford dealers, the aptly named "Midget Mustang" pedal car debuted to nearly as much fanfare as the full-size rendition, with high-profile advertisements appearing in at least a half dozen major magazines, including a full-page ad in *LIFE*.

"Here's a child's gift that'll look just as inviting under a Christmas tree as a 1965 Mustang will look in your driveway," began one such promotion. "Give your child a Midget Mustang this Christmas—for a taste of the fun all Mustangers enjoy!" "Stop in today and order your Midget Mustang," continued another ad inviting Christmas shoppers into their nearest Blue Oval showroom. "And while you're here see all the new Fords."

Like its grownup counterpart, Ford's all-metal pedal car was a real bargain, at least according to ad copy, which proclaimed a "$25 value for only $12.95." Midget Mustangs rolled on a 23-inch wheelbase and measured 39 inches long, 14 inches high. Standard equipment included a working three-speed stick on the righthand doorsill, the coveted Rally-Pac instrument cluster decal, whitewall rubber tires accented with true-to-life deluxe wheel covers, and a steel three-spoke steering wheel modeled after the real thing. Apparently all Ford-marketed Midget Mustangs were red, although rumors claim a few may have been painted light blue/gray. It also was not uncommon to find junior's pedal car repainted to match mom and dad's daily driver.

Yet another variation was created earlier in 1964 especially for the Indianapolis 500 Festival Committee. As expected, these pedal-driven playtoys were painted white with a blue stripe running down the middle of their hoods and decklids, just like the Mustang convertible that paced the Indy 500 that year. They also featured "Official Indianapolis 500 Pace Car" decals and a hand-lettered serial number tag. Reportedly only 100 of these pace car pedal cars were

created, with less than five legitimate examples known to still exist. One survivor sold for $1,700 at a collector auction in the 1990s.

The pedal car idea was first presented to Lee Iacocca by AMF's Patrick Wilkins early in 1964. Iacocca loved the three prototypes he saw and full production quickly followed. Ford dealers sold about 93,000 Midget Mustangs from December 1964 through the 1965 Christmas season, then Dearborn officials opted to drop the promotion in 1966. AMF people, however, weren't deterred; they continued producing and marketing Mustang pedal cars themselves, but only after they removed all "Ford" references.

AMF also added new spinner hubcaps and an updated grille that echoed the 1966 Mustang's. Other upgrades appeared for each succeeding model, beginning with GT-style racing stripes added to the body sides in 1967. A new "finger-molded" plastic steering wheel showed up in 1968, and chrome side scoops, a revised T-handle shifter, and wire wheel covers became part of the package in 1969. The familiar running-horse logo was deleted that year, and the color was switched to yellow in 1971. AMF finally shut down its pedal car assembly line in 1972.

Nearly 120,000 kid-powered mini Mustang convertibles were sold from 1964 to 1972, all using the same stamped-steel body scaled down from the real thing. After the original production line ceased operation, AMF sold off all its tooling to the CIA Corporation in Mexico City, Mexico. Mexican-manufactured Mustang pedal cars were offered in various colors. Fourteen years later the San Diego–based Little Car Company tried to import 1,000 mini Mustangs from the Mexican firm to help commemorate the real pony car's 25th anniversary. But poor quality hampered this plan and only 200 were distributed among dealers in the United States.

All Mustang pedal cars, built south of the border or in Illinois, remain valued collectibles today.

Nearly 120,000 Mustang pedal cars were sold from 1964 to 1972, including about 100 specially adorned with Indy 500 Pace Car graphics in May 1964.

No matter—nothing was going to dim the first pony car's day in the sun. Nor could anything quiet so many satisfied customers, who seemingly couldn't say enough about how much they loved their little horses. More than 4,000 letters of high praise arrived in Dearborn that summer, most of them telling tales of drivers thrilled beyond words. Automotive writers, on the other hand, encountered no such shortage of nouns or verbs, not to mention those all-important adjectives.

"A market which has been looking for a car has it now," announced *Car Life* after testing the hottest thing then on four wheels. "It is a sports car, a gran turismo car, an economy car, a personal car, a rally car, a sprint car, a race car, a suburban car, and even a luxury car." According to *Road & Track*, "the Mustang is definitely a sports car, on par in most respects with such undisputed types as the MG-B, Triumph TR-4 or Sunbeam Alpine." Back in *Car Life's* court, "the car may well be, in fact, better than any domestically mass-produced automobile on the basis of handling and roadability and performance, per dollar invested."

Clearly designers, planners, and engineers had not only met Iacocca's original demands, they'd gone well beyond. "[Ford] has produced more than just a new car," began *Time* magazine's account of America's latest craze. "With its long hood and short rear deck, its Ferrari flair and open-mouthed air scoop, the Mustang resembles the European racing cars that American sports-car buffs find so appealing. Yet Iacocca has made the Mustang's design so flexible, its price so reasonable,

Ford customers were treated during the Mustang's first birthday party, held in April 1965, with the new GT, available as a coupe, fastback, or convertible. Fog lamps and rocker molding stripes were included in the GT package.

and its options so numerous, that its potential appeal reaches towards two-thirds of all U.S. car buyers. Priced as low as $2,368 and able to accommodate a small family in its four seats, the Mustang seems destined to be a sort of Model T of sports cars—for the masses as well as the buffs."

Even more sporty flair appeared in September 1964 after a third available body style, the 2+2 fastback, joined the existing coupe and convertible. Designed under Gail Halderman's watchful eye, the attractive 2+2 featured a trendy sweeping roofline and a rear seat that folded down to open up a large, flat cargo floor extending from the trunk into the passenger compartment. More than 77,000 of these sleek, sexy, ergonomic Mustangs were sold during their first year out. The pot was sweetened further in April 1965 when the Mustang's bountiful options list was expanded to include, among other things, the attractive GT Equipment Group. GT Mustangs (see chapter 4) represented the hottest pony cars available until the Boss models arrived in 1969.

Attractive 14-inch styled steel wheels were optional for V8 Mustangs, GT or not, from 1964 to 1967. They cost $119.71 in 1965.

As for garden-variety Mustangs in 1964, they initially came standard with a truly tame, purely economical 170-cubic-inch inline six-cylinder that made a mere 101 horsepower. That mundane engine was replaced by an improved 200-cubic-inch straight-six, rated at 120 horsepower, when the 1964-1/2 run segued into 1965 production in August 1964. Optional early on was a 164-horsepower 260-cubic-inch "Windsor" V8 topped by a two-barrel carburetor. A larger Windsor small-block, the 210-horsepower 289 four-barrel V8, was also available at extra cost in 1964.

Named for its manufacturing home in Windsor, Ontario, these V8s sprouted roots running back to 1962, the year Ford introduced its first mid-sized model, Fairlane. Initial plans called for the new Fairlane to offer both six- and eight-cylinder power, but Dearborn didn't have a suitable V8 for this downsized platform. The hefty FE-series big-block, introduced four years before, wouldn't fit, and the venerable Y-block V8—which finally replaced ol' Henry's tired "flathead" in 1954—was too heavy, not to mention past its prime. No problem. Engineers simply used the same thin-wall casting technique developed to create a lightweight six-cylinder for the 1960 Falcon to produce a new compact V8.

Ford's first Windsor displaced 221 cubic inches, same as Henry's history-making 1932 flathead V8. This tidy small-block was then bored out to 260 cubic inches in mid-1962 and enlarged again to 289 cubes in mid-1963. The performance-oriented High Performance 289 (see chapter 4) was also introduced as a 1963-1/2 option for Ford's mid-sized line. With its 271 horses, the "Hi-Po" 289 represented just the ticket for drivers who wanted to back up the Mustang's sporty impressions with some real kick after this K-code V8 became a pony car option in June 1964.

"From the outside, the unique styling of the new 2+2 fastback immediately identifies it as a Mustang, with a 'Gran Turismo' sports flair," or so claimed Ford promotional paper work. Total production of 1966 2+2 models (shown here) was 35,698.

The Hi-Po 289 remained the Mustang's hottest underhood choice up through 1966. It carried over briefly into 1967, but by then was overshadowed by the 390 GT big-block V8. The K-code option didn't return for 1968, which incidentally was the last year for the Mustang's 289 V8. A stroked 302-cubic-inch Windsor was released concurrently for 1968, and then superseded its smaller brethren the following year. An even larger small-block, the 351 Windsor, showed up in 1969.

Both the 302 and 351 survived until the 1990s, with the former evolving into its more familiar "5.0" form to again make the Mustang a formidable force on the street. V8 Mustangs

FANCY FRILLS

A main key to the original pony car's success involved what Lee Iacocca liked to call the "three faces of Mustang." This split personality, if you will, guaranteed a scope wider than any ever seen before on the American automotive market. In truth, Iacocca probably sold his baby short; this milestone machine represented so many different cars to so many different drivers. Nonetheless, three appealing identities plainly stood out.

In bare-bones form, a six-cylinder model was a frugal, practical economizer priced at about $2,300. From there it could've been transformed into a relatively luxurious "mini-T-bird" by adding a major collection of comfort and convenience options, which typically included such things as power brakes, power steering, a vinyl roof, and so on. And a third personality resulted after the installation of the optional 289 High Performance V8, Ford's Special Handling Package, and perhaps a limited-slip differential. Introduced in June 1964, the K-code "Hi-Po" 289, rated at 271 horsepower, helped transform Dearborn's polite pony into a wild stallion, though at considerable cost. The K-code V8, priced at $327.92, was the most expensive item found on the Mustang options list in 1964 and 1965.

From the beginning, Mustang buyers found themselves teased with a wide choice of extra-cost additions, and those options just kept piling on as the '60s sped by. Customers who stuck with the budget-conscious six-cylinder and its floor-shifted three-speed manual transmission were in the minority every year. Base six-cylinder models made up 35.6 percent of the production run in 1965 and 41.7 percent in 1966 before optional V8s really started cooking. The six-cylinder's piece of the pie dipped to 30 percent in 1967, then fell to 18.4 the following year. The six's percentage in 1971 was a mere 9.8.

As for the standard three-speed stick, it was installed in 31.9 percent of 1964–1965 Mustangs. The percentage then fell to 17.2 in 1969 and 10.8 in 1971. Total optional additions, meanwhile, went on the rise, with the typical amount spent on extras going from $358 per car early in 1964 to more than $500 in 1967.

Optional transmissions were among the pricier options listed in 1964–1965. The only gearbox offered behind the Hi-Po 289, a four-speed manual transmission cost $113.45 in six-cylinder applications, $184.02 when bolted up behind a V8. Ford's Cruise-O-Matic automatic transmission was priced at $175.80 behind the base six-cylinder, $185.39 when paired up with either the 200-horsepower 289 V8 or its 225-horse running mate. Trading the standard six for the optional 200-horse 289 two-barrel meant spending an extra $105.63. Adding another $52.85 to that total allowed a customer to install the 225-horse 289 V8 with its four-barrel carburetor.

The second most expensive option in 1964–1965, at $277.20, was air conditioning, which was only offered in rather clunky underdash form during the Mustang's early years. A fully integrated in-dash air conditioning system didn't arrive until 1967. The price that year for this option, called "Selectaire," was $356.09. Ouch.

Two more options appeared in April 1965 to help up the ante even further. Most prominent was the GT Equipment Group, which included a nice array of sporty image enhancements along with a decent dose of performance-enhancing hardware (for more on this package, see chapter 4). The other new choice, the Interior Decor Group, spruced up the Mustang's interior with unique luxury trim, the GT's sporty five-dial instrumentation, padded visors, simulated walnut accents, and special seat inserts featuring an embossed herd of galloping horses. It was that latter touch that inspired Mustangers to call this option the "pony interior." The work of designer Damon Woods, the pony interior cost $107.08 in 1965. The tab for the GT deal was $165.03.

Front disc brakes were included in the GT package or could've been added separately at a cost of $56.77. Attractive styled-steel wheels fit the GT image to a T—that is as long as a buyer had an extra $119.71 to spend on them. Done in dazzling chrome, these coveted 14-inch five-spoke rims were only available for V8 models. Various stylish wheel cover options mimicked wire wheels or incorporated spinners like competition-type knock-off rims or both. Basic spinner covers and their wired counterparts cost $17.82 and $44.83, respectively.

A full-length console, priced at $50.41, could've been added inside between the Mustang's standard bucket seats. Another shorter console costing $31.52 was also offered for air-conditioned cars—remember, the 1964–1966 optional air conditioner bolted up beneath the dashboard, filling the space otherwise occupied by the typical console's storage compartment. Preferred interior enhancements also included a $31.52 deluxe steering wheel with faux wood rim (included in the pony interior deal) and the $69.30 Rally Pac, a combination clock/tachometer unit that attached to the steering column.

The Rally Pac's tachometer read up to 8,000 rpm when ordered along with the 271-horsepower Hi-Po V8, but maxed out at 6,000 revs in all other applications. And two different Rally Pac styles appeared: one for the standard Mustang's Falcon-based dash, another for the GT/Interior Decor's five-dial instrumentation. The latter unit was of special low-profile design to allow an unobstructed view of the five-dial dash's round, centrally located speedometer. Basic Mustang instrumentation featured a speedometer that typically ran from left to right in a wide rectangular layout.

Various lesser baubles also helped enhance an early Mustang's asking price: backup lights, tinted glass, power operation for a convertible's soft top, even a standard full-width front seat with center armrest. Boosting that bottom lineup around $3,500 was no problem as long as the ink in your pen held out—checking off options easily qualified as a day's work 40 years ago.

Listed on the options list in April 1964, the High Performance 289 V8 didn't become available until June that year. Output for the "Hi-Po" 289 was 271 horsepower.

Base price for a Mustang convertible in 1966 was $2,652.86. Total droptop production that year was 72,119. Springtime Yellow is the color appearing here.

gained more muscle each year during the 1980s, and the 5.0-liter legacy truly emerged after carburetors were replaced by electronic fuel injection in 1987. The redesigned 1994 Mustang GT retained the popular 5.0-liter V8, but this veteran pushrod mill finally was retired the following year, replaced in 1996 by Ford's 4.6-liter overhead-cam V8.

Back in August 1964, the Mustang's optional V8 choices changed, along with its standard power source, as the 260 small-block was replaced by a 289 two-barrel Windsor rated at 200 horsepower. The optional 289 four-barrel V8 also was boosted up to 225 horsepower, thanks to more compression, after the traditional 12-month production run began for 1965. The presence of a 260 V8 is yet another quick clue to a 1964-1/2 Mustang's identity.

Only minor trim updates announced the arrival of the 1966 Mustang, with the most noticeable being a revised grille fitted with a "fully floating" running-horse centerpiece, sans the chromed crossbars seen on 1965 models. No worries, though. Not fixing something that obviously wasn't broken proved to be the right move. After rolling out 559,451 Mustangs during that

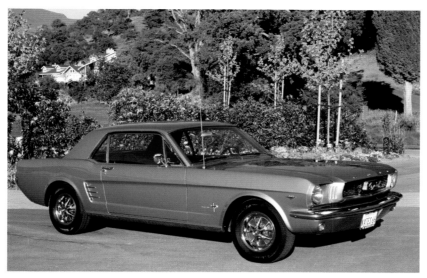

The simulated louver trim on each rear-quarter panel (directly behind the doors) was revised with three horizontal bars for 1966.

A restyled grille represented one of the easiest ways to differentiate a 1966 Mustang (shown here) from its 1964–1965 forerunner. Notice the optional wire wheel covers.

Sixteen exterior shades were available for the Mustang coupe, convertible, and fastback in 1966. Total coupe production that year was 499,751.

first 18-month production run, Ford produced another 607,568 nearly identical pony cars for 1966, a record for the breed that still stands.

And it always will. Just as all of us will never be young again, there is no way we will ever see another Mustang like the first.

GALLERY

CHAPTER TWO

Shelby Mustangs, 1965–1970

What goes around apparently does come around. In August 2003, Ford officials proudly announced they were back in business with an old friend. Carroll Shelby, the racing legend from Texas who, more than any other contributing player, defined Dearborn's Total Performance reputation during the 1960s, would once again help Fords go fast.

"It would be an understatement to say that Shelby Fords from the 1960s are coveted classic automobiles," said Advanced Product Creation Vice President Chris Theodore while introducing the new deal between Ford Motor Company and the man he called "a legend in the field of performance automotive products."

SNEAKY SNAKES

"Our [latest] partnership with Carroll and his team will create modern-day, world-class performance products that are as potent and coveted as the Shelby Fords from 40 years ago."

"Throughout my career, I have had the privilege of working with several manufacturers in the development of some great

PAGES 64–65: The familiar "Cobra" logo appeared in the center of the GT 350's steering wheel in 1969. Full instrumentation also was standard.

All GT 350s were 2+2 fastbacks finished in Wimbledon White. The Guardsman Blue racing stripes were optional, as were the five-spoke Cragar wheels seen here. Silver-painted 15-inch stamped-steel rims were standard. Notice the cutout exhaust exiting directly in front of the rear wheel.

automobiles," added Shelby, who turned 80 in 2003. "But my energy and passion for performance products has always been strongest when it involved vehicles from Ford Motor Company. I couldn't be more proud than I am today to have the opportunity to re-create history with the only automotive company that holds the key to my heart."

Shelby's involvement with Detroit's original pony car dates back to late 1964 when Lee Iacocca came to him with a simple request. Founded in June 1962, Carroll Shelby's company, Shelby American, first concentrated on making its Ford-powered Cobras race-winners here and abroad. Iacocca now wanted to see his newborn Mustang muscled up into a real racehorse, a hot-to-trot street car that, like Chevrolet's strongest Corvettes, also could become a Sports Car Club of America champion with minimal fuss or muss. Shelby obliged even though, as he later admitted, he "wasn't real high on the project," primarily for two reasons: he didn't think he "could make a decent car out of the Mustang" and he preferred creating all-out racing machines by the handful, not street-legal hot rods by the hundreds.

"That was the real idea—to go racing," said Shelby in a 1971 *Sports Cars of the World* interview. "I never wanted to build a lot of automobiles to make a lot of money. At the time my intention was to build 100 [Mustangs] a year, because that was what you had to build in order to race."

But Iacocca wanted more than that, and what he wanted he usually got. He also was Shelby's best friend in Dearborn; turning him down would've more or less represented a bite on the hand that had been feeding his racing fix from the outset. "It was Lee Iacocca who really stayed behind us all the way, encouraged us and then he got us into the Mustang program," Shelby added.

So Shelby found himself turning out GT 350s for customers who may or may not have planned to enter them in SCCA B/Production competition. Shelby production began in October 1964, with the official public debut following on January 27, 1965, to the utter joy of Walter Mitty types left disappointed by the relatively tame pony car introduced the previous April. "The GT 350 is all that most of us wanted the original Mustang to be in the first place," exclaimed *Car Life* magazine's Jim Wright, who echoed the thoughts of some Mustang watchers who had expected to see Ford introduce a true American sports car. Shelby himself later called his original GT 350 "a no-compromise car built to get the job done."

That job started in 1965 after Ford began delivering bare-bones fastbacks from its San Jose plant south to Shelby American's original shop in Venice, California. From there, according to *Motor Trend*, the recipe was simple enough: "take a 2+2, inject some Cobra venom, tone up the leg muscles [and] add lightness." *Add* lightness? Shelby truly was a magician. Seriously, though, what he did was eliminate nearly 200 pounds by, among other things, removing the backseat and replacing Ford's stock steel hood with a scooped fiberglass unit. Rear seating had to go anyway because SCCA B/Production specifications demanded that the car be a two-seater.

Production of 1965 Shelby GT 350s began in October 1964. The model was introduced in January 1965.

Fitted at the San Jose plant, the brake system incorporated big-car discs in front, Fairlane station wagon drums in back. Already included as well in the Mustangs delivered to Shelby American were aluminum-case Borg-Warner T-10 close-ratio four-speed manual transmissions and big, burly nine-inch rear ends incorporating gnarly Detroit Locker differentials. All Shelby GT 350s also began life in San Jose with white exteriors and black interiors. Remaining equipment was installed at Shelby American, as was the name.

"We were going to call [our] Mustang a 'GT-something,'" recalled Shelby in a 1995 *Mustang & Fords* magazine interview. "[But] I couldn't think of what [exactly] to call it. Ford sent about 15 people out trying to decide what to name it. I finally got upset one day and said, 'How far is it over there to that building where we're assembling the Cobra?' They looked at me like I was silly, then one of the guys walked over there and said, '349 paces.' I said, 'Good, we'll call it the GT 350. Get on an airplane, get back to Detroit, and do some work.'"

Venom came from a High Performance 289 V8 treated to various Cobra-style upgrades. Feeding this savage snake was a 715-cfm Holley four-barrel on an aluminum intake. "Tri-Y" headers brought up the exhaust end, and behind those converging tubes were glass-packed mufflers that bellowed through short, race-car-style cutout tailpipes exiting directly in front of each rear

A full exhaust system was added in place of the competition-style cutouts in 1966, and stylish rear-quarter glass appeared as well. Color choices also expanded to five that year: Wimbledon White, Guardsman Blue, Candy Apple Red, Ivy Green, and Raven Black. The optional stripes were Guardsman Blue on a white model, white on the other four.

wheel. Cast-aluminum "Cobra" valve covers and a matching-style oversized oil pan completed the package. Shelby's dyno-tested output rating for this warmed-over Windsor was 306 horsepower.

Toning up those leg muscles involved adding a thicker one-inch sway bar up front, override traction bars, and suspension-travel-limiting cables in back, and Koni adjustable shock absorbers at all four corners. Handling was enhanced further by lowering the upper A-arms' mounting points by an inch, a modification that in turn required special Pitman and idler arms. A one-piece export brace (in place of the stock two-piece setup) also was incorporated to guarantee suspension geometry precision by tying the shock towers together more rigidly. A "Monte Carlo" bar tightened things up even further, spanning the gap between shock towers across the engine, thus triangulating underhood bracing.

Blue rocker panel stripes, incorporating appropriate "G.T. 350" identification, were added at Shelby American. Standard wheels were 15x5.5-inch station wagon rims wearing 7.75x15 Goodyear Blue Dot rubber. Snazzy 15x6 five-spoke Shelby wheels, supplied by Cragar, were available at extra cost, as were Guardsman Blue LeMans racing stripes that ran from nose to tail.

Taking on the GT 350 assignment forced Shelby American to trade its original home in Venice, California, for roomier digs adjacent to the Los Angeles International Airport in March 1965. Counting the first street-going prototype, Shelby American built 561 GT 350s that year. That figure originally was listed as 562 before research in 1994 determined that one of those cars,

Various changes were made to the 1966 GT 350, shown here, to make it more civilized and thus widen its scope.

TALL TEXAN: CARROLL SHELBY

Who knows what might have become of Ford's high-performance reputation during the '60s had Carroll Shelby made it big in chicken ranching. Born January 11, 1923, in Leesburg, Texas, Shelby decided to try his hand raising poultry in 1949 but soon fell into bankruptcy after disease wiped out his winged inventory. A friend then suggested an avocation that almost immediately demonstrated his true talents. It turned out Shelby was a natural behind the wheel of a race car.

His earliest amateur hot-shoe experiences came on local dragstrips early in 1952. Next he borrowed a friend's MG and won his first road race in Norman, Oklahoma. Additional successes on this country's fledgling Sports Car Club of America championship circuit soon attracted the attention of both sponsors and big-time race teams, and at the same time he made a name for himself with his "meat-and-potatoes" manner.

In August 1953, in a hurry to get to work, he took to a track in the striped bib overalls he always wore while wrenching on his cars. Early guffaws then were traded for reverence after that garb became a trademark for one of the world's top sports car drivers. Later, a 1966 magazine ad for Shelby's Ford-powered hot rods proclaimed, "It's [sic] been a long time since bib overalls." The man behind those machines was shown confidently standing in a suit and tie next to a GT 350. Meanwhile, line art below this photo depicted his old work wear hanging by its suspenders from a hat tree, along with his familiar Stetson, another Shelby standard.

Carroll Shelby stuck steadfastly with his overalls even after making it big-time on the international racing stage. His break came in January 1954 when Aston Martin competition team manager John Wyer invited him to drive one of his DB3S roadsters. He made his first appearance at Le Mans that June, then helped Aston Martin earn 24-Hour laurels in France five years later. In between, he copped back-to-back Sports Car Club of America championships in 1956–1957 and was named *Sports Illustrated*'s "Driver of the Year" for 1957. He also earned "Sportscar Driver of the Year" honors from *The New York Times* in 1957 and 1958 and copped his final driving championship, in United States Auto Club terms, two years later.

Shelby took to the Formula One circuit in 1958 but encountered comparatively meager Grand Prix success before his career abruptly came to a close. Major chest pains first experienced in February 1960 disclosed a congenital heart defect that ruled out any further on-track adventures. His last race was a GP event held in Los Angeles in December 1960. He finished fifth in his "Birdcage" Maserati Tipo 61.

With his driving days done, Shelby found more time to concentrate on business. He had opened Carroll Shelby Sports Cars in Dallas early in 1957, but selling someone else's products wasn't exactly what he had in mind. He was running a high-performance driving school and distributing Goodyear racing tires in 1961 when he contacted the AC Cars firm in England about the possibility of using its tiny Ace roadster as a foundation for an American-powered road rocket he wanted to bring to market on this side of the Atlantic. AC responded positively in October that year and the rest is history.

That same month he made a deal with Ford to supply him with new Windsor small-block V8s. As for naming his V8-equipped AC Ace, a suitable tag reportedly came to Shelby in a dream: "Cobra." A proto-

type Ford-powered Cobra was hastily cobbled together in February, and the man with a plan then opened his Shelby-American firm the following month in Venice, California.

The aluminum British body fit Ford's 260-cubic-inch V8 like a glove—a boxing glove, that is. Shelby-American's 260 Cobra packed a punch like nothing seen before from a U.S.-based manufacturer. Then Shelby replaced the 260 with a notably hotter 289-cube small-block, followed by the completely outrageous 427-cubic-inch FE-series big-block. High-performance legends loom no larger than Shelby's 425-horsepower 427 S/C Cobra, easily the meanest, nastiest "production" vehicle ever to set rubber on American pavement.

Shelby-American teamed up again with Ford in 1965 to market truly wild pony cars, inspiring more than one witness to marvel at how quickly Shelby's latest career had taken off. "Fast-moving

ABOVE: Shelby American built the 1965 GT 350 in a shop adjacent to the Los Angeles International Airport.
OPPOSITE, TOP: Shelby Mustang production moved east to Detroit for the 1968 model .
OPPOSITE, BOTTOM LEFT: A cowboy hat was Texan Carroll Shelby's trademark, as were bib overalls early on during his racing career.
OPPOSITE, BOTTOM RIGHT: Shelby got back into the Mustang-building business with the GT500 in 2007.

Carroll Shelby does things at such a pace, by the time the news is in print, it's ancient history," explained a May 1965 *Car Life* report. "And the news recently has been important enough to make him America's fifth largest auto producer. The Texan's successful mid-wifery to all sorts of Ford-powered performers since his original Cobra has resulted in elevation to almost division-within-a-division status at Ford, a sort of Bureau of Racing for Dearborn. [His] projects have multiplied to such an extent, [the] three-year-old Shelby-American firm has had to move into the big hangars at Los Angeles International Airport."

At LAX, Shelby not only built GT 350s and venomous 427 Cobras, he also took Ford's GT-40 race car in after early results with this expensive, British-built racer left Henry Ford II disappointed to say the least. One year later, Ford's 427-powered GT-40 became the first American entry to win the 24 Hours of Le Mans.

Unfortunately, Henry II lost all enthusiasm for racing not long after-ward. Ford undid its competition ties with Shelby in February 1970, leaving Carroll to concentrate on his chili recipe, which he had begun marketing in August 1969. He was back working with the father of the Mustang in October 1982 after Lee Iacocca's move to Chrysler, and five years later began contributing to the Viper's development. Shelby drove the Viper prototype that paced the Indianapolis 500 in May 1991.

He began marketing his Shelby Series 1 sports car in 1997, and then hooked up with Ford again to help roll out the Ford GT sports car, introduced in 2005. He began marketing the Ford Shelby GT500 in 2007—talk about your circle of life.

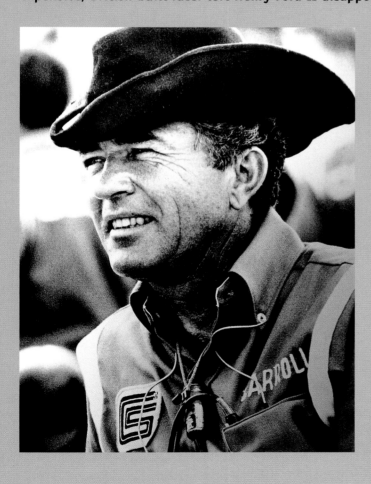

though planned, was never built. This missing model initially was slated to be part of a special run of "R-models," with that 'R' standing for one thing: racing.

Shelby American actually began building two types of race-ready Mustangs in 1965, those R-model road racers and nine other GT 350s set up specifically for the dragstrip. Four more of these drag cars were built in 1966. GT 350R production in 1965 was 36, counting two prototypes. Even more rude and crude than a garden-variety GT 350, an R-model was delivered from San Jose truly stripped: no headliner, carpeting, or upholstery. No sound deadener or insulation. No side glass or rear windows. And no gas tank.

Spartan GT 350R interiors featured one bucket seat, a four-point roll cage, sheet aluminum inner door panels, and a fiberglass shelf in place of the backseat. A six-gauge instrument panel replaced stock instrumentation, and the Mustang dashpad was deep-sixed, too. Plexiglass side windows in aluminum frames (without cranking mechanisms) went into the doors, helping drop about 25 pounds of unwanted weight. Another 20 pounds went away after the stock rear window was traded for more plexiglass.

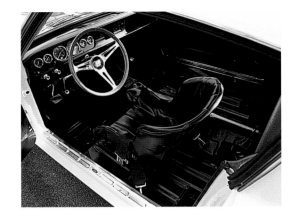

The 1965 GT 350R's interior was spartan to say the least: one bucket seat, aluminum door panels, and a fiberglass shelf panel in the space commonly occupied by a backseat in stock Mustang applications.

The stock gas tank was replaced by a special 34-gallon fuel container created by joining two bottom halves from standard 16-gallon Mustang tanks. Inside went baffles to prevent sloshing; on top went a three-inch snap-open filler (surrounded by a large "splash cone") to expedite fuel loading during pit stops. Joining the tank in the trunk of a GT 350R was the battery and an electric fuel pump.

Additional modifications included covering the rear quarter roof vents and fuel filler in back with aluminum panels. Wheel openings also were re-radiused and flared to supply ample clearance for a set of wide 15x7 American Racing five-spoke mags shod in Goodyear racing rubber. A special fiberglass apron was added up front, and bumpers were left off at both ends. Behind that apron's central opening was a large three-core Galaxie-based radiator and external oil cooler.

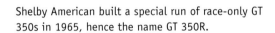

Shelby American built a special run of race-only GT 350s in 1965, hence the name GT 350R.

Powering the GT 350R was a specially prepared High Performance 289. All assemblies were balanced and blueprinted, the ported/polished heads and manifold were port matched, and the whole works reassembled to precise specs. Dyno tests showed from 325 to 360 horsepower. The price for the entire package was a hefty $5,995.

On the track, the GT 350R quickly proved its worth, with Shelby American driver Ken Miles piloting one to victory in its first SCCA outing in Texas on Valentine's Day 1965. Shelby GT 350s copped the B/Production championship that year, followed by two more SCCA titles in 1966 and 1967. As for the "standard" 1965 GT 350, it was, in *Road & Track*'s words, "pretty much a brute of a car." *Hot Rod* reported a 0–60 time of 5.7 seconds for a rough rider that was hard on both the ears and the seat of the pants.

But was it too rough? Demand for a two-seat, thinly disguised racer was limited, and a production run of barely 500 cars, each requiring extensive and expensive modifications, clearly wasn't supplying Ford with the exposure Dearborn officials were hoping for, at least not on the street. Thus, Shelby was directed to widen the GT 350's appeal, aiming it more at drivers who took their hot cars a little less seriously.

Dilution of Shelby's original ideal, per Dearborn's direction, began right away as the 1966 GT 350 emerged in kinder, gentler form. For starters, the second edition featured a backseat. An optional C4 automatic transmission appeared too for those who preferred resting their right arms, and color choices expanded from one to five, with Wimbledon White joined by blue, red, green, and black.

More attention was also given to exclusive imagery in 1966 as rear-quarter windows and body side scoops appeared. Among customer complaints in 1965 was the fact that this $4,500

A 34-gallon gas tank (top), complete with a competition-style fuel filler, went into the GT 350R's trunk. Dynamometer tests of the model's 289-cubic-inch V8 put output between 325 and 360 horsepower.

race car didn't look like much more than a stock Mustang. Along with being fully functional—the glass aided rear visibility and the scoops cooled the rear brakes—these additions clearly set a 1966 Shelby apart from a typical, mild-mannered pony car.

Save for substituting full exhausts for 1965's loud cutouts, the GT 350's power source carried over into 1966 unchanged. Underneath, however, things were quite different as costs were cut and harshness was lessened. Lowering the front suspension's upper A-arms was discontinued and those rear over-ride torque control arms were traded for simpler under-ride traction bars. Stiff Koni shocks and that noisy Detroit Locker remained part of the deal but only if a customer paid extra for them. They were no longer standard.

These changes actually were made in "running" fashion in 1966. The first 252 GT 350s sold as 1966 models were 1965 leftovers still fitted with many of the previous year's features. Unadorned 15-inch wheels remained standard for those 252 cars, as did the Koni shocks before they became a dealer-installed option. Beginning with GT 350 number 253, 14-inch five-spoke Magnum 500 rims became standard and new 14-inch aluminum-alloy 10-spoke wheels were optional. These Cragar-supplied 15-inch five-spokers remained optional for the early leftover models.

Not all 1966 GT 350s had backseats, either. As many as 82 of the 1965 leftovers reportedly were shipped to Shelby American as two-seaters, with some apparently fitted with rear seats as dealer options. The 1965 model's override traction arms, with their welded-on brackets, remained in place too until the supply evaporated, apparently after about 800 1966 GT 350s were completed. Traction-Master bolt-on traction bars were the norm from then on.

An optional Paxton supercharger appeared in 1966 to reportedly boost output by 46 percent. According to a *Motor Trend* test, a blown GT 350 could do the quarter-mile in 14 seconds flat. Shelby American also introduced a GT 350 convertible in 1966, although all six either stayed with Shelby or were given as gifts to valued friends. Each painted a different color— yellow, green, blue, red, white, and pink—these topless models were the last six GT 350s off the line that year. Five of the six featured automatic transmissions and all had under-dash air conditioners. Their rear quarter scoops also didn't deliver any cooling air to the rear brakes because the top mechanism precluded the installation of the internal ductwork.

A much more socially acceptable automobile overall, the 1966 GT 350 attracted nearly 2,400 customers, including the Hertz Rent-A-Car company, whose employees were already putting some of their most preferred customers into Corvettes when Shelby American General Manager Peyton Cramer approached them late in 1965 with a proposition: why not add 100 or so Shelby Mustangs to their rental catalog, too?

Hertz officials liked the idea and requested delivery of a prototype on October 26, 1965. The Shelby American crew took a Wimbledon White GT 350, repainted it black with gold striping, and added an "H" to the name. A second "GT 350H" prototype was requested in November, and Hertz ordered 100 cars shortly afterward. When the dealing was finally done, another 902 Hertz Shelbys were created for 1966.

As much as 80 percent of that run was painted gold on black, but perhaps as many as 200 GT 350H models featured typical Mustang colors. It was long believed that all GT 350H Mustangs had steel hoods in place of the fiberglass lids used on earlier Shelbys. Not so: only a few were built using an all-steel bonnet. Most accounts have said too that Magnum 500 wheels appeared in all cases. Again not true: some had Cragar mags. And while most GT 350Hs had automatic transmissions, some were also delivered to Hertz with four-speeds. Like all 1966 Shelby Mustangs, the Hertz cars were fitted with a 595-cfm Autolite four-barrel carburetor when equipped with an automatic transmission. Four-speed models stuck with the proven 715-cfm Holley four-barrel.

Most of the 1,002 GT 350H models created for Hertz Rental Cars in 1966 were black with gold accents.

MIDDLE AND ABOVE: Typical Mustang colors, like the traditional Wimbledon White, also appeared on the 1966 GT 350H, as did Shelby American's optional Cragar wheels. Magnum 500 rims (shown here) were used in most cases. Some also featured stock steel hoods in place of Shelby's scooped fiberglass lid (bottom).

Color choices were new for all GT 350 Shelbys in 1966, Hertz-delivered or otherwise.

Most Hertz Shelbys in 1966 featured automatic transmissions and smaller four-barrel carburetors. The few manual transmission models retained the GT 350's big Holley four-barrel.

Renting the GT 350H Shelby to Hertz customers instantly created one problem: inexperienced drivers didn't get along well with the GT 350's metallic brakes, which worked best when hot. Complaints of excessive pedal pressure were common. The addition of a brake booster was tried on some, but not all cars. Instead, the only real solution ended up being a sticker applied to the dash that read, "This vehicle is equipped with competition brakes. Heavier than normal brake pedal pressure may be required."

Though Ford people surely were pleased about 1966's increased numbers, Carroll Shelby still saw only a downward slide. The original Shelby Mustang legacy rolled on from there into early 1970 before winding down, but its zenith came that first year as far as the main man behind the machine was concerned. "Big corporations tend to destroy the cars they create," said Shelby in an interview 20 years later, and from his perspective Ford Motor Company execs wasted little time starting their teardown.

"All of the corporate vultures jumped on the thing and that's when it started going to hell," he explained in 1971. "I'm not knocking Ford, because when you get into bed with a big company they're all the same. I started trying to get out of the deal in 1967 and it took me until 1970 to get production shut down. I asked Lee [Iacocca] all the time, you know, 'Let's knock this off.'"

Further design influences from back east came along, again to Shelby's dismay, in 1967 in the form of various fiberglass body parts. The third-edition Shelby was three inches longer than a typical 1967 Mustang, thanks to an extended fiberglass nose that incorporated a deeply recessed grille sporting twin driving lights. Those lights were mounted in two different positions, together in the middle or at opposite ends of the grille, depending on which state the car was originally delivered to. Statutes in some states required minimum distances between headlights, thus the reason for the variation.

Both a new valance panel below the grille and the stretched hood were also done in fiberglass. The panel incorporated a large cutout that both allowed cooling air an easy route into the

radiator and enhanced frontal impressions. The hood featured a wide scoop with twin inlets, and functional louvers were added on each side of the openings when optional air conditioning was ordered in 1967. Also functional were the restyled rear-quarter side scoops, which came in two pairs; lower scoops for brake cooling, upper for extracting bad interior air.

Rear impressions were equally bold thanks to the addition of Mercury Cougar sequential taillights and a fiberglass deck lid incorporating a large ducktail spoiler. Fiberglass quarter panel extensions formed the spoiler's end caps, while a pop-open gas cap and a valance with cutouts for chrome exhaust tips completed the look. Without a doubt, no one could ever mistake a 1967 Shelby for just another Mustang.

Beauty beneath the skin in 1967 included the Mustang's heavy-duty suspension with a thicker front stabilizer bar, adjustable Gabriel shock absorbers, and variable-rate front coils thrown in for good measure. The export brace was again added between the shock towers, but the Monte Carlo bar was eliminated. Fifteen-inch steel rims wearing Thunderbird mag-style full wheelcovers were standard. Optional on early 1967 Shelbys were 15x7-inch Kelsey-Hayes MagStar wheels. Cast-aluminum 10-spokers became an option later that year.

Hands down the biggest news for 1967 involved the introduction of the GT500, a big-block running mate for the small-block GT 350. The GT 350's 289 remained rated at 306 horsepower that year even though the Tri-Y headers were traded for Ford's cast-iron High Performance 289 exhaust manifolds. A standard oil pan also was used in place of the oversized Cobra unit seen in 1965 and 1966. Standard beneath the new GT500's hood was a 355-horsepower 428 FE-series

Extra fiberglass bodywork was added front and rear in 1967 to help enhance the Shelby's exclusivity. Also new that year was the GT500, powered by a 428-cubic-inch big-block V8.

Fog lamp location differed in the grille of the 1967 Shelby (foreground) depending on varying state laws that mandated a minimum distance between headlights.

V8 topped with twin Holley four-barrel carburetors, an engine that appeared intimidating but really wasn't. Undoubtedly more to Shelby's liking was the 427-horsepowered "Super Snake" prototype, which reportedly reached 170 mph during testing in Texas, an event that more or less stood as Shelby's last stand in the Mustang world. For then, that is.

From there his name carried on in figurehead form only as GT 350/500 production was transferred from California to the A.O. Smith plant in Livonia, Michigan, in 1968. Shelby American's LAX lease was up by then and Dearborn officials needed little excuse to bring the Shelby Mustang fully into the corporate fold. Although they did have another rationale—there were no high-quality fiberglass sources in the Los Angeles area, but there were in Canada, not far from Detroit.

Michigan-built models were officially renamed "Shelby Cobra GT 350" and "Shelby Cobra GT500," and the lineup was expanded in 1968 to include a new convertible, this one actually offered for sale to the public. Also new for 1968 was the optional 428 Cobra Jet big-block, which added "KR" (short for King of the Road) to the GT500's name (for more on the 428 CJ V8, see chapter 4). Styling changes were minor, with the most noticeable involving the substitution of

ABOVE: Shelby Mustang production moved from California to the Smith Plastics division of the A.O. Smith company in Livonia, Michigan, in 1968.

BELOW LEFT: A large Holley four-barrel carburetor fed the 428 Cobra Jet, which was fitted with cylinder heads borrowed from Ford's race-proven 427-cubic-inch V8.

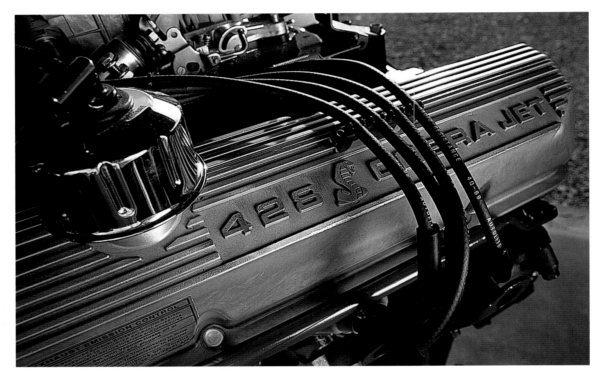

larger 1965 Thunderbird sequential taillights in place of the 1967 Cougar units installed the previous year. Federally mandated side marker lights also appeared in 1968.

Though officially rated at 20 horsepower less than the garden-variety GT500's dual-carb 428, the 335-horsepower 428 Cobra Jet easily outran its FE-series cousin. "It's big and strong and very highly tuned," claimed a *Car Life* review. "At 6,000 rpm, the Cobra Jet will pull a semi-trailer up Pikes Peak." GT500KR quarter-mile performance registered in the mid-14-second range, which was truly great news, especially considering that GT 350 standard power in 1968 dropped down to 250 horses, these supplied by Ford's 302 Windsor small-block.

The KR reference was dropped in 1969 because all GT500s featured Cobra Jet V8s that year. The GT 350, meanwhile, again traded engines; this time it was a 290-horsepower 351 Windsor. Housing either engine, 351 or 428, was an all-new fiberglass façade that both heightened exclusivity and predicted some of the frontal impressions to come for the 1971 Mustang. NACA ducts abounded on the 1969's glass hood; two up front that supplied cooling air into the engine compartment, two in back to let the hot air escape, and one in the middle for the engine's ram-air equipment. The fiberglass fenders incorporated brake-cooling ducts ahead of the front wheels, and another set of scoops allowed cooling breezes to blow on the rear brakes. Two different types of rear scoops were used depending on body style: fastback scoops were inset up high, convertible scoops protruded and were lower to avoid a conflict with the top mechanism.

A ducktail spoiler again brought up the similarly styled rear, as did 1965 Thunderbird taillights. New were the side-by-side aluminum exhaust outlets that exited through the center of the rear valance panel. Equally new five-spoke wheels were standard at the corners; no optional rims

ABOVE: Ford introduced the awesome 428 Cobra Jet V8, conservatively rated at 335 horsepower, in April 1968, and it immediately became the heart of the GT500KR. Those last two letters stood for "King of the Road."

OPPOSITE, TOP: A padded roll bar was standard for all Shelby convertibles in 1968. Production of GT500 convertibles that year was 402. The "KR" tag was dropped in 1969 after all GT500 models were converted to 428 Cobra Jet power.

Shelby built a handful of GT 350 convertibles in 1966 for friends of the company. The public finally got a chance to buy a topless Shelby in 1968.

ABOVE: A 428 Police Interceptor V8 topped by dual four-barrel carburetors was standard for base GT500 models in 1968. Though rated at 360 horsepower, this FE-series big-block was no match for its 335-horse Cobra Jet cousin.

A radically restyled nose, done in fiberglass, graced the 1969 Shelby, offered again in small-block GT 350 and big-block GT500 forms.

or wheelcovers were offered in 1969. Some early models, however, apparently were fitted with Magnum 500s after defects showed up in those five-spokes.

All that fiberglass helped make the final Shelby turn heads with ease, but not in the fashion originally envisioned by its creator. As *Car and Driver*'s Brock Yates explained, "The original Shelby GT 350 was a fire-breather, it would accelerate, brake and corner with a nimbleness only a Corvette could match. [But] the GT 350, 1969-style, is little more than a tough-looking Mustang Grande—a Thunderbird for Hell's Angels—certainly not the car of Carroll Shelby's dreams."

Shelby finally went to Ford Vice President John Naughton in the fall of 1969 and asked that the niche market Mustang bearing his name be discontinued. Not only was the car no longer the road rocket originally concocted, it also was competing with its own brethren, the Boss 302 and Boss 429 Mustangs. Naughton agreed, and the case was closed. But there still remained many models left in the pipeline. About 3,200 GT 350s and 500s were built for 1969 before the axe fell, and nearly 790 of these were still hanging around as the model year came to a close. The decision was then made to simply update these 1969 leftovers with chin spoilers,

black hood stripes, and 1970 serial numbers before the breed quietly rolled off into the sunset.

Features Editor Joe Scalzo was among the first to publish an obit in *Car Life*'s October 1969 issue. "The Shelby, most enthusiasts agreed, had been dead, or close to death, for years," he wrote. "Each year since its 1965 inception [it] had become more of a compromised car; and even by Shelby's own admission it had lost its identity as a Supercar. As the stylists heaped on more chrome, they at the same time removed more and more of the car's performance features. At the time of its death it had entered a never-never land where it had neither the luxury of, say, the Mustang Mach 1, nor the performance and handling of the Boss Mustangs." Ending the story then and there was only right. After all, last call for the two Boss Mustangs was also just around the corner.

Yates' opinion aside, many Ford fans still feel the Shelby Mustang story closed on a relatively high note. Carroll Shelby's opinions too have since softened, if only because the small-block originals and their big-block brothers have been put on such high pedestals by the Mustang faithful. Today, Shelby himself resides on an even higher perch, so why would he want to rain on anyone's parade by taking pot shots at the cars they love so dearly? Nearly 40 years later, Shelbys still impress with their sensuality and strength; in their heyday they were among the coolest cars on Main Street, U.S.A.

And, as they still say, image is everything.

ABOVE: Plans apparently were in place in 1968 to continue the Shelby Mustang legacy into the 1970s. Notice the 1969 Shelby behind this mock-up vehicle.

LEFT: Leftover Shelby Mustangs from 1969 were simply repackaged and sold as 1970 models. Twin black stripes were added to the hood, as was a chin spoiler below the bumper.

OPPOSITE, BOTTOM LEFT: Only 194 GT 350 convertibles were built for 1969.

OPPOSITE, BOTTOM RIGHT: 1970 Shelby GT500.

Chevrolet already had five widely differing model lines up and running when Ford rolled out its groundbreaking pony car in April 1964. The fifth Chevrolet, the mid-sized Chevelle, had debuted just months before, joining the Corvair, Chevy II/Nova, Corvette, and full-sized (Impala, Bel Air, Biscayne) group. As fate would have it, Chevrolet chief designer Irv Rybicki had proposed yet another model a few years before, an upscale Nova-based "personal coupe," a machine that mimicked much of the upcoming Mustang's makeup at a time when no one at General Motors even knew Dearborn's earth-shaker was in the works. But Chevy General Manager Bunkie Knudsen said no way, pointing out that the

MOVIN' ON UP

division simply didn't need one more line, certainly not with Chevelle development just getting underway.

Knudsen turned an about-face, of course, after the Mustang hit the road running in 1964, as did everyone else at GM.

PAGES 90-91: Ford introduced a patriotic spring Mustang in February 1972. Two different packages were offered, both featuring special red and blue accents on a bright white finish. The 15-inch Magnum 500 wheels seen here were included in one of the two deals.

Fortunately, for Chevrolet, design studio head Henry Haga already had various suitable sketches to show his boss when Knudsen received the directive from above in August: forget about the numbers, get a sixth car ready posthaste! Withering deadline pressure notwithstanding, Bunkie's people had their Mustang response finalized for public sale by the fall of 1966, as did John DeLorean's staff over at Pontiac.

Like DeLorean's new Firebird, Chevrolet's 1967 Camaro followed in the Mustang's hoof prints in nearly all aspects. Its hood was long, its rear deck short, and overall impressions were truly sporty. What set GM's copycat apart was its softly contoured shape, which instantly made Ford's original pony car look stiff and boxy in comparison. As for basic dimensions, the Mustang's new challenger was longer, lower, and wider, and predictably featured a little more passenger room inside. Last, but certainly not least, both Camaro and Firebird also incorporated ample space up front for optional big-block V8s, performance-conscious equipment that wouldn't fit between early Mustang fenders no matter what size shoehorn was used.

Such facts remained secret right up until the Camaro debuted in September 1966. Sure, the guys in Dearborn knew full well two years before that GM would come back at them with something new. They just had no idea what "new" would entail. In the meantime, they got busy preparing their response to GM's response with little clue as to what exactly they needed to do. That Ford had its own bigger, hopefully better, pony car ready for 1967, also with available big-block power, was almost as much blind luck as it was perfect planning. Then again, maybe not.

While Ford's chief engineer Tom Feaheny, product planner Ross Humphries, and the rest may not have had a clue as to what form GM's reply would take, they did discover some guiding

light coming from another Pontiac product, the big-engined GTO, introduced the same year as the Mustang. Big-block muscle cars became all the rage around Detroit after Pontiac showed the way, leaving Ford officials little choice but to jump on this fast-paced bandwagon or learn to like dust for dinner. From there the progression became plainly predictable: making more muscle meant more engine, and more engine meant making more Mustang.

But that wasn't all. According to Humphries, his boss, Hal Sperlich, wasn't about to let the Mustang team rest on their laurels, and in his mind the best way to "keep the momentum going" was to improve upon the original pony car in all facets. More brute force was only the beginning. Sperlich also wanted more braking, more handling, more comfort, more convenience, more quietness, and so on. Making more Mustang not only allowed the installation of big-block muscle, it also resulted in a more substantial platform as a whole, which in turn allowed designers and engineers to dial in, among other things, increased interior space, better ride characteristics, and much improved roadworthiness.

TOP: Final front-end appearances for the restyled 1967 Mustang were all but fully developed by December 1964.

ABOVE: The 1967 fastback was still taking shape in January 1965.

Work on this new and improved pony car began even as confetti still filled the air in the early summer of 1964. Lee Iacocca, who later bemoaned the path his baby took after 1966, kept daily watch over the project, which featured four main focuses. Primary was an overall refinement that concentrated especially on the aforementioned ride and handling improvements. Assisting greatly in that department was the revised front suspension layout—adapted from Ford's new-for-1966 mid-sized chassis—that represented the second area of attention. Predictably next on the list was the resizing and reinforcement required to handle all that planned big-block performance. The final point, and probably the most vexing, involved styling updates.

Designer Gail Halderman knew going in that his group faced the toughest task, and they all soon had the clay under their fingernails to prove it. As Light Car design exec Don Kopka explained before a Society of Automotive Engineers gathering in October 1966, "Our mission was to refine and improve the breed without losing any of the Mustang's personality and without any sheet metal changes that would destroy the strong identity established by the million-and-a-half Mustangs that were expected to be on the road before the 1967 model first saw the light of day." Countless proposals came and went, many of them thankfully, before Halderman's

THE FIELD FILLS OUT

Talk about running free. Prior to 1967, Ford's wildly popular Mustang had no rival, or at least nothing in Detroit that was capable of stealing its thunder. Sure, Plymouth's Barracuda was around, but just consider the numbers. The 60,000 Barracudas that made their splash in 1965 represented the high-water mark for this breed, offered from 1964 to 1974. By 1966, Ford was building that many Mustangs about every six weeks. Dearborn also established its own all-time pony car production standard that year, with the final tally reading an amazing 607,568.

Big Three responses finally began to arrive the following year. Chevrolet Chief Designer Irv Rybicki had proposed a small, sporty Chevy, a machine similar to Ford's original two-seat T-bird, early in 1962, but Division General Manager Bunkie Knudsen shot it down. Knudsen changed his mind two years later after Lee Iacocca and crew

"Banshee" dream machine. DeLorean continued promoting this sports car ideal after taking over the division's general manager post following Pete Estes' move over to Chevrolet in July 1965. Chevy's F-body was already in process by then, but Pontiac's tall, thin general manager would have nothing to do with it. He was still working on his beloved Banshee in February 1966. Then GM Executive Vice President Ed Cole took matters into his own hands.

In March 1966 Cole directed DeLorean to forget the Banshee and "make a car out of the Camaro." Pontiac's new Firebird debuted on February 23, 1967, and like the Camaro, it too was offered with optional big-block power. The hot-looking, hot-running Firebird 400 was more than capable of leaving a 390 Mustang in the dust.

And as if GM's new thoroughbreds weren't competition enough, Ford Motor Company introduced its own in-house copycat, a slightly longer, more prestigious pony car from Mercury called Cougar. Unlike its Mustang cousin, the Cougar was not available with six-cylinder power; eight cylinders made up the only way to fly for the machine *Motor Trend* called its "Car of the Year" in 1967. Both small- and big-

forced his hand. Chevrolet people were instructed to develop their own pony car in August 1964 and they responded with their F-body platform, which mimicked the Mustang in every way. Pete Estes, Knudsen's successor, introduced Chevrolet's all-new F-body, the Camaro, to the automotive press on September 12, 1966.

Estes called the 1967 Camaro a "four-passenger package of excitement." Like the Mustang, the new Camaro was meant to represent various different cars to various different drivers, a fact not missed by admiring journalists. "The problem is not whether to buy the Camaro," began a *Car Life* report, "but what kind of Camaro, for [this model] probably wears more faces than any other single car now made." The big-block SS 396, announced in November 1966, plainly showed off its meanest façade. Ford's first big-block pony car, the new-for-1967 390-powered GT, simply was no match for this muscle-bound Clydesdale.

Chevrolet also rolled out its legendary Z/28 Camaro a few weeks after the SS 396 to help stir a pony car buyer's blood even further. Nothing in the Mustang corral even came close to matching the Z/28 as far as open-road excitement was concerned, at least not until Dearborn's first Boss 302 arrived two years later. Suddenly it seemed the horseshoe was on the other hoof.

Pontiac made it a three-car race in the "Trans-Am pony car" field in 1969 by introducing its aptly named Trans Am Firebird. From 1969 to 1978 it was a big-block or no block at all beneath a Trans Am's hood, which was typically decked out in those so-called "screaming chicken" graphics. Before its cancellation in 2002, the feared and revered T/A was Detroit's only muscle car able to boast of an uninterrupted trip from the 1960s into the new millennium.

Pontiac's F-body Firebird story dated back to early 1963, when engineer John DeLorean first began toying with his two-seat

blocks were installed, including the rare 427 FE-series V8. A truly savage Cougar, the Eliminator, showed up in 1969 to run with Chevy's Z/28 and Ford's Boss 302 Mustang.

Two more Trans-Am pony cars arrived in 1970 after Chrysler unveiled its all-new E-body platform, home to Plymouth's latest, greatest Barracuda and Dodge's original Challenger. Hemi-powered E-bodies ranked among the meanest muscle cars of their day, but the best all-around performers were the SCCA-inspired Barracuda AAR and Challenger T/A, both built for 1970 only. Standard power in each case came from a 340-cubic-inch small-block V8 topped by three two-barrel carburetors.

Even once-stoic Kenosha-based American Motors entered the pony car race, introducing its new Javelin in the fall of 1967. A unique two-seater, AMC's AMX, followed in February 1968. Called "the hottest thing to ever come out of Wisconsin" by *Mechanix Illustrated*'s Tom McCahill, the truly small, definitely fast AMX was offered in original form up through 1970, then was marketed as a gussied-up Javelin beginning in 1971. American Motors' last Javelins were built in 1974, as were Chrysler's final E-bodies.

Though obviously challenging, all of these rivals still couldn't stop the Mustang in its tracks. Not even close. And when GM's F-body did finally retire in 2002, Ford's pony car stood tall as the lone survivor in its field. Dodge's Challenger did return for 2008, and a reborn Camaro waits in the wings as these words go to press. But both will have a long way to run to catch the car that started it all.

Chevrolet marked the Camaro's 30th birthday with a special anniversary model (left) in 1997. Also include above are, from left to right, 1969, 1968, and 1967 models.

team achieved the final product showcased before the SAE. "We think it is obviously Mustang, yet a definite improvement of the breed," added Kopka.

Most press critics agreed. "Detroit has cobbled up so many fine designs in the last twenty years that when Ford decided to change the Mustang, everybody held their breath," wrote *Hot Rod*'s Eric Dahlquist. "But it's okay people, everythin's gonna' be all right." "Anyone who likes the old Mustang ought to go nuts for the '67," added a *Car and Driver* review. "We think the styling is tougher than last year's. It's heftier, and more substantial looking."

Road & Track's staff, on the other hand, didn't think that being "substantial looking" was necessarily a good thing. "The [new] facelift has retained all the identifying characteristics of the first series but has fattened up the Mustang in all directions," read a March 1967 *R&T* report. "It still has that chunky look about it and, frankly, looks a bit old-fashioned beside its new competitors."

Save for wheelbase, which remained at 108 inches, nearly all dimensions went up in 1967. Overall length (183.6 inches) and width (70.9 inches) were stretched by 2 and 2.7 inches, respectively, overall height went up nearly an inch to 51.8, and the track increased 2 inches to 58 at both ends. As expected, interior and trunk space in turn grew along with the engine bay. All this growth meant more weight; about 85 extra pounds in the base six-cylinder coupe's case. At least that model still cost less than a dollar a pound.

Taking possession of Dearborn's first big-block Mustang required shelling out an extra $263.71 for the 320-horsepower 390-cubic-inch "Thunderbird Special V8," one of various FE-series engines offered by Ford that year. Born in 1958 at 332 and 352 cubic inches, the FE family included the 390, introduced in 1961, the 406 (1962), the famed 427 (1963), and the 428 (1966). The 390-cube FE was a passenger car option through 1971 and also appeared in 1968–1976 Ford trucks.

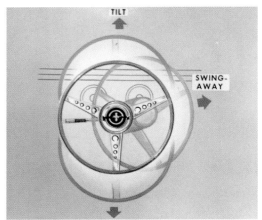

As for its debut between Mustang flanks in 1967, reviews were mixed as to whether or not bigger meant better in this case. According to *Car and Driver*, "The Mustang 390 GT is as hot as spit on a griddle." But most other magazines didn't agree. "Once regarded as a high-performance engine, the 390 must now be thought of as a mid-range powerplant," explained *Car Life* after experiencing the new big-block pony car. "It is, nowadays, a relatively slow-turning engine, limited at the top end by breathing restrictions, but reliable. It makes an admirable power source for the demands of sustained, power-assisted travel in an air-conditioned atmosphere tinctured by the outpourings of the stereotyped Ford Family of Fine Music—for such is the forte of the [390 GT] Mustang."

A tilt steering wheel was a new option for 1967. Pushing the turn signal lever forward allowed a driver to choose from nine different positions.

Well, at least an admirable big-block was better than no big-block at all. Much mightier FE-powered Mustangs would show up soon enough; in the meantime the bloodline had to start somewhere.

OPPOSITE, TOP: Designers enlarged various dimensions for the 1967 Mustang to offer more comfort and more convenience. More engine was also a consideration, and to that end the engine compartment was enlarged to accept the Mustang's first big-block V8.

RIGHT: Ford made big news when it rolled out its one millionth Mustang in February 1966. Fanfare was nowhere near as loud when the two millionth model appeared two years later.

ABOVE: The 1967 convertible's top was available in black or white. The vinyl top boot was color-keyed to the interior.

Ford's Southern California dealer network put together the Mustang GT California Special in 1968 using various Shelby touches. A six-cylinder was standard; all Mustang V8s were available at extra cost.

A luxury-conscious Mustang, the Grande, debuted in 1969 with special interior trim and deluxe interior appointments. This 1970 Grande appears with an optional vinyl roof.

Another Mustang makeover in 1969 added more heft to the body as width, length, and weight increased even further. Height dropped about a half-inch, and this decrease, coupled with that extra length, helped enhance overall sleek impressions. Especially aesthetically pleasing was the new "SportsRoof," which was a fastback by another name. SportsRoof accents included simulated rear-quarter air intakes and a ducktailed spoiler in back. Showing off this renamed, restyled body best in 1969 were three new high-profile models: Mach 1, Boss 302, and Boss 429. (For more on the two Boss Mustangs, see chapter 4).

A fourth new Mustang also debuted for 1969, the luxury-conscious Grande. Available as a hardtop only, the Grande featured special exterior trim and a deluxe interior with simulated wood accents. Underneath, voided rubber bushings were installed into the leading mounts of each leaf spring in back, with the goal being to better absorb road shock. A special insulation package with 55 pounds of extra sound deadening material was also installed to help make the Grande, in Eric Dahlquist's words, "as quiet as Jack Benny when the check comes to the table."

The 1969 Mach 1, on the other hand, looked like "a blend of dragster and Trans-Am sedan," according to *Car and Driver.* But don't be fooled; it arguably represented the best combinations of comfort, class, and performance Detroit had to offer 40 years back. Standard interior features included high-back bucket seats, a console with a floor shifter, a deluxe sport steering wheel, loads of simulated woodgrain appointments, and the Grande's sound insulation. On the outside went dual racing mirrors, distinctive striping, a pop-open gas cap, and a blacked-out hood with a non-functional scoop and competition-style tie-down pins. A Mach 1 also could have been jazzed up even further with three sporty options: the front chin spoiler, rear window slats, and a rear spoiler made most popular on the Boss 302.

Beneath that super-sweet icing was some seriously tasty cake. Also standard was the road-hugging GT handling suspension with four bright styled steel wheels shod in fat Wide Oval rubber at the corners. Dual exhausts and V8 power were standard as well—no wimpy six-cylinders would do. Though the base engine was a mild 351 Windsor fed by a frugal two-barrel carburetor, the options list included four stronger V8s, all topped by four-barrel carbs.

Kicking off the optional V8 lineup was the 290-horsepower 351 small-block. Next came the 320-horsepower 390-cubic-inch FE, followed by two 335-horse 428 Cobra Jet big-blocks; one with Ram Air, one without. Ford's new Ram Air equipment for 1969 featured the legendary "Shaker" scoop, which attached directly to the top of the air cleaner and protruded up through an opening in the hood. When the 428 CJ (see chapter 4) started shaking side to side, so did this black scoop, hence its name. As for function, a vacuum-controlled bypass flap inside the Shaker automatically opened wide whenever pedal met metal, allowing cooler, denser outside air to rush through the scoop into the hungry Holley's four throats below.

Calling the 1969 Cobra Jet Mach 1 "the quickest standard passenger car we've ever tested," *Car Life* magazine simply couldn't say enough about how this big-block pony car apparently redefined the breed. "Are you ready for the first great Mustang, one with performance to match its looks, handling to send imported-car fans home mumbling to themselves, and an interior as elegant, and livable, as a gentleman's club?" Quarter-mile performance was a sensational 13.86 seconds for this smokin' showboat.

Raves continued for Ford's greatest pony yet in 1970. "Even though the Boss 302 has to rank as the ultimate in Mustangs, the Mach 1 runs a close second," claimed a *Sports Car Graphic* report that year. "And for the difference in bucks and cop-attraction, you might want to take another look at the Mach 1." While the 250-horse 351 Windsor remained standard in 1970, the optional lineup changed slightly, with the old 390 FE dropped and a new 351 small-block added. Named, like the Mach 1's base V8, for its home—in this case Ford's engine plant in Cleveland, Ohio—that engine shared only its displacement with the existing 351 Windsor. A product of Ford engineers' efforts to create lighter, cleaner-running, more efficient V8s, the 351 Cleveland featured the free-breathing canted-valve cylinder heads first seen atop the Boss 302 V8 the year before. The Mustang's 351 Cleveland four-barrel V8 was advertised at 300 horsepower in 1970. Ford also offered a two-barrel version that year rated the same as the 351 Windsor, creating even more confusion for customers not in the know.

"Man, you've got to have a mind like a data processor to keep track of which engine is today's 'hot one,'" wrote *Sports Car Graphic*'s Paul Van Valkenburgh concerning Ford's 1970 engine roll call. "Call up E&F (Ford's Engine and Foundry) to ask how many different engine designs they've built recently and they'll say, 'You mean right now, or by quitting time?'"

All Cleveland small-blocks were considered performance engines, yet they used two-bolt main bearing caps instead of the preferred, more durable four-bolt caps normally designed into

McQUEEN'S WILD RIDE

Mustang fans still can't get enough of this famed car chase, easily one of the greatest in Hollywood history, if not *the* best from the days before computer-generated cheats began dominating modern filmmaking. For about 12 of the 113 minutes that make up Warner Brothers' 1968 crime drama, *Bullitt,* movie-watchers are sent screeching and squealing down, around, and even over the streets of San Francisco as Detective Frank Bullitt's Highland Green 1968 Mustang fastback flies off in pursuit of the bad guy in a sinister Dodge Charger. Cutting-edge (for its day) camera work makes you feel as if you're riding in the back seat—or nearly on the verge of being run over as the two cars speed past, at some points doing nearly 120 mph. When Lieutenant Bullitt's Mustang finally slides out of control into a ditch, shattered front spindle and all, it does so right into your lap.

More than one channel surfer nowadays probably clicks in just in time for those 12-odd minutes then cuts back in search of other golden oldies—*Vanishing Point,* perhaps? Some car-crazy movie nuts have nothing but those 700 or so seconds on pre-TiVo tape. Why not? Academy-award-winning editing, superior sound synchronization (also Oscar-nominated), sensational stunt driving, and a really cool explosion at the end—could it possibly get any better from a chick-flick-hating, red-blooded American male's perspective?

Released nationwide in December 1968, *Bullitt* starred Steve McQueen rather appropriately as the too-cool-for-school, turtleneck-wearing police detective on the trail of a government witness murderer. Other major players included Robert Vaughn, Norman Fell (Mr. Roper in television's *Three's Company*), and a really young Jacqueline Bisset. Don't forget Robert Duvall, who got a bit part as a cab driver.

Unforgettable performances also came from the two not-so-identical pony cars supplied by Ford for the film. While both Mustangs were powered by 390-cubic-inch V8s, one of the dark green fastbacks was a GT, the other wasn't, explaining perhaps why all external identification (including Ford references) and trim were removed from each vehicle. Eagle-eyed viewers, however, might notice the GT-style rear valance, with its twin exhaust cutouts, that shows up in some frames.

Noted California hot rodder Max Balchowski was tasked with making sure *Bullitt*'s four-wheeled stars were up to snuff, and he began by massaging the cylinder heads and tweaking the ignition and carburetors on both Mustangs' big-blocks. Front shock towers were reinforced to help stand the strain of all those sharp corners and, particularly, the airborne leaps planned for San Francisco's hilly pavement. Koni shock absorbers and Firestone tires were bolted on at the corners, as were four American Racing Torq-Thrust wheels. McQueen reportedly was fond of Italian Nardi steering wheels, so Ford's stock piece was traded for a customized wood-rimmed unit inside.

And as much as McQueen liked people to think that he did his own stunts, he shared that wooden wheel with professional stuntman Bud Ekins, a good friend who doubled for him during those sensational motorcycle jumps (over barbed wire) in 1963's *The Great Escape*. Veteran stunt driver Carey Lofton, hired to stage the classic *Bullitt* chase, did some driving during its filming, too. That scene alone required two weeks of camera work, amounting to one-sixth of the movie's complete filming schedule.

At scene's end, the Charger, piloted fearlessly up to that point by Bill Hickman—ranked by many at the time as Hollywood's most talented wheel man—was attached side-by-side to the Mustang via a special tow bar released by Lofton to career into a specially constructed, rigged-with-explosives roadside gas station. Though the driverless Dodge didn't mow down the gas pumps as planned, the station went up in a triggered fireball anyway, taking with it the killer wanted by Frank Bullitt. If you're quick with a freeze frame, you just might catch a glimpse of that towing apparatus protruding from the Mustang's side during these climactic frames.

And if you really want to get picky, you'll also probably count as many as eight hubcaps detaching from the Charger during the chase, the result of the many varied camera angles shot during the scene, coupled with Oscar-winning editor Frank Keller's willingness to make use of as much of that film as possible. A pesky VW Bug also keeps making encore appearances thanks to Keller's cuts, but who cares when the main action is so damned exciting?

Not to mention violent. Only one of the two movie cars is known today, probably because the Mustang that performed the jumps was damaged so severely it surely ended up in a crusher. Used for quieter, slower scenes, the second fastback was sold to an editing department man in much better condition following the film's completion. Various resells followed (McQueen himself reportedly tried and failed to buy it at one point in the 1970s), and at last check the car was in the hands of an owner who preferred to steer clear of the limelight. "No" has been his vehement response every time he has been contacted about either selling it or showing it off in public.

At least *Bullitt* fans found themselves treated to a nostalgic reminder just after the new millennium arrived. First unveiled in concept car form in Los Angeles in January 2000, a reborn Bullitt

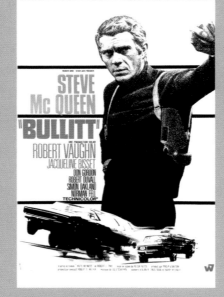

Mustang went on sale in April 2001. Heavy-duty suspension upgrades were again the norm, as were five more horses compared to that year's garden-variety GT. Helping release those extra ponies was a specially tuned exhaust system that emitted a rumble reminiscent of the growls that damn near earned *Bullitt* a second Academy Award in 1968. Retro-style instrumentation inside also helped take drivers back to 1968, as did the Bullitt Mustang's wheels—American Racing mags, what else?

Steve McQueen surely would've been proud.

A Highland Green Mustang fastback starred along with Steve McQueen in the Warner Brothers' 1968 crime drama, Bullitt.

high-revving, high-horsepower engines. Cylinder heads also varied between the two- and four-barrel variations. Two-barrel heads had small valves (2.04-inch intakes, 1.66-inch exhausts) and were of the "open-chamber" design. Four-barrel Cleveland heads featured wedge-shaped combustion chambers and larger valves (2.19-inch intakes, 1.71-inch exhausts).

Being an engine created with future considerations in mind, the 351 Cleveland had a future, something Ford's other high-performance engines couldn't claim as the 1970s opened for business—especially after Dearborn shut down its race shops. On November 20, 1970, Ford Motor Company sales group Vice President Matthew McLaughlin announced that Ford was pulling out of all motor-sport activities with the exception of limited support for drag racing and off-road competition. Dearborn's once mighty racing program was history. "The greatest peacetime non-governmental competitive effort to occur in this century has quietly drawn to a close—the victim of progress," wrote *Motor Trend*'s Jim Brokaw.

Another victim of those changing times was Bunkie Knudsen, who had jumped ship at GM and moved over to Dearborn early in 1968. Though he was only Ford Motor Company president for a scant 19 months, he managed to make a lifetime's worth of enemies there, including Lee Iacocca and Henry Ford II. After warning him more than once that he needed to change his aggressive ways, Henry II fired Knudsen in September 1969, to the delight of Iacocca, who seemingly disagreed with his archrival as often as he could.

Bunkie valued racing big-time and loved horsepower, and he apparently felt the Mustang needed to show off only one face, a strong one. Iacocca, however, recognized the handwriting was on the wall for the great American muscle car, with safety crusaders, insurance agents, and tailpipe sniffers supplying all the ink. Seemingly everyone in Detroit, except, apparently, Knudsen, knew the end of an era was awaiting them just around the corner as the 1960s wound down.

By then Henry Ford II had grown especially conscious of automotive safety and emissions issues. "In 1969, Henry II pledged the assets of the company to help whip the pollution problem," wrote Brokaw. "He wasn't fooling. Shortly after his speech, Ford announced the allocation of $18 million for the installation of anti-smoke equipment on the factories' smoke stacks. Two months later, the racing budget for 1970 was drastically reduced by about 75 percent."

Ten years before, Iacocca had begun pushing Ford to run with the youth market. But by 1970, that group had grown older and wiser, and Dearborn's sales-conscious marketing marvel was paying close

TOP LEFT: Conventional dual headlights reappeared for the Mustang in 1970. New that year was the Grabber SportsRoof, which featured reflective C-stripes. Technically limited to 1970 Boss Mustangs, the 15-inch Magnum 500 wheels seen here were added easily enough to any model.

ABOVE: Bunkie Knudsen wanted an even bigger Mustang for 1971 and he got it, much to the dismay of Lee Iacocca. Even more room was designed up front to make room for even more engine. Notice the resemblance to the 1966 Thunderbird in the top photo.

BELOW: Many press critics were quick to point out the uselessness of the 1971 SportsRoof's almost flat rear window.

The 429 Cobra Jet V8 superseded its 428 CJ forerunner in Ford's mid-sized muscle car ranks in 1970, then became a Mustang option in 1971 after Knudsen enlarged the pony car platform. Output for the 429 CJ in 1971 was 370 horsepower.

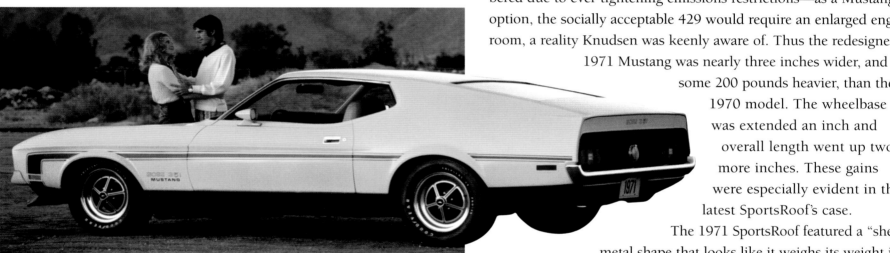

The Boss 351 was a one-hit wonder, built for 1971 only. Standard was the 351 High Output small-block V8, rated at 330 horsepower.

Three body styles remained available in 1971: the ever-present coupe (shown here), the sleek SportsRoof, and the sexy convertible.

attention to changing attitudes. Once completely behind Ford's Total Performance campaign, Iacocca no longer considered race cars a good investment. "It's no secret that Iacocca questions the value returned for each racing dollar [spent]," announced a January 1971 *Motor Trend* report. "It is also no secret that deposed former president Bunkie Knudsen was a staunch supporter of racing, and anything that was in to Bunkie is currently out."

Out as well were Bunkie's babies, the Boss 302 and Boss 429, both cancelled in 1970. Not all was lost, however. One last Boss Mustang remained, if only thanks to the Cleveland small-block's availability. Using a special 351 Cleveland V8, the 1971 Boss 351 (see chapter 4) was every bit as impressive as its two race-bred forerunners while offering more in the way of tractable street manners. But it lasted only one year.

One other last stand for Mustang performance came in 1971, this one courtesy of Bunkie Knudsen. In February 1968, Henry II's newly hired president had needed just one look at Gail Halderman's mock-up to give the go-ahead for a final expansion on Dearborn's pony car theme. No other candidates mattered; Knudsen had made up his mind. The next Mustang, planned for 1971, would be bigger and better—not to mention potentially faster—than ever.

While a perceived need to offer even more interior room did have something to do with the 1971 expansion, the main impetus came from Ford's new cleaner-running 385-series big-block V8, introduced in 1968. This 429-cubic-inch V8 was lighter than its FE predecessor, yet wider thanks to its canted-valve cylinder heads. To replace the Mustang's 428 Cobra Jet—its days numbered due to ever-tightening emissions restrictions—as a Mustang option, the socially acceptable 429 would require an enlarged engine room, a reality Knudsen was keenly aware of. Thus the redesigned 1971 Mustang was nearly three inches wider, and some 200 pounds heavier, than the 1970 model. The wheelbase was extended an inch and overall length went up two more inches. These gains were especially evident in the latest SportsRoof's case.

The 1971 SportsRoof featured a "sheet metal shape that looks like it weighs its weight in better ideas," according to *Sports Car Graphic*. "The new body gives one the feeling of being buried in a bunker. Gone is the light, airy feeling of lots of glass and a high seat with commanding view. We have returned to the bulbousity of the '49 Merc. The hood bulges into your line of sight from the force of thousands of pounds of pressure from styling, and the flat, miniscule rear backlite gives a beautiful view of the stars for two in the rear, but little else."

Sure, rearward visibility was exceptionally poor. But who needed to look back when that bulging hood in front was hiding the optional 429 Cobra Jet V8? Built only for 1971, this 370-horsepower Mustang represented Knudsen's lasting legacy and also stood tall as one of the quickest Fords ever built. (For more on the 1971 CJ Mustang, see chapter 4).

Both Grande and Mach 1 rolled over into 1971 and remained on the market until this platform retired two years later. Grande production figures demonstrated how much Mustang buyers grew to love the car's softer side, especially after its tougher persona started fading away. After building 22,182 Grande hardtops in 1969, Ford rolled out another 13,581 in 1970. The count then jumped up to 17,406 in 1971, 18,045 in 1972, and 25,274 in 1973. The last figure represents 19 percent of that year's total Mustang run, while those first 22,000 Grandes made up only 8.4 percent of 1969's complete tally. Clearly something had changed the way customers looked at Mustang—the death of the muscle car perhaps?

At least buyers still had the Mach 1 to play with after 1970, though the game was no longer as fun in standard trim. A 210-horsepewer 302 Windsor two-barrel V8 became the base engine in 1971; in Ford's words, "to broaden the Mach 1's potential market appeal." The two Cleveland small-blocks (two- and four-barrel) were optional, as was the awesome 429 Cobra Jet, with or without Ram Air. Included in the latter package was a blacked-out "Dual Ram Induction" hood that incorporated two functional scoops.

ABOVE: The quickest way to differentiate a 1972 Mustang (shown here) from a 1971 involved a quick peek in back, where tiny "Mustang" script appeared above the right taillight. Block lettering, running across the rear deck lid, was used the previous year.

RIGHT: The Mustang's grille didn't change for the first time in the car's history in 1972. Frontal appearances remained identical for the 1971 model (shown here) and its 1972 successor.

A small-block Cobra Jet based on the 351 Cleveland V8 appeared late in 1971. A cross between the four-barrel Cleveland and the Boss 351's HO small-block, the 351 Cobra Jet was rated at 280 horsepower.

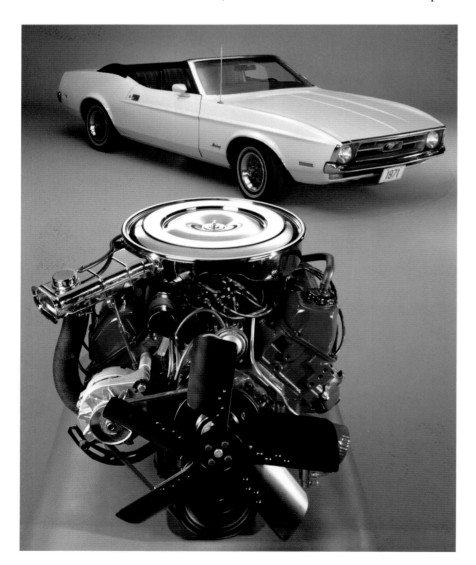

Ford promotional people erroneously called this a "NASA hood," undoubtedly because they figured more Americans would relate to the National Aeronautics and Space Administration than its predecessor, the National Advisory Committee for Aeronautics, known to test pilots and race car builders alike for the aptly named "NACA duct." This air inlet was specially designed to maximize flow in high-speed situations—like flying at the speed of sound. Once discovered by automobile racers, NACA ducts began showing up in all locations where brakes (and drivers) needed cooling and hoods needed scooping. NACA was forgotten by the time those two NACA-style scoops were added to the Mach 1 hood in 1971. On the flipside, practically every human on this planet, and certainly all those on the moon, knew what NASA was. Realizing this, Ford's label makers transformed the NACA scoop into the NASA scoop.

Such silly name-dropping aside, the twin NACA ducts on Ford's 1971 NASA hood funneled cooler air into a plastic housing underneath. This housing, in turn, was sealed to the air cleaner by a large rubber "doughnut." Vacuum-controlled diaphragms inside the plastic ductwork opened up at full throttle to allow denser outside atmosphere to flow directly to the air cleaner, which relied on a conventional snorkel to breathe in underhood air during normal operation. Dual Ram Induction was available at extra cost for the 1971 Mach 1's two optional Cleveland small-blocks.

A heavy-duty foundation with front and rear sway bars, now called the Competition Suspension, remained standard beneath the 1971 Mach 1. Also included were E70-14 tires for small-block models, F70 for the optional big-blocks. Truly fat F60-15 rubber was available at extra cost in all cases, and these tires required another option, the attractive 15x7-inch Magnum 500 wheels. Standard at the corners in 1971 were 14x7-inch rims dressed with flat center caps and deep-dish trim rings.

Appearance items included typical tape striping, a black honeycomb grille mounting a pair of rectangular "sportslamps" just inboard of each headlight, another black honeycomb panel in back, and a competition-style pop-open gas cap. While a conventional chromed bumper remained in back, the front unit was molded out of urethane and colored to match exterior paint. Twin racing mirrors also were color-keyed. The standard interior was typical Mustang in this case, but the upscale Mach 1 Sport Interior could've been added as an option.

A nearly identical Mach 1 Mustang returned for 1972. All standard equipment carried over, including the base 302 small-block, now net-rated at 141 horsepower. As in 1971, the NASA hood wasn't included atop the 302 unless specified as a no-cost option. It was added automatically along with the three optional Cleveland small-blocks, the 177-horse

351 two-barrel, the 351 Cobra Jet, and the top-dog 351 HO. The HO was a tame version of the 1971 Boss 351's exclusive Cleveland V8, also labeled a High Output small-block.

According to engineer Tom Morris of Ford's Special Engine Group, "the basic guts" of those two 351 HO small-blocks were the same, with different cylinder heads, pistons, and camshafts incorporated in 1972. The Boss 351's beefy short-block assembly carried over for the durable 1972 HO, and so did the aluminum dual-plane intake manifold, which sported a big Autolite four-barrel carburetor. Like its Boss forerunner, the 1972 HO's cam was a mechanical unit, but it was tamed considerably to work with less compression. Output was 275 horsepower.

The 351 Cobra Jet was another Cleveland small-block derived from the Boss 351's heart. Actually introduced very late in 1971, this little CJ mill represented, in *Popular Hot Rodding*'s words, "an attempt at 'cross-breeding' the standard Cleveland [four-barrel] and the truly high-performance Boss 351." Like the 1972 HO, the 351 CJ borrowed the Boss 351's burly cylinder block with its four-bolt main bearing caps. The crankshaft, however, was the same cast-iron unit bolted up by those two-bolt caps at the bottom end of a typical 351 Cleveland. And instead of the forged-aluminum pop-up pistons stuffed into the HO, the 351 CJ was filled with cast-aluminum flat-top slugs.

Cobra Jet cylinder heads were based on the two-barrel Cleveland's open-chamber design,

The popular Mach 1 returned for 1972 in similar fashion. A dual-scooped hood was still standard along with familiar graphics and black lower body accents. Trim rings and small hubcaps were again included in the package.

but used the 351 four-barrel's larger valves (2.19-inch on the intake, 1.71 on exhaust). The cam was a hydraulic grind. Ignition was supplied by a dual-point distributor that was basically a recalibrated version of the 351 HO unit. The Cobra Jet's dual-plane intake manifold also was similar to the one used by the Boss 351's HO small-block, but it was cast in iron instead of aluminum. This intake was topped by an Autolite four-barrel.

The 351 CJ was rated at 280 horsepower in 1971, 266 in 1972 due to a few minor changes. Apparently the Cobra Jet label was dropped from official references that year, probably to avoid any unwanted attention from those darned insurance agents. Advertised output for this hot small-block, called a Cobra Jet or not, dropped to 259 horsepower in 1973.

Curiously neither the Cobra Jet nor HO could've been topped by the optional Dual Ram Induction hood in 1972. That the NASA hood was no longer available for the Mach 1's top performance engines was a matter of meeting Washington's tougher emissions standards. Appar-

Thin-shell high-back bucket seats were standard for the 1972 Mustang convertible, as was a power-operated top. Curb weight was a healthy 3,210 pounds.

ently a Ram Air 351 four-barrel V8 couldn't be emissions-certified, while the tamer two-barrel could. The same situation existed in 1973, when 26.3 percent of the Mustang pie consisted of Mach 1s, a high for the proud breed. A 302 two-barrel was again standard, and two 351 Clevelands, the two-barrel and the four-barrel CJ survivor, were optional.

Ford continued marketing a Mach 1 during the Mustang II years, but it just wasn't the same. Many felt exactly the same about the Mustang in general after the first-generation run came to an end in 1973.

GALLERY

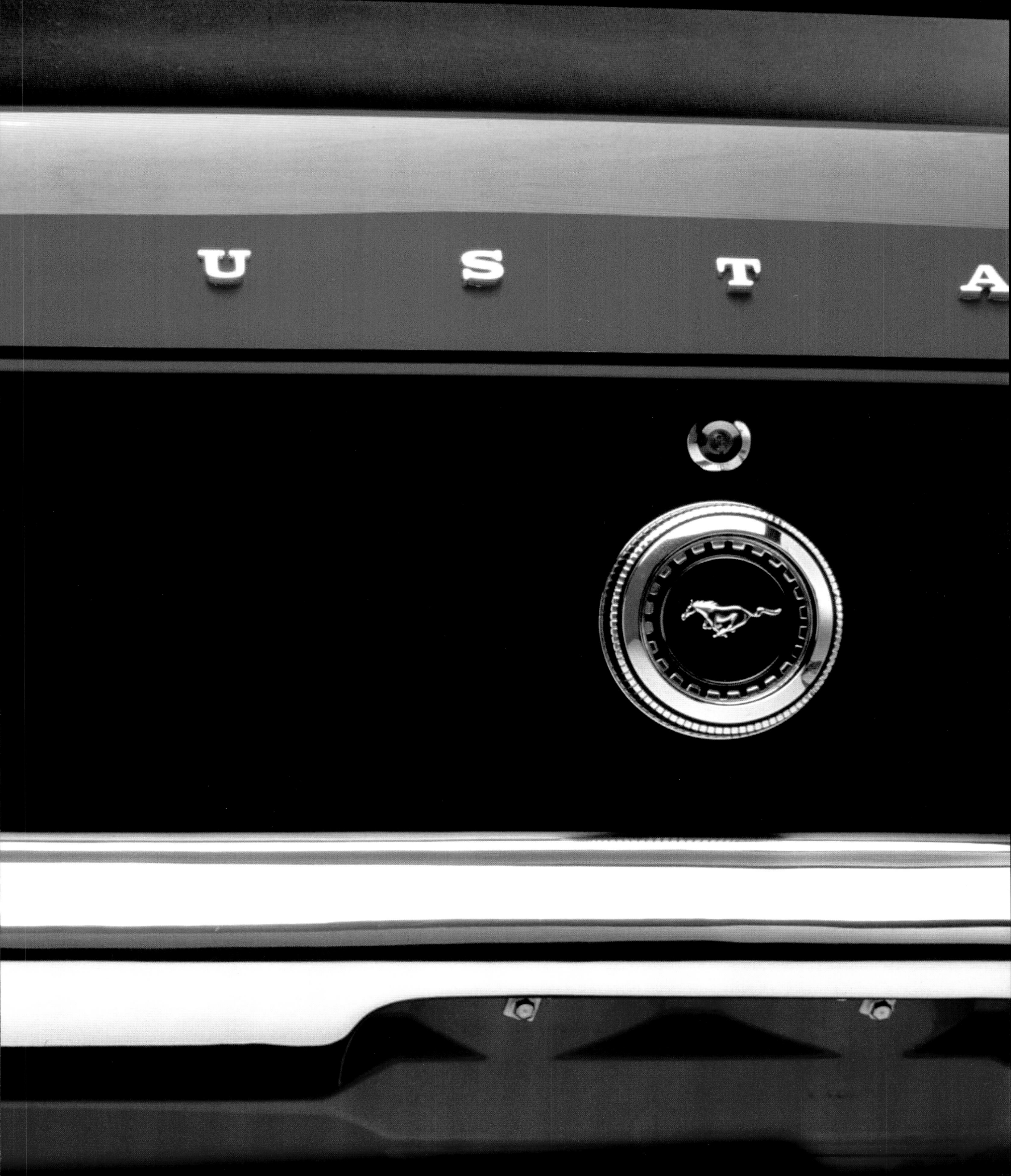
U S T A

Two memorable automotive breeds were born in Detroit in 1964: the pony car and the muscle car. Ford, of course, gets credit for conception of the former, General Motors the latter. Officially released in October 1963, Pontiac's original GTO, like the Mustang, appealed to both young buyers as well as those young at heart, but in this case a sporty image was always fully reinforced by real sportiness. The idea was so simple: stuff a lot of engine into not a lot of car and keep the price down where blossoming Baby Boomers could afford it. Though high-performance automobiles certainly were nothing new when the so-called "Goat" made the scene, this much horsepower had never before come so affordable, so practical,

RACE HORSES

and so easy to handle. And that reality represented reason enough to bestow milestone status on Pontiac's new-for-1964 muscle car.

Once this ground was broken, various other companies wasted little time following in Pontiac's tire tracks with similarly

PAGES 116–117: Ford's 271-horsepower High Perform-ance 289 small-block V8 was a Mustang option from 1964 to 1967. A chromed open-element air cleaner was part of the package.

This badge identified the hottest Mustang available up until the optional 390-cubic-inch big-block appeared in 1967.

Deluxe wheelcovers with simulated knock-off "spinners" were available at extra cost for the Mustang up through 1966. Shown here is the 1964–1965 style; the 1966 unit differed slightly between the six spokes.

muscled-up mid-sized machines. Oldsmobile introduced its 4-4-2 late in 1964 and Buick's Gran Sport and Chevrolet's Chevelle SS 396 appeared the following year. Soon everything from compacts to full-sized models were turning into "Supercars," a nickname used by the press early on. Slipping red-and-blue tights and a cape on a pony car was only natural considering its lightweight nature.

Obviously not all Mustangs were muscle cars. But some were, and some of these were far tougher than their buff brethren. The GT class, offered from 1965 to 1969, included many com-paratively mild-mannered characters, while the Boss 429 lineage, built in small numbers in 1969 and 1970, consisted of nothing but superhuman brutes. In Mustang terms, the muscle car era may have come to a close in 1971, but not before Ford's pony car had made its fair share of entries in Detroit's high-performance history books.

The Mustang's rise to power began just a few months after its introduction in April 1964. Ford's High Performance 289 V8 became a pony car option in June, and the "Hi-Po" Windsor small-block's 271 horses went a long way toward hauling off some of the slings and arrows left about after Dearborn didn't release a true sports car along the lines of the Mustang I two-seater. *Car Life* critics couldn't say enough about the Hi-Po's "obvious superiority" compared to the "more mundane everyday Mustang." They continued on to say, "Where the latter has a style and a flair of design that promises a road-hugging sort of performance, and then falls slightly short of this self-established goal, the HP Mustang backs up its looks in spades." A *Hot Rod* road test claimed a decent 0–60 run of 6.9 seconds.

The Hi-Po 289 was introduced as a 1963-1/2 option for Ford's mid-sized Fairlane, morph-ing it into what Ford promotional people called "the Cobra's cousin." "Tie this savage little winder to a four-speed floor shift, tuck it into Fairlane's no-fat body shell, and you've got a going-handling combo that's mighty hard to beat," went a 1964 ad pitch. Built up through 1965, Ford's 271-horse Fairlane never did attract anywhere near as much attention as its pony car counterpart did. The Hi-Po Mustang stood as Ford's wildest little horse up through 1966. Though it appeared one more time in 1967 it was overshadowed that year by the new 390 GT big-block model.

Identified with a "K" code in Ford's engine lineup, the High Performance 289 was carefully created from top to bottom with high-rpm operation in mind. Its block featured strengthened main bearing caps (fastened down by two bolts, not four) holding a nodular-iron crankshaft. Inside were cast-aluminum pistons tied to that crank by beefed-up rods, and an enlarged harmonic balancer went on up front to help the K-code 289 rev up as smoothly as possible.

Durable valvetrain pieces included stiffer dual valve springs; hardened pushrods, spring retainers, and keepers; and screw-in rocker studs. Among other rev-conscious components was a larger pulley for alternator-equipped Hi-Po 289s and a special, stronger fan that also featured increased pitch to maximize cooling capabilities. Like all 1964 Ford V8s, early K-code renditions used generators.

Supplying fuel and air was a 600-cfm Autolite four-barrel on a standard 289 cast-iron intake. The cam was a solid-lifter unit, the distributor was a dual-point type with mechanical advance. Dual exhausts sent spent gases on their way, and topping everything off was a chromed, low-restriction, open-element air cleaner.

Ford's Special Handling Package (quicker steering and stiffer springs, shocks, and sway bar) and "Red Band" tires were included in the Hi-Po deal. A manual transmission was the only choice behind the K-code 289 in 1964 and 1965. An available automatic transmission didn't appear for the Hi-Po application until 1966, when Ford's far-from-politically-correct ads proclaimed, "Here, at last, is a memorable high-performance machine that you're not afraid to let your wife drive to the supermarket!"

In 1965, the 271-horsepower 289 could've been combined with the new GT Equipment Group to create the highest of high-performance pony cars. Available for all three body styles, the GT package was only offered with one of the two optional four-barrel V8s, the Hi-Po 289, or its tamed 225-horse cousin. A $327.92 option in other Mustangs, the K-code V8 cost $276.34 when ordered with the GT equipment because the two packages shared the Special Handling upgrades. Front disc brakes also were included in the GT deal, as were low-restriction dual exhausts. As mentioned, all Hi-Po 289s featured duals, but the 225-horsepower 289 relied on a single tailpipe in non-GT applications.

At the ends of the GT's twin pipes were chromed trumpets protruding through chrome-trimmed cutouts in a special rear valance panel. Available beneath any V8 Mustang, the dual exhaust option required the addition of spot-welded reinforcement plates at the tail end of each unit-body "frame rail." While these plates' presence doesn't necessarily help document a true 1965–1966 GT—again, optional duals were installed on non-GTs, too—their absence does mean the car in question is not a factory-built GT regardless of how many other GT features are in place. An early Mustang GT is easily faked today, save for that one clue to the crime underneath. Ford didn't help matters in 1965 by offering nearly all GT image items, save for actual "GT" emblems, as dealer options. Full-page ads even spelled out the situation in no uncertain terms: "Make your Mustang into a GT! Your Ford dealer has the goods."

Those emblems superseded the "Mustang" lettering and running-horse logo found on the front fenders of non-GT models. Additional GT imagery included lower bodyside stripes, which incorporated their own style of "Mustang" lettering at their leading ends. Completing the appearance package were unique grille bars framed by fog lamps up front.

Standard inside a 1965 GT was a sporty five-dial dash in place of the base Mustang's Falcon-style instrumentation. This layout also was included as part of the "pony interior" option, also new that year. Setting the two apart was a simulated walnut appliqué for the pony interior dash; the background for GT instrumentation was done in camera case black. Chrome mylar highlights were common to both.

Most of the GT lineup carried over unchanged into 1966, with a revised blacked-out grille and "GT"-labeled gas cap representing the most noticeable updates. F70-14 Wide Oval tires became part of the package the following year, as did power assist for the standard front disc brakes. For 1967 only, all automatic GT Mustangs wore "GTA" fender badges, with that extra letter framed in red to announce the customer's transmission choice in no uncertain terms. New that year too for GT/GTA models only was the rare Competition Handling Package, an even more rugged suspension option that among other things included big 15-inch wheels and tires. Fourteen-inchers were the norm in all other cases.

Ford announced the new GT Equipment Group one year after the Mustang debuted. A stiffened suspension and various exterior dress-up items, including fog lamps in the grille, were included in the deal, priced at $165.03 in 1965.

The GT option was available for all three Mustang body styles from 1965 to 1969. The Wimbledon White 1965 GT fastback seen here is equipped with optional styled-steel wheels.

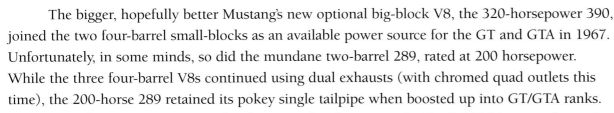

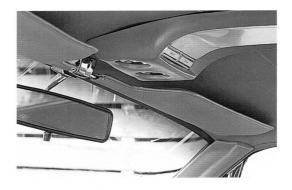

Fog lamps (top left) remained standard for the GT in 1967. New that year was the GTA (bottom left), with the "A" denoting automatic transmission. In-dash air conditioning (top middle), an overhead console (bottom right), and a special rear cove panel (middle right) also debuted on the 1967 options list. An optional 8-track player (top right) was a 1966 carryover.

Ford's famed 427-cubic-inch FE-series big-block V8 initially was listed as a Mustang option in 1968 before the 428 Cobra Jet superseded it in April that year.

The bigger, hopefully better Mustang's new optional big-block V8, the 320-horsepower 390, joined the two four-barrel small-blocks as an available power source for the GT and GTA in 1967. Unfortunately, in some minds, so did the mundane two-barrel 289, rated at 200 horsepower. While the three four-barrel V8s continued using dual exhausts (with chromed quad outlets this time), the 200-horse 289 retained its pokey single tailpipe when boosted up into GT/GTA ranks.

According to some critics, pokey became a fair description for Ford's 390 Mustang after making comparisons with its new big-block rivals from GM. "Perhaps this superburger, if it is a super-burger, needs a little more mustard," was *Car Life*'s analogous take on the situation. Nonetheless, few could deny the 1967 GT's general appeal. "The Ford Mustang started the whole Detroit sporty-car boom three years ago, and the car has been a gold mine for Ford Division ever since," claimed a *Car and Driver* report while announcing that the latest GT copped "best sport sedan over 300 cu. in." honors in its 1967 readers' poll. "The 289 cu. in. version of the Mustang cleaned up in our poll two years running, and now the heftier, heartier 390 cu. in. GT model is doing the same job."

"People are just more aware of the machine than almost anything you can think of being made in America today," added *Hot Rod*'s Eric Dahlquist in honor of Ford's newest GT Mustang. "Whisking along the freeway at speed or slipping through downtown traffic, heads turn and there is a knowing recognition of being with a winner."

The GT Equipment Group's price dropped down below $150 in 1968 due to the deletion of power front discs from the standard package. The GTA didn't return but the two-barrel carb exclusion seen in 1965 and 1966 did, with only the 230-horsepower 302 small-block and 325-horse 390 big-block available for the fourth-edition Mustang GT. Another truly exciting GT, powered by Ford's new 428 Cobra Jet V8, debuted in the spring of 1968.

Most other mechanicals and trim features were familiar that year, save for Ford's restyled styled-steel wheels, the only type available in 1968 GT applications. These 14x6-inch argent-painted slotted rims featured bright trim rings and small center caps sporting red-painted "GT"

Revised styled-steel wheels and bodyside C-stripes were standard for the 1968 GT, as were the traditional fog lamps and appropriate fender badges. Chrome quad exhaust tips were included in the back.

lettering. Trading the argent paint for chrome plating was optional. These same wheels—without the "GT" lettering—were optional for all 1968 Mustangs.

Flashy "C-stripes" were new for the 1968 GT but could've been replaced by 1967-style rocker stripes. Buyers who preferred a truly high profile could also add the Reflective Group option, which made those stripes glow in the headlight beams of other cars. Highly reflective paint was added as well to the styled-steel wheels as part of this deal.

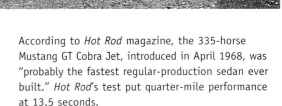

An available two-barrel carburetor returned for the 1969 GT, this time bolted atop the 351 Windsor V8, rated at 250 horsepower. Additional power choices that year included the 290-horse 351 four-barrel, the 320-horse 390 four-barrel, and the 428 Cobra Jet. As in 1967, dual exhausts with chromed quad outlets were included behind the 1969 GT's four-barrel V8s only.

According to *Hot Rod* magazine, the 335-horse Mustang GT Cobra Jet, introduced in April 1968, was "probably the fastest regular-production sedan ever built." *Hot Rod*'s test put quarter-mile performance at 13.5 seconds.

Changes for 1969 included a switch to E70x14 Wide-Oval belted tires and the return of the standard GT rocker stripes, these done in four colors (black, white, red, or gold) depending on exterior paint and interior color choices. Racing-style hood pins were new, as was a non-functional hood scoop with integral turn signal indicators. This fake scoop was superseded by the fully functional, poke-through-the-hood "Shaker" when the ram-air 428 Cobra Jet was installed.

Missing was the typical "GT" identification found on the fenders of earlier models. Only the gas cap in back and the styled-steel wheels' center caps carried "GT" identification in 1969. Few witnesses probably noticed these deletions, however, basically because so few took note of the last GT Mustang as a whole. Less than 5,400 were built, all of them lost in the shadows of Ford's two newest bucking broncos, the Boss 302 and Boss 429.

Far and away the hottest GT was the aforementioned Cobra Jet rendition, the machine that, in 1968, brought Ford's pony car up to speed in resounding fashion. And to think the initial impetus behind this big-block brute came not from within but from New England, with a little extra help supplied by a fast-thinking automotive journalist working across the country in California.

The man with the original Cobra Jet plan was famed Ford dealer Robert F. Tasca Sr. Founded in 1953 in East Providence, Rhode Island, Tasca Ford was, by the early '60s, the East Coast mecca for Blue Oval muscle car buyers. Yet as good as he was at selling fast Fords like proverbial hotcakes, not even Bob Tasca could teach an old pony new tricks. He had eyes, he could see that the new big-block Mustang would never run with Pontiac's Firebird 400 or Chevy's SS 396 Camaro, not without some major rethinking. As Tasca Ford's performance manager Dean Gregson told *Hot Rod* magazine late in 1967, "We found the [390 Mustang] so non-competitive, we began to feel we were cheating the customer. We had to do something about it."

Ford's last Mustang GT—that is until 1982—was treated to nearly no special exterior identification in 1969, save for standard hood pins.

ABOVE: A Mustang GT Cobra Jet, piloted by Al Joniec, copped top Super Stock honors at the National Hot Rod Association (NHRA) Winternationals in 1968, running the quarter-mile in 12.12 seconds.

RIGHT: Too-cool-for-school quad exhaust tips debuted for the Mustang GT in 1967. Ford's original styled-steel wheels were optional that year.

Ford dealer Bob Tasca of East Providence, Rhode Island, was responsible for convincing Ford officials to build the Cobra Jet Mustang in 1968, and his dealership sold their fair share back in the day.

In truth, Tasca's solution was born by accident, literally, after a dealership mechanic trashed the 390 V8 in a 1967 GT coupe while street racing late one night. Instead of simply replacing the blown FE, Gregson's guys decided to build their own brand of Ford power. They began with a 428 Police Interceptor short-block. A GTA 390 hydraulic cam was stuffed inside, reworked 1963-1/2 low-riser 427 heads went on top, and the works were crowned with a big 735-cfm Holley four-barrel. The sum of these parts was basically a "stock" big-block Mustang, created only with available Ford go-fast goodies, that was capable of 13.39-second bursts down the quarter-mile. Tasca called his fast and furious 428 Mustang the "KR-8;" "KR" for King of the Road, "8" for 1968.

In the summer of 1967, *Hot Rod* magazine technical editor Eric Dahlquist got wind of Tasca's work and decided to head east to see for himself. Like Tasca, Dahlquist recognized how easy it would be for Ford to replicate the KR-8 on its own regular production line, and he planned to promote this idea the best way he knew how. His November 1967 *Hot Rod* report on Tasca's 428 Mustang featured a lead page that looked like a ballot. At the top were two boxes marked "YES" and "NO." Below were instructions to "Circle your choice in the box provided and return to: Mr. Henry Ford II, Dearborn, Michigan 48121." Readers' votes then would hopefully help convince Ford's main man that if he built it, they would come.

"It was a real shame," remembered Dahlquist. "Everything was already in the parts bin to make Ford competitive on the street. But it was various managers within Ford that didn't understand the importance of doing this thing—creating the Cobra Jet. The only way to get attention was to let Henry Ford II himself receive the responses, and boy did he get 'em. It wasn't long before a Ford public relations person was calling me asking that I 'turn off the spigot.' 'Enough already, we are going to build it.'"

Dahlquist alone, of course, wasn't responsible for the Cobra Jet's birth, though his efforts certainly didn't hurt. "The next time I went back to Ford I got a nice reception," he said. "The engineers were very happy." Among them was Bill Barr, then principal design engineer in charge of FE-series V8 design and testing. According to Barr it was Tasca who made the CJ thing happen. "Bob likes to say he was the father of the Cobra Jet, and he's right," he said. "When Tasca came to town, he was always immediately given an audience, and this time he flogged the company for what he wanted. He railed for the Cobra Jet. He supplied the political pressure to get this thing going, and that prompted us to do something like he had done."

Barr's team quickly went to work granting Tasca's wish. But why hadn't Dearborn people seen a need to keep up with the Joneses earlier? "Ford was content to be a 'fast follower,'" answered Barr. "They were happy to be the producers of cars for the masses, mass transportation. Ford men recognized what most buyers were like—'so many people want a car that looks like the car that went so fast.' Most didn't really want a race car-type engine."

Mustang customers who did, however, first found the Cobra Jet 428 option available in April 1968 after dealers began receiving notice on March 29. CJ Mustang production had commenced at the Dearborn assembly plant on December 13, 1967, with the first 50 consisting of

MORE MUSCLE

Ford engineers wasted little time putting the Blue Oval back into the street performance race after the guys at Tasca Ford showed them the error of their ways late in 1967. "We didn't have anything then that ran very well and we wanted to do this thing quickly," explained big-block development engineer Bill Barr. "Our advantage was that the FE had been around since the '50s. We had a lot of parts to pick from."

Barr's team began with a passenger-car 428 block recast in nodular iron alloy that featured thickened main bearing bulkheads and extra reinforcing ribbing. Typical two-bolt main bearing caps were retained to keep things simple and cost-effective, and lower-end durability was enhanced by bolting in a strong nodular-iron crankshaft and beefy Police Interceptor (PI) connecting rods. Taking things to an even higher level on top were free-breathing big-valve 427 cylinder heads. Added as well was a cast-iron copy of the aluminum PI intake manifold, Tasca's big 735-cfm Holley four-barrel carburetor, and less restrictive cast-iron exhaust manifolds.

The sum of these parts was the 428 Cobra Jet V8, rolled out as a midyear 1968 option for Mustangs, Fairlanes, Torinos, Cougars, and mid-sized Mercurys. Advertised output remained at 335 horsepower whether or not optional ram-air equipment was installed in these cars because, as Barr pointed out, dyno testing was accomplished in a static situation with no forced induction variable available to affect the results.

Federally mandated emission controls, however, were forced upon Barr's baby. Standard on the 428 Cobra Jet was Ford's Thermactor air pump, an environmentally friendly addition that left some customers choked up in 1968. Barr's engineers, on the other hand, "weren't overly concerned" about this perceived nuisance. "The Thermactor didn't make that big of a difference in performance. It was not as sophisticated a design as you might think, and it did of course induce slightly more back pressure in the exhaust manifold at the exhaust valves, but I don't believe it even made as much as a five horsepower difference."

As for the Cobra Jet label, Barr wasn't really sure who deserved credit for first uttering it, although it was plainly obvious where the "Cobra" part of the equation originated. According to Bob Tasca, Lee Iacocca had paid a high price for the rights to Carroll Shelby's pet name and wasn't about to miss a chance to maximize his investment. The official moniker then basically morphed itself into existence.

"We already had the snake idea in our heads," added Bill Barr. "And we didn't do this like we normally did. We didn't just roll out the product with everyone standing around it scratching their asses trying to name it. The idea was already rolling by that stage. Some artist in Styling had already created a drawing of the Cobra emblem—the snake with the wheels and exhausts coming out of its tail. We had the drawing, then the name came from there."

Some witnesses figured the Cobra Jet moniker was probably a rip-off of the various "Turbo-Jet" tags applied to Chevy's hotter V8s. Barr, however, doesn't buy this. "The sales guys didn't necessarily try to one-up Chevrolet," he continued. "They just might have misinterpreted that drawing, thinking those exhausts in back were jets." Either that or "jet" just plain and simply fit a machine that really could light your fire.

"The Cobra Jet [Mustang] was so strong we had a hard time keeping the tires on the road," claimed Barr. "Once you went down on the loud pedal, this baby could really fly. On the street, the Cobra Jet was absolutely awesome. For stoplight Grands Prix, the 428 Cobra Jet was the bee's knees because nothing could stay with it." In Bob Tasca's humble opinion, "the Cobra Jet began the era of Ford's supremacy in performance. It was the fastest, in my opinion, the fastest production car built in the world at that point."

Barr's tests of a box-stock Cobra Jet Mustang pilot car produced a best quarter-mile time of 13.4 seconds. According to him, all CJ pony cars sold in 1968 were potentially that quick. "When we saw the magazine test scores of about a '13.6,' we figured they must have had a poor driver," said Barr.

Ford Motor Company's famously fast 428 Cobra Jet remained running hard up through 1970, but only for the corporation's two pony cars, the Mustang and its Cougar cousin, during that final year. Mid-sized Mercury and Ford muscle cars were treated to a new CJ V8 in 1970, this one based on the 429-cubic-inch 385-series big-block V8, and this major mill rolled over into 1971 as the top option for all Ford Motor Company high-performance models, including Mustangs.

Even though he also contributed to the 429 Cobra Jet's development, Bill Barr wasn't necessarily convinced that bigger was better in this case. "A 429 Cobra Jet never beat a 428 Cobra Jet" in in-house tests, he claimed. He also felt that no other accomplishments he managed during his 35-year career at Ford could compare to those he achieved during the sizzling '60s. "From 1962 to 1970, it was nonstop fun, more fun than people should be allowed," he said.

Fortunately, loads of fun also awaited the folks who bought the Mustangs Barr helped build.

Conservatively rated at 335 horsepower, the 428 Cobra Jet put Ford right up front in Detroit's muscle car race after debuting in April 1968.

stripped-down, lightweight super-stock models meant to go right to the drags. Regular production of street-going Mustang CJs—available as fastbacks, coupes, and convertibles—began after the factory drag cars were completed.

All "civilized" Mustang CJs built in 1968 featured a functional ram-air hood with distinctive black striping, which didn't appear on the hoods of the super-stock cars. All also were GT models loaded down with various mandatory options. Among other things, power front discs, braced shock towers, and a beefy nine-inch rear end fitted with rugged 31-spline axles were included in all cases. Both four-speed manual and automatic transmissions were installed.

The heavily loaded 1968-1/2 Mustang Cobra Jet wasn't for everyone, considering its $3,600 bottom line. But for that money, a CJ buyer received an equally heavy dose of cutting-edge Blue Oval muscle. Testing a specially prepared Cobra Jet prototype, Dahlquist reported a sizzling 13.56-second quarter-mile pass. Duly impressed, he concluded that "the CJ will be the utter delight of every Ford lover and the bane of all the rest because, quite frankly, it is probably the fastest regular production sedan ever built." Dahlquist's words, in turn, inspired Ford promotional people to quote his *Hot Rod* review in their Cobra Jet ads. Rascals as they were, however, Dearborn's admen substituted "is the fastest running Pure Stock in the history of man," a line used separately near the end of Dahlquist's article, in place of his actual conclusion.

Mustang Cobra Jets made their own history in 1968, taking the National Hot Rod Association Winternationals by storm as a wave of white CJ fastbacks driven by Al Joniec, Dyno Don Nicholson, Hubert Platt, and the boys dominated Super Stock competition. In 1969, the 428 CJ then became the standard engine in the new Fairlane Cobra and remained optional for all other mid-sized models, as well as Mustangs. The GT options group was no longer a required option in the latter case, nor was ram-air equipment automatically included.

New for 1969 was the optional Shaker scoop and the Super Cobra Jet package, which was installed whenever a buyer checked off the Drag Pack rear axle option, made up of either

Available as a coupe, convertible, or fastback, the 1968-1/2 Cobra Jet Mustang came standard with all GT equipment. The black hood stripe was exclusive to the CJ-equipped GT.

OPPOSITE, TOP: Two really hot Mustangs: North American's P-51 fighter plane and Ford's Cobra Jet-equipped 1969 Mach 1. Neither was capable of the reaching the speed of sound, but taking either for a spin remained a serious thrill nonetheless.

Mustang Cobra Jets arrived in Pomona, California, in February 1968, and took the NHRA Winternationals by storm, dominating the Super Stock drag racing class.

Among the Mustang CJ drivers who punished the competition at the 1968 NHRA Winternationals were (left to right) Gas Rhonda, Jerry Harvey, Hubert Platt, and "Dyno" Don Nicholson.

a 3.91:1 or 4.30:1 strip-ready axle ratio in a Traction-Lok limited-slip differential. Further SCJ enhancements included tougher forged aluminum pistons, beefy LeMans rods, an external engine balancer, and a racing-style external oil cooler.

The Cobra Jet 428 remained running strong up through 1970, but only for Mustangs and Mercury's Cougars. A notable SCJ change in 1970 involved the arrival of the gnarly, no-spin Detroit Locker differential, which became part of the Drag Pack option along with the 4.30:1 ratio. The Cobra Jet 429 then replaced the CJ 428 in Ford's pony car corral in 1971.

Introduced the year before for Ford and Mercury's mid-sized muscle cars, the Cobra Jet 429 was a $372 option for the 1971 Mustang. The price was $436 for the "CJ-R" rendition, with that extra letter referencing the ram-air equipment included in this package. As was the case with the Cobra Jet 428, the CJ 429 was rated the same with or without optional ram-air. And, at 370 horsepower, the new Cobra Jet was only

Introduced for 1969, the Mach 1 combined all kinds of class with lots of performance imagery. Performance potential was maximized once the optional Cobra Jet 428 V8 was installed.

10 horses stronger than the mundane Thunder Jet 429 passenger car big-block it was based on. On paper, sure; in truth, the upgrades made while trading Thunder for Cobra undoubtedly

SPEED MERCHANT: BUNKIE KNUDSEN

Henry Ford's experienced production manager, William S. Knudsen, left his executive position and his $50,000 salary behind in 1921 after clashing with his overbearing boss. In 1922, he hooked on with General Motors' Chevrolet Division and later became GM president. Nearly 50 years later, a Knudsen and a Ford were back working together, only this time it was William's son and Henry's grandson.

A 1936 Massachusetts Institute of Technology engineering graduate, Bunkie Knudsen basically retraced his father's footsteps in reverse, moving to Dearborn after first making a name for himself at General Motors. He went to work for GM in 1939 and 17 years later, at age 43, became Pontiac Motor Division general manager. Next was a stay at Chevrolet's top office, beginning in 1961, then came a promotion to GM vice president in 1965.

Knudsen had presidential aspirations at GM, but before he knew it, he found himself being passed over for the position. Reportedly he resigned his high post in a fit of pique after his archrival, veteran engineer Ed Cole, took over GM's top corporate office in October 1967. But Henry Ford II wasted no time bringing Knudsen into the Dearborn fold. On February 8, 1968, he made Semon E. "Bunkie" Knudsen president of Ford Motor Company, a job that, up to that point, Lee Iacocca had thought would surely be his.

Knudsen missed nary a beat after switching allegiances. His prime motto always was "You can sell a young man's car to an old man, but you'll never sell an old man's car to a young man," and it was this kind of thinking that had helped him transform Pontiacs almost overnight from dull, boring cars into exciting factory hot rods. "When Mr. Knudsen came from GM he brought along a strong belief in the value of performance," wrote *Motor Trend*'s Eric Dahlquist about Bunkie's move to Ford. Knudsen also loved competition. "Any opportunity you have to show off your product in front of prospective buyers is good," said Knudsen in a 1968 *Motor Trend* interview. "Racing certainly has a visible effect; our sales increase somewhat every time a race is won."

True, perhaps. But by 1968, Iacocca and others among Ford's executive elite were convinced an expensive competition program, something Henry Ford II himself had wholeheartedly supported as late as 1966, wouldn't remain viable as the '60s rolled into the '70s. "[Knudsen] was a racing nut, but he failed to understand that the heyday of racing had passed," said Iacocca of his own archrival in his autobiography.

And, though he was the main man behind Ford's Total Performance promotional campaign early in the decade, Iacocca had no love left for Detroit's muscle car genre as the '60s wound down. "He was probably ready to get out of performance," said designer Larry Shinoda, who, like his boss, defected from GM to Ford in 1968. "Then Knudsen came in and sort of took over. The performance thing was starting to ebb, but Knudsen pumped in a new spark."

Both the Boss 302 and Boss 429 Mustangs debuted in 1969 thanks to Knudsen's enthusiastic support. But both also remained on the scene only into 1970, basically because the main man behind those machines was no longer around to help keep them running. On September 11, 1969, Henry Ford II fired Bunkie Knudsen. Why? "It's obvious [the move] stemmed from differences between Knudsen and Henry Ford," claimed *Car Life*'s Charles Malone. "One of these differences was how aggressive Ford should be in racing. Knudsen favored an aggressive program, but [Henry II] and other company officials wanted de-escalation."

Other sources put at least some of the blame for Knudsen's rapid-fire demise on Iacocca. As one Ford exec told *Time* magazine, "Lee had chewed his way through ten layers of management to get where he was, and he was determined to chew his way through anyone who was placed above him."

Iacocca, on the other hand, felt Knudsen didn't need his help to fall from grace. "The press has often reported that I led a revolt against Knudsen, but his failing had little to do with me," he later recalled. "Bunkie tried to run Ford without the system. He ignored existing lines of authority and alienated top people. In the slow, well-ordered world of GM, Bunkie Knudsen flourished. At Ford, he was a fish out of water. Henry had achieved a great publicity coup by hiring a top GM man, but he soon learned that success in one car company does not always guarantee success in another."

Though Iacocca plainly wasn't sorry to see Knudsen go, he wasn't the only one. "The day Bunkie was fired there was great rejoicing and much drinking of champagne," he added 15 years later. "Over in public relations, someone coined a phrase that became famous throughout the company: 'Henry Ford once said that history is bunk. But today, Bunkie is history.'"

The way was then left clear for Iacocca, who finally became Ford Motor Company president in December 1970. As for his predecessor, Bunkie Knudsen resurfaced in 1971 as president of the White Motor Corporation, Cleveland's long-standing truck-maker. He retired from White in 1980. He died in July 1998.

Known to friends and foes alike as "Bunkie," executive Semon Knudsen resigned from General Motors in a tiff late in 1967 and was hired by Henry Ford II in February 1968.

produced more output than that, but the idea was to fool the insurance cops with an overly conservative advertised rating.

Engineers took the comparatively tame 360-horsepower Thunder Jet and added a 715-cfm Rochester Quadra-Jet four-barrel on a cast-iron dual-plane intake for starters. Big-valve, free-breathing cylinder heads and a potent hydraulic cam also were incorporated, as were four-bolt main bearing caps (for the crank's three inner journals) and a rev limiter. A close-ratio four-speed manual or heavy-duty Cruise-O-Matic C6 automatic transmission went behind the Cobra Jet 429, and mandatory options this time included power front discs, the Competition Suspension, and F70 tires.

The Cobra Jet 429's Drag Pack option offered a buyer a choice between a 3.91:1 Traction-Lok differential or a 4.11:1 Detroit Locker. Adding the Drag Pack again made a Super CJ, but the transformation was more dramatic in the 429's case. Heavy-duty forged aluminum pistons went inside a 1971 Super Cobra Jet, as did a truly radical solid-lifter cam. On top, the Cobra Jet's Q-Jet carburetor was replaced by a larger 780-cfm Holley four-barrel bolted to a specially machined cast-iron intake. An external oil cooler again was installed, but not in all SCJ cases.

The heavier Mustang CJ 429 was predictably a tad slower than its 428 fore-runner. According to *Super Stock & Drag Illustrated*, the far end of the quarter-mile arrived in 13.97 seconds. Trap speed was 100.2 mph. Too bad this big-block pony went as quickly as it came. Only 1,250 Mustang CJ/SCJ 429s were built for 1971 before the option was unceremoniously dropped midyear. Ford officials hoped to keep the legacy alive by rolling out the Cobra Jet 351 small-block late that year, but this 280-horsepower Cleveland V8 wasn't quite worthy. Many Mustangers today don't even remember the rarely seen CJ 351. No one, on the other hand, will ever forget the big-block Cobra Jets.

A huge functional scoop, equally large chin spoiler, and special fenders with rolled lips were all standard for the Mustang Boss 429 in 1969. Beneath that scoop was the awesome Boss 429 V8, token rated at 375 horsepower.

Same for those two Bosses. As for the main man behind them, one only had to look into the office of Ford Motor Company's boss. When Bunkie Knudsen took over at Ford in February 1968, he needed only one look at the Mustang to decide it was time for some serious changes. In his words, the popular pony car was "a good-looking automobile, but there are a tremendous number of people out there who want good-looking automobiles with performance. If a car looks like it's going fast and doesn't go fast, people get turned off." He then put his people to work making more Mustangs go fast. Really fast.

The certainly strong Mustang Cobra Jet already was in the works when Henry Ford II hired Knudsen. But, in Bunkie's not-so-humble opinion, there was no reason to stop there, not with GM's year-old pony cars still kicking up most of the dust in Detroit. Along with its big-block SS 396 Camaro, Chevrolet also had its nimble small-block screamer, the legendary Z/28. Created in 1967 with SCCA Trans-Am road racing in mind, the Z/28 was quickly recognized as the best all-around performer in the pony car field. The Mustang CJ may have been unbeatable down the straight and narrow, but no way it could stick with the road-handling, better-balanced Z/28 in the twisties.

Knudsen apparently wasn't above "borrowing" things from his former employer; witness the 1970 Thunderbird and its pronounced beak that reminded many people of Pontiac's trade-mark pointed prows. More than one GM genius also jumped over to Dearborn at the new boss's invitation and, like him, they also brought various ideas along with them. Among those defectors was designer Larry Shinoda, the man who had sketched up the 1963 Corvette Sting Ray. The early Z/28's humble image was his work as well.

Shinoda joined Ford in May 1968 and was immediately tasked with creating a new look for Bunkie's Z/28-beater, which was being hurriedly developed for 1969. Up until then the former GM man had not been impressed with Ford's pony car. "Initially [we] thought—well, all it is is a Falcon," said Shinoda in a 1981 *Mustang Monthly* interview. "Then it started selling like crazy. We said, well we have our Monza. The Monza did sell better than the basic Corvair, but it was still a sewing machine against the Mustang. The Mustang had the right image, and Chevrolet was forced to build the Camaro." One year after he'd helped dress up the Z/28 for its racy debut, Shinoda found himself doing the same for Ford's rival response.

Shinoda's contributions to Knudsen's new Mustang included the car's eye-catching stripes, slats, and spoilers, as well as its name. "They were going to call it 'SR-2,' which stood for 'Sports Racing' or 'Sports Racing—Group II,' which I thought was a dumb name," remembered Shinoda in 1981. "I suggested they call it 'Boss.' Chevrolet had already named their Trans-Am Camaro the Z/28, but to try to emulate them by calling the new Mustang the 'SR-2?' Well, it was sure not going to help the image of the new vehicle."

As mentioned, two Boss Mustangs were introduced in 1969, and both of these SportsRoofs were developed concurrently by Ford's performance contractor, Kar Kraft Engineering, in Brighton, Michigan, beginning in August 1968. The first Boss 302 prototype went together in only three weeks after Knudsen demanded that his engineers produce "absolutely the best-handling street car available on the American market." The Boss 429, on the other hand, was an entirely different animal created to legalize the "Blue Crescent" 429 V8 for NASCAR competition. Like the Mustang CJ, this big-block beast was best suited for straight-line speed.

These two polar opposites went their separate ways after prototype development was completed. The Kar Kraft team, led by Roy Lunn, built the Boss 429, while Ford Engineering handled the Boss 302 in-house. Matt Donner, the principal ride and handling engineer for both the Mustang and Cougar lines, was responsible for the latter's chassis, which quickly impressed critics with the way it hugged the road. "Without a doubt the Boss 302 is the best-handling Ford ever to come out of Dearborn and may just be the new standard by which everything from Detroit must be judged," claimed a *Car and Driver* report.

Donner's suspension involved, in his words, "mostly adjustments." Stars of the show were super fat F60 Wide Oval tires on wide 15x7-inch Magnum 500 wheels. To make room for all that extra tread, the Boss 302's front wheel arches were re-rolled to increase clearance, and beefier front spindles were added to handle the increased cornering loads produced by the Wide Ovals' stronger grip. Upper control arm mounting points also were initially taxed beyond their limits in prototype applications, so extra bracing was added to the shock towers. This bracing soon became a standard feature for any Mustang fitted with F60 rubber and the Competition Suspension option.

Remaining Boss 302 chassis tweaks included typically stiffened springs and shock absorbers, the latter coming from Gabriel. Rear shocks were staggered (one mounted in front of the axle, the other behind) to help control axle windup. Race-car quick 16:1 manual steering was standard, as were big 11.3-inch front disc brakes.

BELOW: Boss 302 graphics included a special bodyside C-stripe incorporating appropriate model identification. The Magnum 500 wheels seen here were optional in 1969.

BOTTOM, LEFT AND RIGHT: Boss 302 exterior graphics in 1969 included a black-out hood. A chin spoiler up front was also standard.

Four engines were available for the 1969 Mach 1: the base 250-horsepower 351 Windsor small-block, a 290-horse 351 four-barrel, a 320-horse 390 big-block, and the top-dog Cobra Jet 428, showcased here.

Power came from a 290-horsepower 302-cubic-inch small-block V8 based on a modified Windsor block featuring four-bolt main bearings. On top of that went the new free-breathing canted-valve cylinder heads then being readied for the 351 Cleveland V8, the hot small-block Ford would introduce for 1970. Valve gear included an aggressive solid-lifter cam, hardened pushrods with guideplates, 1.73:1 rocker arms with screw-in studs, and single valve springs with dampers. The crank was a hardened forged-steel piece that was cross-drilled for better oiling, pistons were forged-aluminum TRW domed pieces, and the distributor was a dual-point unit with vacuum advance. A rev limiter shut down the juice to that latter equipment whenever rpm reached 6,150. A windage tray went inside a five-quart oil pan, both the fuel and oil pumps were of the high-volume variety, and topping everything off was a huge 780-cfm Holley four-barrel on an aluminum high-rise intake.

Behind the Boss 302 V8 was either a wide- or close-ratio Top-Loader four-speed. Automatics were not available. A heavy-duty nodular 9-inch rear end with 3.50:1 gears and super-strong 31-spline axles was standard. A Traction-Lok differential was optional, as were 3.91:1 and 4.30:1 gears. Adding either of these two ratios mandated the installation of an auxiliary oil cooler.

Shinoda's high-profile touches completed the package. His front chin spoiler was standard; the rear wing and groovy rear window slats were optional. Complementing those quasi-functional touches were various blacked-out paint treatments and reflective C-stripes that incorporated appropriate "Boss 302" identification up front. Shinoda also cleaned up profile impressions by deleting the standard SportsRoof's fake rear-quarter scoops and roof pillar medallions.

Ford's first Boss 302 rolled off the Dearborn line on April 17, 1969. How did it compare to Chevy's Z/28? "I really couldn't say the Boss 302 was dramatically better," concluded Shinoda while letting his Bow-Tie bias show. "I've driven both cars, and I don't think the Mustang handled that much better. In showroom trim, car for car, the Mustang was close, but I can't really say [it] was superior." On the track, it was a tie. The Camaro claimed the SCCA Trans-Am title in 1969, the Mustang in 1970.

Meeting SCCA minimum production mandates, Ford built 1,628 Mustang Boss 302s in 1969. Trans-Am rules then changed for 1970, specifying this time that a manufacturer build at least 2,500 cars or a number equal to 1/250th of that company's total production for the previous year, whichever was greater. In Ford terms, this translated into 6,500 Boss 302s for 1970. The true final tally for the year was 7,013.

Changes and additions for 1970 were minor, with a new rear sway bar, revised tape stripes, more color choices, and Ford's optional Shaker hood scoop standing most prominent. The Magnum 500 five-spoke rims went to the options list that year as conventional 15-inch wheels wearing flat center caps and trim rings were made standard. Apparently another set of updated stripes was readied for 1971 before Dearborn officials cancelled the Boss 302 V8, along with most

Revised bodyside stripes appeared for the Boss 302 in 1970. Notice the optional Magnum 500 wheels, with painted instead of chromed spokes, in this factory photograph.

WHO'S THE BOSS?

NASCAR speedways have long served as proving grounds for the Big Three, at least as far as their main model lines have been concerned. But when it came to pitting pony car versus pony car back in the 1960s, it was Sports Car Club of America road courses that supplied all the proof as to who truly was the boss.

Pioneering sports car fanatics in Boston founded the Sports Car Club of America in February 1944. The group's first organized time trials were held in July 1945, its first official race followed in October at Watkins Glen, New York, and an SCCA seasonal championship was first decided in 1952. Big proof that this sport was here to stay arrived three years later when Road America—this country's first closed competition course dedicated solely to road racing—opened near Elkhart Lake, Wisconsin.

As expected, Chevrolet's Corvette stood tall as America's main representative during SCCA stock-class road racing's initial decade. Nothing else built in the U.S.A could compare until Carroll Shelby started waving his "Powered By Ford" banner in the early '60s. Among his hot little Cobra's various claims to racing fame was an SCCA Class A Production championship in 1964. Shelby's GT 350 then proceeded to run off three consecutive B/Production titles, beginning in 1965.

Ford also led the way during the SCCA's inaugural Trans-American Sedan Championship season. The so-called Trans-Am circuit was born in 1966, with its initial event (called the Four Hour Governor's Cup Race for Sedans) held in Florida on March 25 as a prelude to that year's running of the 12 Hours of Sebring. Factory-backed Plymouth Barracudas and Dodge Darts proved formidable early on that first year, but various independent Mustangs quickly moved to the forefront, attracting the attention of Ford folk up in Dearborn, who turned to Carroll Shelby once more late in the seven-race schedule. Shelby American's involvement then iced the deal for the pony car that seemingly couldn't be beaten.

"Seemingly" was right. Driven by former Corvette man Dick Thompson, *Sports Car Graphic* editor Jerry Titus, and Ronnie Bucknum, Shelby's two "Terlingua Racing Team" (named so to disguise Ford's financial ties) Mustangs won back-to-back Trans-Am titles in 1967. But that was where the domination ended, thanks to General Motors' retaliation.

Introduced to the press on November 26, 1966, at Riverside International Raceway in California, Chevrolet's sizzling Z/28 Camaro was created entirely with Trans-Am competition in mind, its exclusive

302-cubic-inch V8 itself put together specially to stay within the SCCA's maximum 305-cube displacement limit. Street-legal Z/28s had yet to begin finding buyers when Chevy entered the Trans-Am fray in February 1967 at Daytona, where a 302-powered Camaro finished second to a Dodge Dart. Mark Donahue, driving for Roger Penske, managed three wins that year at the wheel of a Z/28, including the season's last two races. Ford may have won the war in 1967, but Chevrolet was clearly gaining battle experience.

Penske Racing's beautiful blue Sunoco Camaros won 10 of 13 Trans-Am races in 1968, with Donahue himself taking eight straight checkered flags after finishing fourth at Daytona in February. A Shelby Racing Mustang was the Daytona winner, but Ford's pony car

stumbled badly from there, allowing Chevrolet to clinch its first SCCA title upon completion of the season's ninth event. Making matters worse was the experimental 302 Tunnel Port V8 that Ford deployed in 1968. Inherent oiling problems led to more than one Tunnel Port's disintegration that year, not to mention the cancellation of this persnickety race-only powerplant by year's end.

Switching to plan B, big bossman Bunkie Knudsen helped put his company back into the Trans-Am race in 1969 after demanding that his people outdo the Z/28. The result, of course, was the Mustang Boss 302, also powered by an exclusive 302-cubic-inch V8. The superb Boss 302 small-block promised greater things for Ford on Trans-Am tracks, considering what a disaster the experimental 302

Mustang coupes (above), campaigned by Carroll Shelby, dominated Sports Car Club of America (SCCA) Trans-Am racing prior to the emergence of Chevrolet's Z/28 Camaro in 1968. Ford's Boss 302 then appeared in 1969 (opposite, top) to battle the Z/28, and the 1970 model (opposite, bottom) took the Trans-Am title back from the Camaro.

Tunnel Port had been in 1968. Throw in the fact that the 1969 Mustang Boss 302's sleek SportsRoof shell cut the wind far better than the notchback coupes used previously and Ford fans couldn't help but get excited as Trans-Am racing's fourth season got underway.

Facing off this time against Roger Penske's formidable Sunoco cars were two Ford teams, the existing Shelby Racing group and a second shepherded by Bud Moore, who had built Mercury's Trans-Am Cougars in 1967 and 1968. Driven by Parnelli Jones and George Follmer, the two Bud Moore Engineering Boss 302s made the most hay in 1969, and by year's end it was relatively clear that Shelby's time in Trans-Am competition was coming to a close. Too bad the same couldn't be said for Penske Racing's dominance. The Mustang Boss 302 closed the gap, but it couldn't quite catch Chevy's Z/28, which won eight of 12 Trans-Am races in 1969. Donahue alone claimed six of those wins, compared to Jones' two and Follmer's one.

As predicted, Bud Moore Engineering's two Mustangs returned for the 1970 Trans-Am season but Shelby Racing's cars didn't, due to Henry Ford II's decision that year to slash his corporation's spending at the track. Meanwhile, Roger Penske jumped from GM to American Motors, leaving Jim Hall to run Chevrolet's Trans-Am program, and Chrysler returned to SCCA tracks (after a three-year hiatus) with its AAR Barracuda from Plymouth and Challenger T/A from Dodge. All

this extra competition, however, didn't deter Bud Moore's Mustangs, which battled Penske's Javelins—not Hall's Camaros—closely before finally clinching the 1970 Trans-Am championship at Kent, Washington, in September.

Ford announced a near-total withdrawal from motorsports two months later, and Chrysler and Chevrolet dropped their SCCA support in 1971, leaving AMC to have its way with what was left of the road-racing field. Trans-Am competition would never be the same, but at least the Mustang went out the same way it came in—as a winner.

Ford built 857 1969 Boss 429 Mustangs to legalize the big "semi-hemi" V8 for competition on the NASCAR circuit.

Also called the "Shotgun Motor" or "Blue Crescent" V8, the Boss 429 big-block featured aluminum cylinder heads with sewer-sized ports. Feeding this beast was a big 735-cfm Holley four-barrel carburetor.

BELOW: Shoehorning a Boss 429 V8 between Mustang flanks required reshaped shock towers and a redesigned, thinned power brake booster. The battery also was relocated to the trunk.

of Ford's legendary motorsports support, late in 1970. At least the Mustang Boss 302 was replaced by the Boss 351 variety the following year.

No successor appeared for the Boss 429, also cancelled unceremoniously in 1970, its sole reason to be no longer present after Henry Ford II decided to get out of racing. The last Boss 429 Mustang rolled off the Kar Kraft assembly line a few months after Henry II fired Bunkie Knudsen in September 1969. Such was life in Dearborn's fast lane.

NASCAR tracks had represented the big Boss's main focus, per another of Bunkie's competition-conscious mandates. "It was in the days just after Knudsen came onboard," said Kar Kraft chief Roy Lunn about the rush to get the Boss 429 up to speed. "He was a real stock car enthusiast, and so stock car racing was being given a big thrust again. To remain competitive, we had to get that 429 hemi-head engine qualified, and the requirement was that you had to build a minimum of 500 in production vehicles."

That production standard didn't specify the vehicle, just the engine. As long as Ford let loose 500 Boss 429 V8s on the street, it didn't matter how they were packaged on NASCAR speedways. So this exotic big-block was homologated between Mustang flanks. On the NASCAR circuit, it appeared behind the extended nose of Ford's Fairlane-based Torino Talladega, which incidentally came standard in regular-production form with the 428 Cobra Jet. Go figure.

The Boss 429 V8's roots ran back to 1968 when Ford introduced its 385-series "thin-wall" big-block engine family for its luxury models. Engineers immediately began considering ways to take this big baby racing, casting a reinforced iron block with four bolts holding the bearing caps on four of the five mains. Huge, heavy cylinder heads with sewer-sized ports, massive inclined valves, and hemispherical combustion chambers were also cast out of iron. But by the time this engine reached production, the iron heads were traded for weight-saving aluminum units with revised combustion chambers. These chambers weren't quite hemispherical, thus the commonly used "semi-hemi" designation. Ford people preferred the "Blue Crescent" moniker, while racers liked the "Shotgun motor" nickname.

A healthy 735-cfm Holley four-barrel, mounted on an aluminum dual-plane intake, fed the coals to this fire-breathing beast, while a Drag Pack-style oil cooler helped keep lubricants within their effective temperature range. As for advertised output, jokers once again simply picked a token figure. Horsepower was listed at 375. Who was kidding whom?

Determining the true number, however, became more or less a moot point after one magazine road tester called the NASCAR-engine pony car "a stone." According to Larry Shinoda, the semi-hemi big-block "was kind of a slug in the Mustang." *Car Life* critics did call the Boss 429 "the best enthusiast car Ford has ever produced" after watching it toast the quarter-mile in 14.09 seconds at 102.85 mph. But most other witnesses were quick to point out that such performance, while nothing to sneeze at, was nothing short of disappointing for such a mean machine. It should have run well into the 13s, if not almost into the 12s. After all, the Boss 429 was a full-fledged race engine unleashed on the street.

But therein lay the rub. Engineers were forced to defeat their own purposes while morphing this monster into a regular-production pet. Those expansive valves and ports were designed to make mucho power at high rpm, yet the compromising street cam was no match for all that free-breathing potential. Same for that Holley four-barrel, which qualified as "big" by most standards, but not the Boss 429's. Adding insult to injury was that darned electronic rev-limiter, which shut off ignition voltage just as the Shotgun was really starting to load up. Such were the pitfalls whenever any manufacturer tried to tame a race car for stoplight-to-stoplight travel.

The Boss 429 Mustang first hit the streets in January 1969, nearly three months ahead of the Boss 302. Stripped-down Mach 1s, minus their engines and stock shock towers, had started showing up at Kar Kraft in December 1968. Once in Brighton, they were fitted with specially reinforced shock towers that widened the engine compartment by two inches to make room for the humongous Boss 429 V8. Upper A-arm location points in turn were moved outward an inch and lowered another inch. Beefier spindles also were installed, as was a modified export brace on top to firmly tie the restructured shock towers to the cowl.

After building 1,628 Mustang Boss 302s in 1969, Ford followed up with another 7,013 in 1970. The window slats and rear spoiler seen on this 1970 model were options that year, as they had been in 1969.

The Boss 429's front fender lips were rolled under like the Boss 302's as fat F60 rubber on 15x7-inch Magnum 500 rims were standard in this case, too. Standard front discs carried over from Boss 302 to 429, too, but power assist was included, along with power steering, in the Boss 429 package. Power brakes and steering were optional for the Boss 302. Additional suspension upgrades included super-duty Gabriel shocks (staggered in back, of course) and thick sway bars at the nose and tail. Behind the semi-hemi V8 went a close-ratio four-speed that delivered torque to a Traction-Lok differential with 3.91:1 gears.

Even with its modified shock towers, the Boss 429's engine compartment remained a crowded place, forcing engineers to create a thinned-down power brake booster to supply driver's side clearance for the Shotgun motor's huge valve cover. The battery was moved to the trunk—just where it belonged as far as drag racers were concerned. Transferring weight from the front wheels to the rear is always a good idea when improving traction off the line is the goal.

Boss 429 exterior modifications weren't as plentiful as the Boss 302's. The 1969 SportsRoof's rear roof pillar medallions and fake rear-quarter scoops were retained and nothing was blacked-out. Simple "Boss 429" decals went on each front fender and a gaping functional hood scoop was added, and that was about it. Dual color-keyed racing mirrors and a front chin spoiler (shaped differently than the Boss 302's) were standard, while a rear wing and Shinoda's window slats were optional.

Kar Kraft rolled out 857 Boss 429 Mustangs in 1969, then kept the line running oh-so-briefly for 1970. Like its small-block running mate, the second edition Boss 429 was offered in more colors. The most noticeable update involved the hood scoop, which was painted low-gloss black instead of matching the rest of the body as it had the year before. A Hurst shifter was added inside in 1970 and the rear sway bar was relocated from below the axle to above.

The first 1970 Mustang arrived at Kar Kraft for conversion late in August 1969. Bunkie was booted three weeks later, leaving no one to save the Boss 429 from its fate. The last Shotgun-motored pony car left the Brighton works on January 6, 1970. Only 499 1970 Boss 429s were built.

Although Ford Motor Company axed nearly all motorsports involvement in November 1970, not all news that month was bad as far as horsepower hounds were concerned. The Boss 351 debuted at the same time to keep the Mustang muscle car legacy running strong for at least one more year.

Powering the 1971 Mustang Boss 351 was Ford's 330-horse 351 High Output (HO) Cleveland small-block with its free-breathing, canted-valve heads that, save for revised cooling passages, were essentially identical to those worn by the Boss 302 V8. Various valvetrain parts carried over, too, but the 351 HO's solid-lifter cam was a bit lumpier than the Boss 302's. Its lower end also featured four-bolt caps, but for all five main bearings, not just three. The HO crank was cast instead of forged, and on top was a 750-cfm Autolite four-barrel carb on an aluminum dual-plane manifold. Included too was that darned rev-limiter (also supplied by Autolite) to once again help keep the lid on tight whenever the pedal merged with metal for extended periods.

As usual, no automatic transmission was available in 1971 for Ford's latest Boss Mustang, only a Hurst-shifted wide-ratio four-speed manual. Standard mechanicals also included the Competition Suspension, F60 tires on 15x7 wheels, power front discs, a ram-air hood, a special cooling package (with a flex fan), and a Traction-Lok 9-inch rear end with 31-spline axles and 3.91:1 gears. Along with that functional "NASA" hood, appearance enhancements included appropriate "Boss 351" decals, a Mach 1 honeycomb grille, dual racing mirrors, twist-type hood locks, and either argent silver or black accents depending on paint choice.

It featured a small-block V8, yes, but the Boss 351 impressed many critics with the way it ran like a big-block. As *Car and Driver* reported, Ford's final Boss Mustang "offers dragstrip performance that most cars with 100 cubic inches more displacement will envy." According to a *Motor Trend* test, the quarter-mile zoomed by in a scant 13.8 seconds, making this machine one of Dearborn's quickest muscle cars to date. Unfortunately it also represented the end of the road for Ford high-performance.

Chrome quad exhaust tips were included as part of the Mach 1 package in 1970 when a four-barrel V8 was installed. The striping on the tail and the black-out treatment for the cove panel and rockers were standard in all cases.

Magazine road tests claimed the 1971 Boss 351 could cook the quarter-mile in a sizzling 13.8 seconds. According to *Car and Driver*, Ford's last Boss Mustang offered "drag strip performance that most cars with 100 cubic inches more displacement will envy."

Lots of black-out touches and some series tape striping was standard for the Boss 351 in 1971, as were dual color-keyed racing mirrors.

The Pewter Silver 1971 Mach 1 shown here (top) features a non-functional NASA hood, optional that year for the base 302 V8, standard for all other engines. The optional Ram Air package added a paint stripe (done in black or argent silver) to the NASA hood's center, as demonstrated on the 1971 Mach 1 (above).

"This is probably the last chance you'll have to buy a machine of this kind," began *Sports Car Graphic*'s March 1971 Boss 351 road test. "Ford is now diverting all its racing dollars into solving safety and pollution problems and trying to satisfy government mandates. We have heard from reliable sources that all [1972] Ford products will be detuned to run on regular fuel. Perhaps we'll just learn to live with the situation, like war and taxes, which we accept as facts of life. But we have few years left. We might as well take what we can get and live it up while we can."

Although the 351 HO did survive into 1972 in detuned fashion, the Boss 351 was around for 1971 only, and nothing emerged to keep up the pace after it retired. Beginning in 1972, Lee Iacocca's baby once more looked like it was going fast when it really wasn't. Mustang and muscle car wouldn't be mentioned again in the same sentence for another 10 years or so.

CHAPTER FIVE

The Mustang II Years, 1974–1978

Lee Iacocca never did like what happened to his baby after 1966, and he was especially unhappy about what went on in Ford's pony car corral during Bunkie Knudsen's short stay in Dearborn. "As soon as [he] arrived, he began adding weight to the Mustang and making it bigger," began his lament in his autobiography. "Within a few years after its introduction, the Mustang was no longer a sleek horse, it was more like a fat pig. In 1968, Knudsen added a monster engine with double the horsepower. To support the engine, he had to widen the car. By 1971, the Mustang was no longer the same car, and declining sales figures were making the point clearly."

LITTLE PONY

After hitting its peak of 600,000 in 1966, Mustang production dropped every succeeding year up though 1972. But perhaps Iacocca was being a little too hard on his archrival. At no point during that time was Ford's progenitor ever in danger of losing its

PAGES 150–151: The popular Mach 1 image rolled over into the Mustang II era, which ran from 1974 to 1978. Wide Oval tires and black lower body accents were standard for the Mustang II Mach 1, available only as a three-door hatchback. A 1975 example, base priced at $4,188, is shown here.

In April 1969 Ford took another shot at invading compacts—most coming from Japan—with its Maverick, based on a shortened Falcon chassis. Mavericks were built for the domestic market up through 1977; a 1972 model appears here.

Not even Ford officials predicted such success for their record-breaking Falcon, introduced for 1960. More than 400,000 were sold that the first year.

leading sales position in the pony car field, and the emergence of all that competition itself contributed to the Mustang's downward trend. Though Plymouth's Barracuda never was a threat from 1964 to 1966, General Motors' Camaro and Firebird certainly did infringe on Ford's turf after hitting the scene in 1967. Even so, most Ford people surely remained happy selling 300,000 Mustangs in 1969. No way, however, were they feeling the same after production nose-dived to 190,700 in 1970, then to a tad less than 150,000 after Bunkie's really big body arrived in 1972. The annual count bottomed at 125,000 in 1972 before surging slightly to 134,800 in 1973.

Sure, Iacocca may have been a bit harsh while trying to pile *all* the blame for the Mustang's decline on Knudsen. But he wasn't the only one heard complaining about the once spry pony's growth during the 1960s. Every bit as disgruntled were the loyal customers who started writing Ford in protest as early as 1968, with one horse lover calling the latest Mustang a "luxury bus." At an annual stockholders' meeting that year, another unhappy owner let Henry Ford II have it smack between the eyes: "When the Thunderbird came out, it was a beautiful sports car. Then you blew it up to the point where it lost its identity. The same thing is happening to the Mustang. Why can't you leave a small car small? You keep blowing them up and then starting another little one, blowing that one up and starting another one."

Ford's other compact milestone, Falcon, experienced a similar fate: it began life truly small in 1960 then eventually grew into a mid-sized model before fading quietly away 10 years later. Ford then started another little one midyear in 1969 using the existing Falcon platform as a foundation. Though reasonably successful early on, the new six-cylinder Maverick still wasn't quite the answer to the foreign import challenge, especially the new threat posed by Japan.

Far better suited to do battle against those compacts was the truly diminutive Pinto, introduced for 1971. Fitted with a frugal four-cylinder, the Pinto not only matched up well with the best Datsun and Toyota had to offer, it also proved to be the right car at the right time once gasoline started turning to gold in the wake of the Arab oil embargo of October 1973. With a gallon of fossil fuel doubling in price in 1974, it instantly became clear to most Americans that big, expensive gas-hogs no longer represented smart choices, a conclusion Iacocca had already reached five years before.

"Late in 1969 we began planning the Mustang II, a return to the small car that had been so successful," he recalled in 1984. "A lot of people in Detroit could hardly believe we were doing this, because it violated an unwritten rule that an established car could only be made bigger—never smaller. To put out a smaller Mustang was tantamount to admitting we had made a mistake. Of course we had."

In November 1969—two months after Henry II let Knudsen go—Iacocca let Ford's top brass know exactly how he felt about Mustang progress during a management conference held in Greenbriar, West Virginia. Dearborn officials immediately agreed to begin development of a new sporty small car, code-named "Ohio," using the Maverick platform as a foundation. The scheduled release for this car was 1974. An "Arizona" proposal was also discussed. Planned for 1975, this second small car was more or less an upscale Pinto.

Most opinions early on had the larger Ohio model, which rolled on a 103-inch wheelbase, going into production as the next-generation Mustang. But Ford minds started changing in April 1970 after Lincoln-Mercury began importing its sexy Capri into America. Rolling on a 100.8-inch wheelbase, this sporty little V6 coupe, nicknamed the "European Mustang," had debuted in London in December 1968 and within a year was a jolly good hit in Great Britain, as well as West Germany. American buyers loved it, too, convincing more than one Dearborn executive that getting really small might just be the next new wave.

With the Capri and other sub-compacts selling like crazy in this country as the '70s dawned, those execs made the decision in July 1971 to ditch the Ohio plan and go ahead with the smaller Arizona project. Nat Adamson, the advanced product planning manager who had led

LET'S GET SMALL

Compact cars certainly were nothing new around Detroit when the Mustang II arrived, and the same could be said about the American market in general when the Big Three first started radically downsizing 15 years prior. Crosley, Kaiser-Frazer, Hudson, and Nash all had tried introducing Americans to small, affordable transportation dating back to just before World War II. Another world war earlier, the cyclecar craze swept this country, enticing entry-level buyers into the market with little, lightweight machines that indeed were not much more than a couple bikes bolted together with an engine in between.

Let's not forget the import invasion, which originated in Europe after peace was declared in 1946. Most notable among these pesky little buggers was Germany's Volkswagen, the truly tiny compact that eventually superseded ol' Henry's Model T as the world's best-selling automobile of all-time. VW's beloved "Beetle" on its own was enough to inspire Detroit execs to begin thinking small, which they did in a big way as the 1950s wound down.

General Motors, Chrysler, and Ford each introduced a groundbreaking compact model for 1960, with Dearborn officials being the first to show one off to the press in July 1959. Of this trio, Chevrolet's rear-engined, air-cooled Corvair was the most radical engineering-wise, Chrysler's Valiant perhaps was the most radically styled, and Ford's Falcon was the best seller. Initially conceived as the "XK Thunderbird" project in 1957, the 1960 Falcon featured unitized body-frame construction, a short 109-inch wheelbase, a 90-horsepower six-cylinder engine, and a humble bottom line beginning at about $1,900.

"Similar in size and general concept to the [American Motors] Rambler and [Studebaker] Lark, Ford's tactical approach to the [small car] skirmish carries the weight of simmered-down flashiness, guaranteed economy, and realistically comfortable seating space, stressing 'cost of ownership' as the major selling point," claimed *Motor Trend*'s October 1959 cover story on what many felt represented the biggest news out of Dearborn in about 30 years. "Not since the days of the Model A has Ford concentrated on functional styling and engineering as part and parcel of what it thinks the American car-buying public wants," continued *Motor Trend*'s Steve DaCosta.

Ford's first Falcon established a U.S. industry record for new model sales, but the attraction began to wear off as the model began to move away from its original ideal, evolving into something bigger, something less efficient, something more costly. By 1966, Falcon was more or less a mid-sized machine, a car that dwarfed the various Japanese imports just starting to take their own bites out of the American market's pie. Sales dropped so low by 1970 that Dearborn planners decided to drop its no-longer-so-compact model midyear

and transfer the Falcon nameplate up into the intermediate Fairlane ranks. Both Fairlane and Falcon were deleted entirely at year's end.

That new threat from the Far East forced Ford designers to reinvent their compact, although they still insisted on relying on the existing Falcon platform to roll out their new Maverick in April 1969. Though it did make an initial splash, Maverick obviously wasn't the answer, basically because it was too big to compete with the more efficient, more affordable Datsuns and Toyotas, not to mention the cock of the compact walk, Volkswagen.

"The fact remains Maverick did not make a big dent in VW, they continued along their merry way," said Ford Motor Company Vice President and Ford Division General Manager John Naughton in a September 1970 *Motor Trend* interview. "Maverick had been successful and had attracted an enormous amount of people, but head to head with VW, we weren't taking them on like we had hoped to. We knew we had to have a smaller car."

That vehicle was the Pinto, called "the second part of a 1-2 punch against the imports" by Ford people. Galloping along on a 94-inch wheelbase, driven by a standard four-cylinder, this little pony debuted in September 1970, about the same time Chevrolet rolled out its own pint-sized Bug-zapper, Vega. According to *Road & Track*, the slightly larger Vega was "by far the more interesting design." Yet Ford's sub-compact still won out in a head-to-head battle.

"Pinto happened to be the more pleasant car to drive in everyday use and carries a price tag some $172 less," continued the *R&T* review. "To be sure, there is 'less car' in the Pinto. But thanks to a smoother engine, a superior gearbox, somewhat greater comfort for the driver and better finish throughout, it is subjectively the nicer car." Chevy sold nearly 275,000 Vegas for 1971, while Pinto sales that first year topped 352,000, followed by another 480,000 in 1972.

Few upgrades were made during the Pinto's career, but that wasn't a bad thing. "The Model T lasted virtually unchanged for 19 years, and with that in mind I felt we should try to accomplish the same objective with the Pinto," said Henry Ford II while introducing his new compact to the press in the spring of 1970. "Any changes in the Pinto will be aimed at making it a better car and not just different looking."

Unfortunately, issues related to the car's fuel tank design landed Ford in court and briefly transformed the Pinto into the latest star of Johnny Carson's *Tonight Show* dialogue. Such slings and arrows aside, the Pinto still helped keep Dearborn competitive during tough times and did so for 10 successful years before another new compact, Escort, came along in 1981.

Both the Mustang and the Maverick (foreground) were treated to high-profile Grabber image packages in 1970.

the Arizona design team from the get-go, was promoted to light car planning manager and tasked with developing what would became an all-new pony car. Production start-up was scheduled for July 1973.

Gene Bordinat's studio supplied styling ideas, for both Arizona and Ohio, but none of these tickled anyone's fancies in Dearborn. So Iacocca looked overseas to Alejandro de Tomaso's famed Ghia studio in Turin, Italy. Ford had just bought controlling interest in Ghia in November 1970. Why not take advantage of this deal, not to mention de Tomaso's legendary experience and expertise? Two prototypes, a notchback coupe and a fastback, were fashioned in Italy and these forms greatly influenced the final look that evolved at the hands of Ford designers back in Michigan.

One stumbling block that hindered Bordinat's team early on involved an original specification calling for the installation of Ford's existing inline six-cylinder engine. Obviously way too long for the downsized platform Iacocca and the others had in mind, the straight-six eventually was dropped from the plan in favor of a pint-sized 2.3-liter four-cylinder. An optional V6, an enlarged variant of the Capri's European-sourced six, was also planned.

As for those engines' wrappings, Bordinat felt only one body style was needed this time around. Dropping the convertible model was a given from the beginning considering how rapidly topless sales were falling across the board in Detroit during the late 1960s. Many top people agreed with Bordinat about concentrating on a single shape, but no one wanted to make the final decision as to which body, familiar fastback or traditional coupe, would be transformed from clay into steel.

In August 1971, Iacocca finally directed Bordinat to stage yet another design competition—much like he had during the original Mustang's creative process a decade before—to help make the final cut once and for all. But this idea ended up perpetuating the quandary instead of solving it. Four groups entered the contest this time, with a sharp fastback from Al Mueller's Lincoln-Mercury studio winning out in November. At the same time, however, Iacocca and crew found themselves falling in love with a neat notchback inspired by the Ghia prototype and done by Don DeLaRossa's Advanced Design studio. Witnesses couldn't get over how much this coupe reminded them of the original Mustang, which, as you might remember, appeared as a notchback first in 1964, then morphed into a fastback later that year.

Production of Mach 1 hatchbacks in 1974 was 44,086. A 2.8-liter V6 was the only engine available in the Mach 1 that year.

Two body styles, a notchback coupe and a fastback, were available during the Mustang II years, with the latter model featuring a convenient lift-up hatch in the back—hence its "three-door" status.

Ford sold nearly 390,000 Mustang IIs in 1974, with the two-door coupe (shown here) being the most popular. Coupe production that year was 177,671. A 2.3-liter four-cylinder was standard; the Mach 1's 2.8-liter V6 was optional.

Wanting very much to revive as many 1964 memories as possible, Iacocca surprised his designers in February 1972 with a direct order to put DeLaRossa's coupe back into the mix along with Mueller's fastback. Production was set to commence only 16 months down the road, but Iacocca wanted it his way: it would be two bodies or none at all. In the fastback's case, its sloping rear roof became a third door, making it a trendy hatchback.

Iacocca also demanded from the beginning that his downsized Mustang be "a little jewel." In either form, he wanted to see an upscale, yet still affordable compact, a lively two-door that would leave all rival four-cylinder cars, foreign and domestic, in its shadow. Quality in all aspects—ride, comfort, fit, and finish—was key, and to this end engineers managed to inhibit noise, vibration, and harshness (NVH) like no other unit-body compact creators before them.

Key to keeping NVH factors under control was an isolated U-shaped subframe up front, credited to engineers Jim Kennedy and Bob Negstad. Jokingly tagged the "toilet seat" around Ford Engineering, this clever design helped absorb both road shocks and engine vibrations before they could be transmitted to the passenger compartment. Extra rubber insulation throughout the chassis and a special sound-deadening barrier that melted to the floorboard while exterior paint was being baked ensured a reasonably quiet ride, certainly so for a compact.

Representing such a radical departure from Bunkie Knudsen's Mustangs of 1971–1973, Iacocca's truly compact pony car, in promotional people's opinions, needed a new name. "Mustang II" was the suggestion made in August 1972 by the North American Operations Public Relations office. Reportedly the "II" was meant to announce a notable rebirth, not just a typical rollover into yet another ho-hum model year. Selling this better idea to the big boss was a piece of cake— remember, Henry Ford *II* had wanted to call Iacocca's original pony car the "Thunderbird II."

Curiously, Iacocca claimed later in a 2004 *Mustang Monthly* interview that he himself preferred the Roman numerals because his new-for-1974 pony car didn't deserve direct recognition

Lee Iacocca considered his "little jewel," the Mustang II, a return to his original Mustang ideal, and buyers apparently agreed, buying them up like nobody's business. Motor Trend editors were so impressed they named Ford's first Mustang II (bottom) their Car of the Year for 1974.

alongside his 1964 classic. Apparently he had had 30 years to second guess his "little jewel," to ponder the model's downturn which followed during the '70s once the original sparkle wore off. Funny thing, however: he was more than willing to accept all kudos when the first Mustang II won *Motor Trend*'s "Car of the Year" trophy in 1974.

According to *Motor Trend*, this new breed stood as "a total departure from the fat old horse of the recent past." And considering the "energy crisis" then gripping this country thanks to the aforementioned Arab oil embargo, *Motor Trend* also claimed that the four-cylinder Mustang II's introduction represented "one of the best-timed announcements in auto history."

Calling the Mustang II "a pony for the '70s," *Motor Trend* went on to describe it as "a rebirth of the Mustang of 1964–65—smaller and even more lithe in feel than the original pacesetter." At 96.2 inches, the 1974 Mustang II's wheelbase was 13 inches shorter than the 1973 model's. The new downsized model also was 14 inches shorter, four inches skinnier, and some 300 pounds lighter. While traditional parallel leaf springs held up its tail, the front suspension was revised to put the coil springs between the upper and lower arms, as opposed to their previous location above the upper arms.

Beneath the hood was a small standard engine. By no means this country's first modern four-cylinder, the Mustang II's base power source nonetheless qualified as Detroit's metric pioneer, as well as Dearborn's first modern domestic-built four-holer. A British-built 1.6-liter four-cylinder had been standard for the first Pinto in 1971; a German-built 2.0-liter four had been optional. Both of these were overhead-cam (OHC) engines. When Ford engineers designed their own OHC four for the Mustang II, they kept metric dimensions to preserve parts interchangeability with those Euro-sourced engines. Producing a meager 88 horsepower, Ford's 2.3-liter four-cylinder, manufactured at the company's engine plant in Lima, Ohio, was capable of as much as 23 miles per gallon. In Yankee terms, those 2.3 liters translated into 140 cubic inches.

The Mustang II's optional V6 displaced 2.8 liters (171 cubic inches) and was advertised at 105 horsepower. Early mechanical bugs left many V6 buyers wishing they'd not opted for two more cylinders, and others complained about the absence of an available V8, a first for the pony car legacy. Still, those darned soaring prices at the pump spurred on the new car's popularity. Production for 1974 was nearly 386,000, reminding many at Ford of those heady days 10 years before.

Standard features included a four-speed stick, rack and pinion steering, and front disc brakes. Ford's SelectShift Cruise-O-Matic automatic transmission was optional. Four models were offered: the two-door notchback coupe, three-door 2+2 hatchback, upscale Ghia coupe, and three-

The Ghia coupe picked up where the Grande left off, serving as a luxury-conscious alternative to the base Mustang and Mach 1. A vinyl roof was a Ghia trademark. A 1975 example is shown here.

door Mach 1. The 2.3-liter four-cylinder was standard for the first three; the Mach 1 featured the V6, with the four-banger available as a credit option. Filling the 1969–1973 Grande's horseshoes, the Ghia featured a vinyl roof, wood-tone door panels, shag carpeting, deluxe seat belts, remote-control mirrors, a digital clock, and spoke-style wheelcovers.

Mach 1 basics included typical exterior striping, Wide Oval tires on styled-steel wheels, and dual color-keyed remote mirrors. Enhancing this attraction further was the Rallye Package, also available for other 1974 V6-equipped models, save for the Ghia. This option added steel-belted white-letter tires on styled-steel wheels, extra-cooling equipment, a Sport package exhaust system, a Traction-Lok differential, a digital clock, a leather-wrapped steering wheel, and the beefed-up Competition Suspension.

Though it looked cool, certainly for a budget-conscious compact, Ford's latest performance-oriented Mustang predictably left racehorse fans a little flat. "While the Mach 1's general concept is enthusiast-oriented, its poor acceleration, wide-ratio transmission and overweight chassis leave too much of its undeniably sporting flavor unsupported by nourishment," claimed *Car and Driver*. *Car Craft* called the 1974 Mach 1 "regrettably underpowered" and suggested that Ford offer a V8 version soon.

Optional eight-cylinders arrived in 1975, but sales dropped by 50 percent anyway as buyers began growing dissatisfied with the Mustang II's tight confines. Squeezing Ford's 122-horsepower 5.0-liter (302-cubic-inch) Windsor small-block between downsized flanks resulted in a few major changes. Repositioning the radiator was required, meaning that a new longer hood and a remounted grille were also needed. A revised subframe crossmember was added underneath.

Basically, everything else carried over from 1974. Solid-state electronic ignition and steel-belted radial tires became standard in 1975, while new on the options list was a manually controlled moonroof. New for the Ghia coupe was a special Silver Luxury Group option that added silver metallic paint with cranberry striping and silver bodyside moldings, a silver Normande-grain half vinyl roof, a prominent hood ornament, and a cranberry interior done in velour cloth with color-keyed sun visors and a console. An "MPG" package also appeared midyear to improve maximum fuel economy to 30 miles per gallon.

New for 1976 was the Stallion package, also offered that year for Pintos and Mavericks. Special paint, various black-out touches, and prominent decals were included in the Stallion option, priced at $72.

At about 187,000, 1976's production paled in comparison to 1974's, but it still led the way in the domestic sub-compact field. Nonetheless, Iacocca's little jewel continued to fail to find a suitable identity. All 2.3-liter cars became MPG models in 1976 as Dearborn officials hoped to promote this fuel-saving aspect as the Mustang II's main selling point. Mach 1 popularity, meanwhile, faded away—the 21,000 examples built for 1975 were followed by only 9,200 in 1976.

Fortunately, for performance fans, that latter drop could've been attributed mostly to the appearance of the new Cobra II, created by Jim Wangers, the horsepower hound who had helped Pontiac's GTO get rolling a dozen years before. Wangers' company, Motortown, performed the Cobra II conversion, which added a non-functional hood scoop, accent stripes, rear-quarter window louvers, front and rear spoilers, and various coiled-snake identification. This option was available with all three engines—four, six, or eight—meaning a mundane MPG model could've been a killer-looking Cobra II at the same time. Total Cobra II production that first year was 25,259.

Standard for the Mach 1, the styled-steel wheels (with bright trim rings) on this 1977 Ghia were optional for other models that year.

Another new package, called Stallion, was offered for the 1976 Mustang II along with that year's Pinto MPG and Maverick. Focusing solely on looks, this option group gussied up a base four-cylinder Mustang II with various blacked-out treatments. Later in 1977 the Stallion option was replaced by the 2+2 Rallye Appearance Package, which featured various blacked-out touches, as well as gold accents atop either Black or Polar White paint. Argent styled-steel wheels also came in this package, while a black chin spoiler was a no-cost option.

The total Mustang II count dropped to 153,000 in 1977, but the 5.0-liter's cut of the pie that year was 25 percent, compared to 17.6 percent in 1976. Apparently the pony car's performance appeal wasn't dead yet. Mach 1 production did dip again (to 6,719), and the Cobra II, now created in-house at Ford, also fell off (to 11,948). But Ford introduced another hot option, the Sports Performance Package, for all models. Included in this coveted deal was the 5.0-liter V8 backed by a heavy-duty four-speed manual transmission, power steering, power brakes, and 70-series radial tires.

Even a fashion-conscious Ghia coupe could've been sexed up with the Sport Group option in 1977. In this case, complements included black or tan paint, a blacked-out grille, a vinyl roof done in Chamois Lugano or Black Odense, bodyside moldings with matching vinyl inserts, a luggage rack, and cast-aluminum wheels. A leather-wrapped steering wheel and center console joined color-keyed appointments inside. A trendy T-top roof also appeared on the 1977 options list, as did a four-way manually controlled driver's bucket seat.

Mustang II production surged to 192,400 for 1978, the last year for the little pony car that proved to be too little in many devoted Mustanger's minds. The Mach 1 tally (7,968) also went on the rise that year, but the Cobra II count dipped to 8,009. Perhaps buyers couldn't quite warm up to the new garish graphics that spelled out "Cobra" in huge letters on each door.

Mechanical upgrades included a plastic cooling fan for the V6 and optional variable-ratio power steering. New on 1978's options list was the Fashion Accessory Group, which targeted female buyers with its lighted vanity mirror on the driver's side visor, illuminated entry, striped cloth seat inserts, and a four-way adjustable driver's seat. But by far most notable among 1978's new additions was the King Cobra, a suitable exclamation point for the Mustang II story.

Clearly a product of the disco era, the 1978 King Cobra primarily relied on flamboyance to turn heads. "With the real muscle car era now no more than a memory, cars like the Ford King Cobra are becoming the machismo machines of the late '70s," explained *Car Craft* magazine's

A trendy T-top roof became a Mustang II option for 2+2 hatchbacks in 1977. It was priced at $629 for base models (shown here).

A special conversion, done by Jim Wangers' Motortown crew in 1976, the Cobra II fastback became a full-fledged factory offering from Ford in 1977 (shown here). Splashy graphics, reminiscent of Carroll Shelby's early GT 350s, were standard for the Cobra II.

Easily the most collectible Mustang II is the King Cobra, built only for 1978. Splashy graphics, front and rear spoilers, wheel-opening spats, and sexy wheels were all standard.

John Asher. Included in this costly deal were various body add-ons, most of which reminded more than one casual witness of what Pontiac was then doing to its popular Trans Am. Looking especially reminiscent was the King Cobra's large hood decal, which brought many comparisons to the Trans Am's familiar "screaming chicken" logo. Additional reminders included a rear deck spoiler, wheel opening air deflectors, a front air dam, and a rearward facing hood scoop. Fortunately that air dam wasn't just for show; it did incorporate functional brake-cooling openings.

Straight-line performance was average at best, thanks to a 302-cubic-inch two-barrel V8 net-rated at only 139 horsepower. "Ten years later and the Ford Mustang Cobra has not only lost its 'Jet,' it [has also] lost its venom," wrote *Cars* magazine's Don Chaikin after watching a King Cobra canter down the quarter-mile in 16.59 seconds at 82.42 mph.

Overall impressions, on the other hand, were far more positive due to the presence of a sporty chassis enhanced with heavy-duty springs, adjustable Gabriel shock absorbers, a rear stabilizer bar, power front disc brakes, power steering, and Goodyear radials mounted on 13-inch aluminum "lattice-lace" wheels. A polished dash insert and sport steering wheel spruced things up inside. All this equipment cost nearly $1,300, bringing a 1978 King Cobra's price to nearly $7,000. "The King Cobra is far from an economy car," added Asher. "But for the money, few American cars can match it for looks, handling and overall performance."

"That's performance today," echoed Chaikin. "Going around corners quickly—and looking like you go around corners quickly—is where it's at. And this little King Cobra does just that." He failed to mention how nice it would've looked parked outside Studio 54.

So ended the Mustang II legacy—a truly short tale about a truly small pony car.

OPPOSITE, BOTTOM: Designers arguably went just a bit overboard with revised Cobra II graphics for 1978. Cobra II production that year was 8,009.

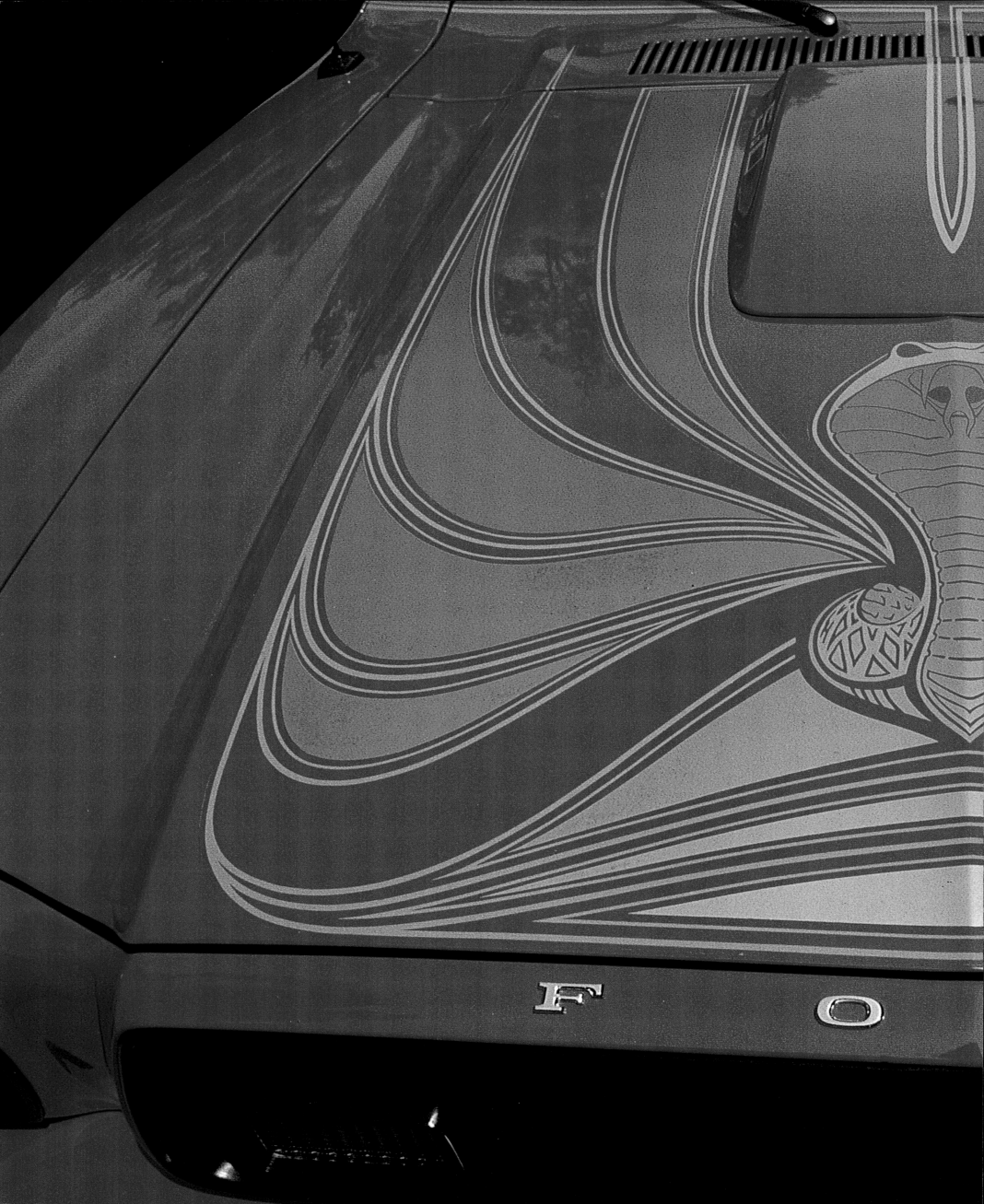

Fox-Chassis Mustangs, 1979–1993

Two chapters in the storied Mustang history came to a close not long after Ford celebrated its 75th birthday in June 1978. As that model year ended so too did production of Lee Iacocca's little jewel. Apparently five years worth of cute-but-cramped Mustang IIs was all the market could stand—few mourned its passing. And, as it turned out, Henry Ford II felt the same about his hard-charging corporate president. A tad more than three decades was all the boss could take.

According to Iacocca, Henry II's true feelings began to boil over in 1975 after he began suffering chest pains. Now facing the inevitable, Henry Ford's grandson suddenly recognized the possi-

BACK ON TRACK

bility of someone-not-named-Ford taking over after his passing. "Iacocca Motor Company" just didn't have the same ring, nor did its forming bode well for the advancement of the proud family's next generation. Iacocca later claimed he never had aspirations

PAGES **176–177:** The Fox-chassis years ran from 1979 to 1993, a few years longer than planned. Ford officials initially considered replacing the third-generation Mustang with an all-new Mazda-based model for 1988 or 1989, but a public outcry halted that plan, leaving the old Fox to roll on until a better idea arrived. A 1982 Mustang, with an optional T-top roof, appears here.

for the corporation's penultimate position, but nothing could belay his boss once he'd made up his mind.

Beginning early in 1975, Henry Ford II made Iacocca's job a living hell. In August that year he even kicked off a Watergate-like in-house investigation of Iacocca's (and others') activities with hopes of finding some dirt that would come in handy—among other things, he actually suspected his Italian executive of having Mafia ties. After spending $2 million (according to Iacocca) on his "witch hunt," Dearborn's top officer was left holding a bag full of nothing. Yet he continued plotting against the once-prized employee who had helped make him a fortune during the 1960s.

Ford's fortunes, however, began to fade during the early 1970s, supplying Henry II with a wholly tangible ammunition source for his fight against Iacocca. A $12 million loss for 1974's closing quarter represented the corporation's first red-soaked quarterly report since 1946. In April 1975 Ford announced first-quarter losses of $11 million, making it back-to-back bad news, for

Like the Mustang II, the new Fox-chassis models initially came only in coupe and three-door hatchback forms in 1979. The optional wheels on this 1979 hatchback were included in the TRX suspension package, which also included Michelin metric tires.

both Iacocca and Ford. An increasingly paranoid Henry II was now fully incensed, and not necessarily due to all the green he was bleeding. His second marriage was coming apart at the time as well, blackening his mood even more.

The plot thickened further in 1976 after Henry II turned his ire on veteran product planner Hal Sperlich, Iacocca's righthand man dating back to the Mustang's earliest development stages. Giving no explanation, he ordered Iacocca to fire a highly talented exec who'd done nothing but great things in Dearborn. Sperlich moved over to Chrysler early in 1977, where his plans for economical front-wheel-drive cars and minivans helped reverse the fortunes of the previously beleaguered third member of Detroit's Big Three.

After Sperlich's canning, Henry II brought in a consultant group to help him restructure Ford's top management offices. In April 1977, the existing two-tiered corporate pecking order, which previously had president Iacocca answering only to chairman/CEO Ford II, was replaced by a "troika" arrangement that added Phil Caldwell into the mix as vice-chairman. An inter-office memo declared that the vice-chairman would be in charge in the absence of the chairman, meaning Iacocca was now third in line. He was pushed down again to fourth in June 1978 when Henry II installed his younger brother, William Clay Ford, in an executive position directly beneath Caldwell. Clearly the plan involved keeping a family member close to the top in the event of Henry II's disability or death.

Iacocca's displeasure mattered not at all, especially after Henry II informed board members on June 12 of his plans to fire his purportedly pushy president. The board talked him out of it for the moment, but a month later he again went before them with the same proclamation. This time he wouldn't be denied. Iacocca got the axe on July 13, though by agreement (to preserve his accrued benefits) he officially "retired" from Ford on October 15, his 54th birthday.

"The best ballplayer in the business is now a free agent," announced an *Automotive News* editorial following Iacocca's firing. Indeed. He was immediately courted by the likes of Lockheed and International Paper, and even Radio Shack. But, as he put it, cars remained in his blood. Though Renault officials tried to bring him to France, in the end it was John Riccardo, Chrysler's board chairman, who managed to snare him. In November 1978 he was officially reunited with his old comrade, Hal Sperlich.

At least the two former Ford men left behind a solid plan for the next new Mustang before being shown the door in Dearborn. That progress dated back to the summer of 1972, a time when Henry II's people were finally getting serious about meeting the growing import challenge. Sporadic gasoline shortages around America that year foretold tougher times to follow and made it even more imperative to explore increased fuel efficiency. The Arab oil embargo, instituted in October 1973, nailed things home and at the same time greatly enhanced the attraction of foreign

compacts. The imports' cut of the U.S. pie prior to 1970 had hovered around 10 percent. Within a few years it had risen to 15 percent and was nearly 23 percent by 1979.

To better meet this threat, Ford officials opted to widen their downsizing approach. First came Granada, their "luxury compact," in 1975. The new Fairmont followed three years later, as did a shrunken Thunderbird in 1977, and an even smaller T-bird in 1980. Along with its Zephyr counterpart from Mercury, the Fairmont was a product of the weight-conscious Fox-chassis project, first mentioned around Ford Motor Company in February 1973. In October 1974, work began on a Fox-based replacement for the Mustang II, and this model was scheduled for release one year after the Fairmont. The slim, trim 1980 Thunderbird also was a Fox-chassis vehicle.

Fox Mustang design work got rolling early in 1975. Contrary to the Mustang II, which was developed first as a fastback, Ford's third-generation pony car was fashioned initially as a notch-back coupe, with a sloping roof added at a later date. Fuel-saving aerodynamics, an entirely new focus around Detroit at the time, were of prime importance as Dearborn designers finally realized that a car could also save on gas by cheating the wind—an efficient vehicle didn't necessarily have to be a smaller one.

Physical laws also were respected when choosing materials. Weight-savings became the order of the day wherever possible, with the goal being to still create a compact pony car that offered more interior space than the painfully small Mustang II. When it was all said and done, Ford's first Fox Mustang appeared to violate those laws in that it looked and felt bigger than its predecessor yet actually was lighter, hence more efficient. Weighing 200 pounds less than the Mustang II, the Fox model was longer, taller, and featured more legroom. A composite front fascia, urethane bumpers, thinner doors and windows, and various lightening holes cut into the unit-body structure all contributed to that weight loss.

ABOVE LEFT: Exterior changes were minor for the 1980 Mustang, which was available again as a three-door hatchback (shown here) or a two-door coupe. Production of base hatchbacks, priced at $5,194 with the standard four-cylinder, was 98,497 that year.

ABOVE RIGHT: Like its Cobra II forerunner, the 1979 Cobra was adorned with splashy graphics. But it also came standard with the specially tuned TRX suspension and its metric Michelin tires mounted on aluminum wheels.

CLASS ACT: JACK TELNACK

John J. Telnack Jr. was destined to be a Ford man. His father worked at the company's enormous River Rouge facility; he was born, in 1937, in Detroit's Henry Ford Hospital; and some of his earliest, fondest memories involve riding wide-eyed by the palatial Ford Rotunda in Dearborn—on his bicycle. He even met ol' Henry once during his youth, and he remembers scaling the wall around Ford's test track to sketch the firm's latest new models as they sped past. At 15 he was treated by his dad to a visit of the firm's Design Center, and he was completely hooked. Six years later he went to work for his favorite automaker after graduating from the Art Center for Design in Pasadena, California. "I couldn't design a Chevy if I tried," said the classy Ford exec with his trademark warm smile in a February 1998 Automotive Industries interview.

Jack Telnack stepped down as Ford Motor Company's vice-president of design in 1997. "We are grateful for Jack's outstanding contribution to Ford's product design over the years," said Ford chairman Alex Trotman after Telnack announced his upcoming retirement that September. "His talents have been recognized far beyond Ford."

Indeed, listing the feathers in his cap after 39 years at Ford can't possibly be accomplished in 25 words or less, not even close. Along with the 1979 Mustang, historic highlights include the rounded 1983 Thunderbird and the sensationally new Taurus, *Motor Trend*'s "Car of the Year" for 1986. All three machines exhibited an unprecedented sense of aerodynamics, certainly from a Yankee perspective, but it was that last milestone (along with its equally stunning Mercury Sable corporate cousin) that really had jaws both dropping and wagging during the Eighties.

"The Taurus is the most significant car introduced by Ford in decades," proclaimed *Motor Trend*'s John Hanson in 1986. "More important, Ford has somehow managed to step away from the stodgy Detroit establishment of sameness and design a car of the future—then show the guts to grab rock-steady middle America by the throat and announce, 'Hey, forget what you know about Detroit iron. This is how it's going to be from now on.'" At 0.32, the Taurus sedan's drag coefficient ranked right up with the world's slipperiest in 1986.

Concentrating on sleek forms that also functioned fabulously against the wind was Telnack's forte, not to mention his claim to fame. "The aero look—with its sweeping lines and fuselage-like curves—has made John J. Telnack one of the most influential designers Detroit has seen since [General Motors'] Harley Earl introduced the 'Torpedo Look' in 1940," announced the *New York Times* in 1987.

Some critics didn't exactly like the "jelly bean" aspects of Telnack's aero look, perhaps explaining the impetus behind his next eye-opening contribution to Ford design history, his "New Edge" approach. First seen on the GT-90 concept car in 1994, then in regular production on the European-market, Fiesta-based Ka (introduced in 1996), New Edge design combined those rounded aero shapes with contrasting, crisp, angular lines. Both Mercury's new Cougar, unveiled in 1999, and that year's restyled Mustang also were products of New Edge thinking, as was Ford's fabulous GT-40 concept vehicle, which debuted in 2002.

Telnack more or less cut his teeth at Ford working on the original Mustang's wheel covers, as well as the new fastback body that showed up in 1965. He was made Lincoln-Mercury studio head that year then served as Ford of Australia's design department president from 1966 to 1969. He came back to work in Dearborn to fashion Mustangs, Mavericks, and Pintos in 1969 but went overseas

again in 1974 after being named Ford of Europe's design president. Telnack was appointed executive director of North American Light Car and Truck Design in 1976 and two years later was renamed executive director of North American Mid-Size Car and Interior Design. From 1980 to 1987 he was the chief design executive for Ford's North American Automotive Operations (NAAO). His promotion to Ford Motor Company design vice-president came in June 1987.

Ford later restructured its design operations to consolidate its various worldwide groups into a new global organization and Telnack was appointed its chief, with the new title of Corporate Design vice president, in July 1993. Yet another reorganization in May 1994, this one ranging corporate-wide, re-titled him as Ford Automotive Operations Design v.p. Wonder how much his employer spent on his business cards.

Among Jack Telnack's last duties at Ford involved choosing his successor, J. C. Mays, simply "J," without a period, to everyone watching Dearborn's latest, greatest designs. It was then left up to Mays to shepherd the next next-generation Mustang, but that's another historic story for later pages.

Ford Motor Company Design Vice President Jack Telnack retired in 1997 after 39 years at the firm he'd loved since childhood.

Base price for a Mustang hatchback in 1979 was $4,436. A four-cylinder was standard; an inline six-cylinder, V6, or V8, was optional.

Total Mustang production for 1980 was 271,322, including 128,893 base coupes, shown here. Another 20,285 Ghia coupes were also built for 1980.

The 1979 Cobra's hood treatment was plainly reminiscent of the artwork that appeared on the King Cobra's lid the year before.

Fox Mustang styling was overseen by Jack Telnack, who had left his position as Ford of Europe's design vice president to become executive director of Ford's North American Light Car and Truck Design department in April 1975. Various studios, again including Italy's Ghia, competed once more against each other for the honor of creating the latest, greatest Mustang, and in the end it was Telnack's team that barely nosed out Gene Bordinat's for that prize. The winning work of art was so refined it rolled right through final production approval in September 1976 with nary a notable revision.

Like the Mustang II, the Fox-chassis pony car was scheduled to appear in public as both a two-door coupe and three-door hatchback. Interestingly, advance press kits mailed out to journalists prior to that debut included a photo showing a proud Iacocca standing in front of Telnack's work. But when magazine people were first allowed to meet up close and personal with pre-production examples (these prototype introductions started as early as May 1978), it was Vice President Bill Bourke who did all the showing off. Proverbial handwriting on the wall? Certainly.

When the resized final product arrived in the fall of 1978 it instantly amazed witnesses with its cutting-edge aerodynamics. According to Telnack, it was the car that kicked off the aero craze in America thanks to its overall wedge shape. "It was the first car with a tapered front end," he said in a February 1998 *Automotive Industries* interview. At 0.46, the 1979 coupe's drag coefficient (Cd) represented a 25 percent improvement compared to its 1978 forerunner. Meanwhile, the new three-door fastback's superb Cd, 0.44, made it one of Detroit's slipperiest offerings.

Revised dimensions included more wheelbase (up 4.2 inches to 100.2), more overall length (179.1 inches compared to 175), and more height (up an inch and a half to 51.8 inches). Inside, the 1979 coupe contained 14 more cubic feet of usable space, while its hatchback running mate offered 16 more. But even with all these changes, Ford's all-new third-generation pony car retained more than enough traditional ties to keep the faithful pony car fans faithful. "The 1979 Mustang will continue to enhance the enthusiasm first generated by the original 1965 Mustang," predicted division General Manager Walt Walla.

As was the case in 1979, the second-edition Mustang Cobra was available with either a 2.3-liter turbocharged four-cylinder (shown here) or a 5.0-liter (302-cubic-inch) V8 in 1980.

The 1979 Mustang Cobra Turbo was powered by a force-fed 2.3-liter four-cylinder that made 140 horsepower.

Priced at $625, the Carriage Roof option made a 1980 Mustang coupe look a lot like a convertible.

Later down the road, Mustang watchers would be amazed at how well Telnack's body reeled in the years. Though a few notable upgrades did occur—most prominently an even more aerodynamic nose for the SVO model in 1984 and a similarly refashioned, fully flush GT facade in 1987—basically the same shell remained looking sharp up through 1993.

"I'm just delighted that the car has had that kind of longevity," said Telnack in a 1994 *Super Ford* magazine interview. "I love the '79 [Mustang] because I was very emotionally involved with that car and I am very definitely surprised [the Fox models] held up this long. I think the main reason [they] held up was because we were able to do a dramatic front end with the aero headlamps to really pull it away from what we've been conditioned to on that car line."

Per Fox-chassis specifications, Telnack's beloved 1979 Mustang incorporated radically revised suspension setups at both ends. Modified MacPherson struts (with coil springs wedged between the lower control arms and subframe instead of being wrapped around the struts themselves) went up front. Bringing up the rear were coil springs (in place of traditional leafs) and a four-link solid axle. A rear stabilizer bar was standard, as were front disc brakes and rack-and-pinion steering. Handling was the car's strong point, as critics quickly noted. According to *Motor Trend*'s John Ethridge, the 1979 Mustang could "now compete both in the marketplace and on the road with lots of cars that used to outclass it."

The new Fox Mustang also outclassed its Pinto-based predecessor in the sales department. By April 1979, Ford's latest pony cars were rolling off the lot twice as quickly as their Mustang II counterparts in 1978. The final production count for 1979 was nearly 370,000.

Standard beneath the hood that year was Ford's 2.3-liter OHC four-cylinder. Optional was a turbocharged four-cylinder and a 130-horsepower 5.0-liter V8. Offered as well early on was a 2.8-liter V6, a problem-plagued option that soon was replaced by Ford's old 200-cubic-inch inline six, which remained available up through 1982. According to *Car and Driver*'s Don Sherman, the 1979 V8 Mustang was "a piece of Detroit iron ready and able to over-rev your pulse rate."

Buyers in 1979 also could've opted for the Ghia package, available this time for both body styles. Mustang Ghias wore various color-keyed body parts, pinstripes, BR78 radial tires, and turbine-style wheelcovers. Low-back bucket seats and color-keyed door panels were standard inside.

Like the Ghia option, the Cobra also rolled over from 1978 and in standard form included the forced-induction 2.3-liter four crowned by a hood scoop adorned with appropriate "Turbo" identification. The 5.0-liter V8, fitted that year with a one-piece "serpentine" accessory-drive belt, was predictably optional. Mustang Cobras came standard in 1979 with the new TRX sport suspension (an option for non-Cobras), consisting of Michelin metric rubber, attractive aluminum wheels, and specially tuned springs and shocks. A third special edition model, an Indy 500 pace car replica, was introduced midyear to mark the Mustang's second appearance at "The Brickyard." This package was offered only for the 1979 hatchback.

The snazzy Recaro bucket seats included inside the 1979 pace car replicas appeared as an option for all Mustangs in 1980 along with a "carriage roof" that covered a notchback's top in diamond-grain vinyl to make it look like a convertible. High-pressure P-metric radial tires and more effective halogen headlamps became standard on all Mustangs that year. Other Indy pace car parts (front air dam, hood scoop, rear spoiler) were added to the 1980 Cobra, which also was treated to a revised tape treatment. Rolling over too from 1979 was the Sport option, available only for the hatchback. Included in this deal were styled-steel wheels with trim rings and various dress-up moldings for the rocker panels, windows, and bodysides.

The base 2.3-liter four-cylinder also carried over into 1980, as did its troublesome turbocharged variant. Gone was the relatively peppy 5.0-liter V8; in its place was an optional, more efficient 119-horsepower 4.2-liter V8, created by reducing the Windsor small-block's bore from 4 inches to 3.68. Only 2.7 percent of the 1980 Mustang run featured this wimpy power source, which initially was available only with an automatic transmission. A four-speed overdrive manual gearbox appeared midyear to at least turn up the excitement a little.

Few changes were made in 1981, the final year for the garish Cobra. The previous year's engine lineup repeated, save for the gremlin-infested turbo option, discontinued early on after first being advertised in Ford literature. Notable new options included a trendy T-top roof (available for coupes and hatchbacks), power windows, rear window louvers (for the hatchback), and a Traction-Lok differential. That latter addition helped cure a problem inherent to the Fox platform: its four-link coil suspension was too willing to "wheel hop" during hard acceleration. Allowing both tires in back to take equal bites greatly inhibited this action.

Overall appearances remained familiar in 1982, and the same could've been said for the engine lineup, with the inline six and frugal 4.2-liter V8 making their final appearances. New that year was a revised model lineup. Starting things off was the base "L," offered only as a coupe. Next up was the more prestigious GL, followed by the upscale GLX, both available as coupes and hatchbacks. At the top was the reborn GT, back after a 13-year hiatus.

Available only in hatchback form, the 1982 GT was paired up with another returning friend, the 5.0-liter V8, also offered that year as an option for non-GT Mustangs. This performance-oriented small-block was prominently promoted as the "HO" V8, with those letters again standing for "High Output." HO upgrades included a larger two-barrel carburetor, a more aggressive cam, stiffer valve springs, and a double-roller timing chain in place of the conventionally linked chain used in earlier 5.0-liters. On top was a low-restriction, dual-snorkel air cleaner wearing a chromed lid; on the exhaust end was a mundane single pipe. The HO's 157 warmly welcomed horses inspired Ford to proclaim, "The Boss is Back!"

Backing up the HO was the carryover four-speed SROD (Single Rail Overdrive) manual transmission. All HO Mustangs, GT or not, also were fitted with bright exhaust tips and welded-on traction bars, with the latter pieces added to further control wheel hop. And stuck on each HO fender as well was the chromed "5.0" emblem that soon would stand tall as a badge of honor among this country's newborn muscle car set.

Typical vinyl covering and the convertible-like Carriage Roof option (shown here) remained available for the 1981 Mustang coupe.

Revised model designations appeared for 1982, with the coupe now available in the basic L (shown here), the dressier GL, or the top-shelf GLX form.

Big news for 1982 involved the return of the hot-to-trot Mustang GT (foreground), which came standard with a High Output (HO) 5.0-liter V8 rated at 157 horsepower. Behind the GT is a special edition McLaren Mustang, modeled after the IMSA concept car created by Ford in 1980 to mark the company's return to organized road racing.

SETTIN' THE PACE

Leading the pace lap around the "Brickyard" prior to the annual running of the Indianapolis 500 has been a prestigious honor dating back to the initial running of the "greatest spectacle in motorsports." A Stoddard-Dayton touring car, driven by Indianapolis Motor Speedway founder/president Carl Fisher, brought the first Indy 500 field to the starting flag on May 30, 1911. That Fisher also piloted Stoddard-Dayton pace cars in 1913 and 1914 was no coincidence—he owned a Stoddard-Dayton dealership in Indianapolis.

Actually, the moniker used most often prior to World War II was "pace maker," though the term "official pace car" did show up a few times on some doors and fenders during the '20s, '30s, and '40s. Prewar pace makers came from well-known firms like Ford, Chrysler, Cadillac, and Lincoln. Long-lost classics like Stutz, Packard, Marmon, Cord, Duesenberg, and LaSalle also took part, as did nearly forgotten Premier, National, Cole, H.C.S, and Rickenbacker. In most cases, these vehicles were stock, regular-production models, save for one notable exception: the 1941 race was paced by Chrysler's exotic Newport, a four-door, dual-cowl phaeton showcar created to demonstrate futuristic styling ideas.

The modern practice of marketing pace car replicas for public consumption didn't start gaining real steam until the '60s. But Ford probably deserves credit for first lighting a fire beneath this still-hot fad thanks to the 2,000 appropriately identified "Official Pace Car" Sunliner convertible demonstrators shipped to dealerships in 1953 to help mark both the company's 50th anniversary and its pace-lap appearance at Indy that year. More than one dealer further enhanced this promotion by reproducing replicas for sale to their customers. The rest is history.

Three times Ford's famed pony car has been picked to pace the Indy 500, and three times the appearance represented a coming-out party of sorts for an all-new Mustang. In May 1994, a Special Vehicle Team (SVT) Cobra convertible did the honors at Indianapolis about six months after Dearborn's latest and greatest fourth-generation Mustang had hit the streets to rave reviews. Fifteen years prior, Ford's first Fox-chassis Mustang led the pack on race day, proudly announcing the third generation's arrival in the process. And the Mustang's initial lap at Indy in 1964 helped mark the breed's birth—it just doesn't come any newer than that.

Iacocca's little pony was barely six weeks old when it hit the bricks on May 30, 1964, with Henry Ford's son Benson at the wheel. Two or three (the exact count is unclear) actual pace cars were specially modified for the 48th running of the Indy 500, with a backup or backups built in case of breakdown or accident. Power was supplied by experi-

mental 289 High Performance V8s stuffed full of forged-aluminum pistons and aggressive solid-lifter cams. Balanced and blueprinted, these high-winding Windsor small-blocks also were carefully constructed to guarantee ample oiling during that one glorious pass around the rack at 100+ mph.

Along with these hot-to-trot pace cars, Ford also put together 35 "festival cars," similarly adorned (white with blue stripes) Mustang convertibles better suited to handle, at much slower speeds, the preferably petite rear ends of various hand-waving race queens. These parade vehicles were stock ragtops fitted with low-compression 289 four-barrel V8s. Both four-speed and automatic versions were delivered to Indy, and reportedly all 35 were sold after the race at a dealer auction held in Louisville, Kentucky.

Mustangs have paced the Indianapolis 500 three times, including the 1964 (top) and 1979 (above) events. A red Cobra convertible (opposite, bottom) made it a trifecta in 1994. Opposite, top: Ford chairman Alex Trotman (middle) poses at The Brickyard with Parnelli Jones (left) and A. J. Foyt.

Festival cars then filtered into John Q. Public's hands from there, as did about 200 pace car replica coupes built in April and early May. These 1964-1/2 Mustangs featured the same lettering and striping seen on the topless parade cars but were finished in Pace Car White instead of the Wimbledon White used on the race-day convertibles. All replica coupes were identically equipped with 260-cubic-inch two-barrel V8s, Cruise-O-Matic automatic transmissions, power steering, and white interiors.

Dearborn officials chose to mark the Mustang's second Indy 500 appearance with quite a bit more effort and flair. This time Ford established a new Detroit record for pace car replica production, rolling out 10,478 copies of the T-top coupe racing great Jackie Stewart drove around the track on May 27, 1979, to kick off the 63rd Indy 500. Unlike Stewart's ride, which was powered by a modified 5.0-liter V8, the replicas featured the 1979 Mustang's optional flip-open roof panel and were offered to the public with either V8s or turbocharged 2.3-liter four-cylinders. All the turbo-four models were fitted with four-speed manual transmissions, while the 5.0-liter cars featured both four-speed sticks and automatics. The production breakdown read 5,970 turbo-fours, 2,402 V8/four-speeds, and 2,106 V8/automatics.

All 1979 pace car replicas looked the same on the outside with their Silver Metallic paint complemented by black accents and red/orange striping. Applying the official Indy 500 commemorative decals was left up to the dealer or owner—some cars got these graphics, some didn't. Additional standard features included Ford's coveted TRX suspension, a front air dam with foglamps, a non-functional rear-ward-facing hood scoop, a rear spoiler, and exclusively patterned Recaro bucket seats.

Adding official pace car exterior identification was again a customer's prerogative in 1994 when the Mustang was invited to Indy for the third time. All 1,000 Rio Red SVT Cobra convertibles built that year were pace car replicas, but not all featured these decals, which

were delivered in the cars' trunks. A special pace car dash plaque was included inside regardless of whether the buyer wanted it or not.

All 1994 pace car replicas also featured tan convertible tops and saddle interiors—both saddle and black appointments were offered inside a 1994 SVT Cobra coupe. Cobra convertible wheels also differed that year compared to their coupe counterparts: convertible units featured black paint in the openings between their five brightly chromed spokes, while the coupe wheels were left natural aluminum inside those openings.

Like its coupe running mate, the 1994 Cobra convertible was powered by a hopped-up version of the Mustang GT's 215-horsepower 5.0-liter V8 that produced 25 extra horsepower. Additional standard equipment included power steering, air conditioning, leather interior appointments, and Ford's mondo Mach 460 AM/FM CD stereo.

As a side note, the five pace cars specially prepared by Jack Roush for the 1994 Indy 500 weren't true SVT models, they were garden-variety Mustang GT convertibles converted into Cobras. And another Ford racing legend, Parnelli Jones, handled pace-lap chores that year, the last for the Mustang at the Brickyard.

Along with an expected Traction-Lok rear axle, the 1982 GT also came standard with a special handling suspension, power steering and brakes, and P185/75 radial rubber on cast-aluminum wheels. TRX wheels and tires were optional, as were Recaro buckets and a T-top roof. Additional standard features included a special grille, a non-functional hood scoop, an exclusive front fascia with foglamps and air dam, a rear spoiler, and a monochromatic exterior done in red, black, or metallic silver.

A *Motor Trend* test of a prototype 1982 5.0-liter Mustang resulted in a rather remarkable 6.9-second 0–60 pass, making this revived street machine one of the quickest cars Detroit had to offer that year. Make it *the* quickest at that price. "It is a vastly improved automobile that goes, stops and handles well enough to outperform many of its more expensive competitors, both import and domestic," wrote *Motor Trend*'s Jim McCraw. "For our money, it's the best-balanced, most capable Mustang ever done." Could praise get any higher?

The 1983 Mustang emerged in even more aerodynamic fashion thanks to a new front fascia. Restyled taillights also appeared that year along with two new optional power sources:

The 1983 Mustang GT featured an even stronger 175-horse HO V8. Note the optional T-top roof, introduced in 1981.

another turbocharged 2.3-liter four-cylinder and Ford's 3.8-liter "Essex" V6. That latter engine produced 105 horses, compared to 87 for the archaic inline six it replaced. The much improved turbo four featured Bosch-supplied electronic port fuel injection instead of an old-school two-sbarrel carburetor.

Ford Motor Company's first electronic fuel-injection system had appeared in 1980 for the Lincoln Versailles. The corporation's innovative Electronic Engine Control (EEC) technology had debuted for carbureted engines two years before. Improved EEC II equipment arrived in 1979, followed by the EEC III the following year. The latter was found on carbureted engines as well as Lincoln's 5.0-liter V8 with its centralized fuel injection. Ford's superior EEC IV computer controls, featuring an onboard self-diagnostic system, arrived in 1984.

Rated at 145 horsepower, the Mustang's first injected, turbocharged four incorporated forged-aluminum pistons, special alloy valves, a lightened flywheel, and an oil cooler. A 90-horse-power carbureted 2.3-liter four-cylinder remained the base engine for the 1983 Mustang, while the optional HO V8 was again the top option. HO output increased to 175 horsepower that year thanks mostly to a revised cam and new four-barrel carburetor, last found atop a Mustang small-block V8 in 1973. Holley supplied that four-holer.

Ford's 1983 GT was available with either the HO V8 or turbo four. New behind both engines that year was a Borg-Warner T-5 five-speed manual transmission, a major upgrade compared to the SROD gearbox it replaced. Most other GT mechanicals rolled over from 1982.

Along with the 5.0-liter HO V8, a 1983 GT also could've been equipped with Ford's turbocharged four-cylinder. The TRX aluminum wheels seen here were optional.

Absent since 1973, a convertible model returned to the Mustang lineup in 1983, to the delight of topless driving fans everywhere.

Ford marked the Mustang's 20th birthday with a special anniversary model, offered in convertible and hatchback forms. Like its original forefather (background), the 20th Anniversary Mustang was dubbed a mid-year model, hence its "1984-1/2" designation.

Additional improvements included wider tires and a thicker rear stabilizer bar. A revised rearward-facing scoop graced the hood, and black trim around the windshield and side glass completed the package. The TRX suspension was again optional.

A Mustang convertible returned from retirement midyear in 1983. All of these topless models began life as full-roofed notchbacks and all were adorned with power tops with glass backlights after their steel roofs were cut off. Both GT and GLX Mustangs were transformed into convertibles that year, with the latter examples making up the bulk of those ordered. Convertible production made up 20 percent of the 1983 pony car run.

The Mustang lineup was revised again in 1984. The base L, now offered in coupe and hatchback forms, remained. But next up the ladder was the LX, available as a coupe, hatchback, or convertible. Again built with or without a roof, the GT once more led the way that year. Standard for the L and LX was the 2.3-liter four-cylinder, but the LX convertible's base engine was the 3.8-liter V6. Available GT engines rolled over from 1983. GTs in 1984 got V-rated tires, good up to 130 mph, and the TRX option was offered for one final time. Also retired at year's end was the GT Turbo.

Ford's efficient EEC IV electronic controls were added to all 1984 Mustang engines. The V6 also got electronic fuel injection to help boost output to 120 horsepower. While the 1984 GT's HO small-block remained carbureted, an EFI 5.0-liter V8, rated at 165 horsepower, appeared for automatic transmission applications. Ford's innovative four-speed automatic overdrive (AOD) transmission was a new Mustang option for 1984. New too were quad shock absorbers in back.

Yet another midyear model appeared in 1984, this one marking the Mustang's 20th birthday. Available as both a convertible and hatchback, the 20th Anniversary pony car could've been fitted with three different powertrain combos: the HO/five-speed, the EFI 302 with AOD transmission, or the 2.3-liter turbo four and five-speed manual. All were 1984-1/2 GT models and all shared the same exterior: Oxford White paint accented with Shelby-style "G.T. 350" striping on each

The Euro-style SVO Mustang, with its asymmetrical hood scoop, debuted in 1984 and wowed Yankees with its amazing 175-horsepower four-cylinder. Turbocharging and electronic fuel injection helped this little four-cylinder really run.

rocker panel. Interiors were done in Canyon Red and featured articulating sport seats and special dashboard badges denoting their limited-edition status.

New for 1984, too, was the aforementioned SVO model with its aero nose, Trans Am–style ground effects, and "bi-plane" rear spoiler. Announced in September 1980, Ford's Special Vehicle Operations department had been formed to create "a series of limited-production performance cars and develop their image through motorsport." Michael Kranefuss, who had previously been competition director for Ford of Europe, was brought across the Atlantic to run SVO, and he wasted little time putting the latest-generation pony car to work on IMSA and SCCA road-racing courses. A "limited-production performance car" then followed four years later.

A major blast of fresh air, Ford's first SVO Mustang wowed critics in 1984 with its hot, high-tech performance and Euro-style sporty flair. Beneath its asymmetrical hood scoop was an intercooled, turbocharged, fuel-injected 2.3-liter engine that amazingly pumped out V8-type horsepower using only four cylinders. Output for this 140-cubic-inch mighty mite was a sensational 175 horses. Throw in a Hurst-shifted five-speed manual transmission, Koni gas-charged shock absorbers, quick-ratio steering, four-wheel disc brakes and 16-inch aluminum wheels, and the sum of the parts equaled a bodacious street racer that even European drivers could love.

Americans, however, couldn't quite warm up to what amounted to perhaps the best balanced performance Mustang to date, a claim echoed by more than one automotive magazine at the time. Such raves did not translate into sufficient sales, however, even after engineers bumped output up

New Goodyear Eagle tires on 15x7 cast-aluminum wheels were rolled out for the Mustang GT in 1985. The HO V8 hit 210 horsepower that year.

to 205 horsepower in 1985 by adding a revised intake, improved turbo housing, a longer duration cam, larger Bosch injectors, and less restrictive exhausts featuring twin tailpipes trailing the single catalytic converter. This intriguing machine, called "Fords future think car" and the "Future Boss" by *Motor Trend*, was cancelled in 1986 after 9,844 were built for its short three-year run.

Along with a second-edition SVO variant (updated with flush headlight covers), LX and GT models made up the 1985 lineup as the basic L failed to carry over from 1984. All Mustangs that year were fitted with a fresh façade featuring an integral air dam and a revised SVO-type grille opening. LX models came standard with power brakes and steering, low-back bucket seats, and an AM/FM stereo. LX engine choices were 1984 repeats.

The 1985 GT was fitted with new wheels and rubber, as well as the SVO Mustang's Y-pipe exhaust system. Those rims were 15x7 cast-aluminum units that incorporated 10 ornamental openings. They were shod in Goodyear Eagle P225/60VR unidirectional Gatorbacks, really wide tires that couldn't help but greatly enhance traction and handling. Additional GT enhancements arrived under the hood, where 210 horses now resided, representing a high for the carbureted HO legacy. New were tubular headers, another revised camshaft, and friction-reducing roller lifters. Also contributing to the 1985 HO's output gain was a redesigned accessory drive system that spun the air conditioning compressor, power steering pump, and alternator slower to reduce parasitic horsepower loss. That year's T-5 five-speed was upgraded too with shorter throws between gears.

Next to no noticeable exterior changes announced the 1986 Mustang's arrival. The LX's engine lineup also carried over save for one notable deletion: gone was the throttle-body-injected V8, replaced in automatic transmission applications by the HO small-block previously limited to manual-trans installations. New for the HO V8 in 1986 was a sequential multi-port EFI system in place of that good, old four-barrel carburetor. The EFI HO also was fitted with true dual exhausts incorporating twin catalytic converters. Additional HO upgrades included high-swirl heads, a

more efficient water pump, and a reinforced engine block. Five-liter V8 output was now 200 horsepower, the same advertised tag found on that year's SVO Mustang four-cylinder. Last on 1986's list of upgrades was the V8 Mustang's beefier 8.8-inch axle, which replaced the wimpy 7.5-inch rear end found beneath earlier HO models.

Fox-chassis styling finally was freshened in a big way in 1987, with the latest LX taking on a new rounded nose featuring flush-covered, wraparound headlights. Much more dramatic was the updated GT, with its ground effect skirts and exclusive lattice-covered taillight treatment. The GT also used those aero-styled headlights but didn't have a grille opening between them like the LX.

Only two Mustang engines were available in 1987: the LX's standard 2.3-liter four-cylinder and the GT's 5.0-liter HO V8. Once again the HO was an option for the LX. Transmission choices too were simplified as both engines could've been backed up by either the AOD automatic or five-speed manual. New turbine-style 15x7 wheels were exclusive to the Mustang GT that year. Standard for the 5.0-liter LX models were the 1986 GT's 15-inch alloy rims.

New for the base four-cylinder was a multi-port fuel injection system that brought maximum power up to 90 horses. HO output, meanwhile, peaked at 225 horsepower in 1987 thanks to better breathing cylinder heads (copped from Ford's truck line) and revised EFI equipment with enlarged (up from 58mm to 60) throttle body bores. Tube headers and a roller cam carried over from 1986.

According to *Hot Rod*, those 225 horses, hitched up to the lighter LX Mustang body, could gallop through the quarter-mile in an impressive 14.17 seconds. In the same test, Ford's heavier, pricier 1987 GT posted a 14.60-second dash. No matter which body you chose, Dearborn's latest HO pony car was a certified Camaro-killer. And it cost less, too, making it Detroit's so-called biggest bang for the buck.

Nothing notable set the 1988 Mustang apart from its restyled predecessor, and much the same could've been said the following year. HO Mustangs delivered in environmentally conscious California in 1988 were fitted with a mass-airflow sensor in place of the speed-density fuel control system used in all other cases. In 1989 the superior mass-air system was installed on all models in all states. The LX/HO combination was renamed "LX 5.0 Sport" in 1989, and a 140-mph speedometer replaced the GT's 85-mph unit midway through that year's run.

Introduced for 1984, the Mustang LX became the base model the following year after the L failed to return. Available as a coupe, hatchback, or convertible, the LX came standard with a four-cylinder engine, but the hot 5.0-liter HO V8 was an option. A 1987 5.0-liter LX hatchback is shown here.

Mustang fans anticipated a special model to mark their beloved pony's 25th birthday, but all Ford did was bake them a cake.

Mustangers hoping for another special anniversary model, this one commemorating 25 years on the road, were left empty-handed in 1989, probably due to Ford's original plan to retire the Fox-chassis pony car that year in favor of an all-new Mazda-sourced front-wheel-drive model. But instead of superseding the long-running Fox, that front-driver was morphed into the new 1989 Probe, this after a customer outcry the likes of which Detroit had never heard before. Then, after missing the big birthday party in 1989, a "25th Anniversary" Mustang did show up in limited numbers the following year, apparently because the Mustang began life, in Ford officials' minds, as a 1965 model, not a 1964-1/2 as enthusiasts long have claimed. All of these 1990 anniversary cars were Emerald Green LX convertibles with white interiors.

Minor updates for 1990 were of a safety-conscious nature as rear seat shoulder belts and a driver's side airbag became standard Mustang fare. Adding that airbag meant a tilt steering column could no longer be installed. The console's center armrest structure was deleted, too, and new map pockets went into the door panels as consolations.

New for 1991 were enlarged 16-inch wheels for the GT, which had rolled on those same, tough-to-clean turbine rims since 1987. Installing these 16-inchers required revised fender lips for added clearance. News on the mechanical front included a redesigned cylinder head (with two spark plugs per cylinder) that helped 1991's base four-cylinder make 105 horsepower. Minor updates for 1992 included new color-keyed bodyside moldings and bumper strips. Introduced too was a four-way power driver's seat option.

Ford's last Fox-chassis Mustang finally showed up in 1993, and engineers marked its arrival by dropping advertised HO output to 205 horsepower. Go figure. New on the options list that year was a trendy compact-disc player. Much more impactful was the Special Vehicle Team's new Cobra, introduced as a hatchback only. Powered by a stock GT V8, the 1993 Cobra relied on various chassis modifications to make hay. A race-ready Cobra R also appeared in 1993 to help kick off the SVT Cobra legacy in proud fashion.

Both the SVT Cobra and GT rolled over into the Mustang's next new generation, which arrived just a couple years late in 1994. Most pony car lovers agreed that the wait was more than worth it.

TOP: What a difference a quarter-century makes! Nonetheless, the 1989 GT (foreground) still looked unmistakably like a Mustang—and it also differed little from its 1987 and 1988 forerunners.

ABOVE: Tabbed the "LX Sport" in 1989, the HO-powered base Mustangs carried over into 1990 all but unchanged. The 225-horse 5.0-liter V8 was available again that year in all three LX bodies—coupe, hatchback (shown here), and convertible.

RIGHT: Ford may have missed the party in 1989, but they came back in 1990 with a special 25th Anniversary LX 5.0-liter convertible, painted Emerald Green and complemented with the GT's turbine wheels.

New 16-inch wheels appeared for the GT in 1991, and these five-spoke rims were also installed on the 5.0-liter LX. Total production of the latter, including all three body styles, was 27,880 that year.

BELOW: Ford's Special Vehicle Team introduced its first Cobra for 1993. A tweaked chassis and 235-horsepower 5.0-liter V8 were standard for the original SVT Cobra, sold only in hatchback form that first year.

GALLERY

983 JCB

The longest-running generation in Mustang history, the Fox-chassis legacy, lasted 15 mostly good years, five more than planned. Dearborn officials originally hoped to end the Fox run after a decade or so and probably would have, had their initial next-generation proposal not gone over like a proverbial lead balloon once the Blue Oval faithful got wind of it. The resulting public outcry, expressed through mail by the truckload in 1987, convinced Ford not to roll out the ill-advised front-wheel-drive Mustang that was nearly fully developed by then. Instead of a Mazda-based pony car, loyal customers then got a leftover Mustang that sure looked a little long in the tooth as the '90s started rolling.

NEW AND IMPROVED

Work on plan B understandably didn't begin until after Ford people decided to rename their Japan-sourced front-driver "Probe," a move announced in the summer of 1987. But even then, early progress on a more suitable replacement for the Fox Mustang was painfully slow. That project didn't really get rolling until Alex Trotman became executive vice-president of Ford's North American Automotive Operations (NAAO) in 1989, after which time he asked two NAAO directors, Ken Nabroski and Steve Lyons, if they had any better ideas.

Nabroski in turn looked to Mustang engineering manager John Coletti in August 1989. Coletti's assignment involved pulling together a special brainstorming team tasked with concentrating solely on this project. His so-called skunkworks was formed in September, with its nine members initially meeting informally every Thursday to hopefully formulate both a business plan and viable design parameters. Skunkworks design man John Aiken, working with Dennis Reardon and Pat Schiavone, began developing early styling proposals in November, and their initial clay mockup was submitted, along with a basic plan, for Trotman's approval in February 1990. The resulting program, code-named "SN95," was officially underway by May.

Coletti's band of pioneers was then superseded by "Team Mustang," an equally dedicated group that would eventually peak at 450 members during SN95 development. Team Mustang made an old warehouse in Allen Park, Michigan, its home in June 1990, and this facility was soon renovated into Ford's Danou Technical Center. Program manager Will Boddie was originally in charge in Allen Park before moving on to serve as director of Ford's Small and Midsize Car Segment. Mike Zevalkink replaced Boddie atop Team Mustang in April 1991.

PAGES 208–209: A prominent hood scoop (for both V6 and V8 models) and a bright "corral" for the grille's galloping pony logo marked the arrival of the restyled 1999 Mustang, the first to exhibit design chief Jack Telnack's "New Edge" ideal.

Reportedly 1,350 of the vehicle's 1,850 components were new when the 1994 Mustang debuted in December 1993. The LX designation didn't carry over into the fourth generation; the 1994 lineup consisted of the base Mustang V6 (shown here) and the GT 5.0-liter.

One strategy Team Mustang used to help create its next-generation pony car image involved a series of consumer clinics, or "gallop polls," held in 1990. A long hood and short rear deck were givens going into these polls, but what about other facets and family ties? "The people we interviewed wanted galloping horses on the car," explained design manager Bud Magaldi. "But they also said that, even if you took the horses off, the car should still look like a Mustang." Also prioritized was an "American" feel. "Our research clinics proved to us that a car could be perceived as too European or too Japanese," added Magaldi.

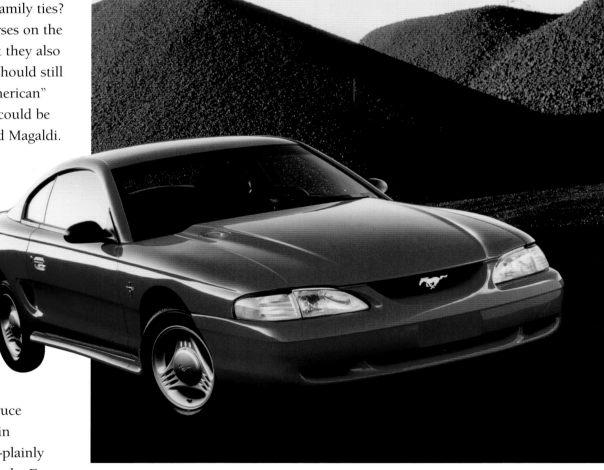

Such thinking ran all the way to the top. "What I was really fighting for on the car was a strong Mustang identity," added design vice-president Jack Telnack in a 1994 *Super Ford* magazine interview. "I wanted it to be the pure American, red-blooded Mustang. Not European, not Asian, just plain American Mustang and that's why I insisted on the horse in the grille where God intended it to be; scoops in the sides; triple taillights; and the twin cockpit interior. These are the things we have to have to make it a Mustang."

One early design proposal—nicknamed "Bruce Jenner" in honor of the Olympic legend because, in Magaldi's words, "it was a trim, athletic vehicle"—plainly looked way too much like Ford's new 1989 Probe, the Far East–flavored Mazda-in-disguise that already had turned loyal Mustangers way off. Bruce Jenner also was, again according to Magaldi, "too smooth, too clean and friendly, too nice."

Far more patriotic and bold were two themes that resulted from a design competition staged in September 1990. Leading one team was John Aiken, the man behind Bruce Jenner; captaining the other was Dave Rees. Rees' group created "Rambo," named for its gutsy, macho impressions, which proved to be a bit too tough-looking according to those gallop polls. Contrarily, Aiken's latest proposal apparently appeared just right: not too soft, not too hard. "It was called 'Arnold Schwarzenegger' because it looked like a Bruce Jenner that went down to the gym and put on some muscle and bulk," said Magaldi.

The Schwarzenegger design was approved for production in November 1990, and from there the project began gaining real momentum due to a new process at Ford called World Class Timing. Streamlining as many procedures as possible to save cost and time, Ford's new WCT plan

Like its V6 running mate, the 1994 GT (shown here) was offered in traditional sports coupe and convertible forms—no more notchback sedans or three-door hatchbacks.

NOT SO FAST

Mustang fans certainly are a devoted lot, which helps explain why Ford still had a pony car riding around in 2003 and General Motors didn't. Chevrolet's Camaro and Pontiac's Firebird no longer had a leg left to stand on, both literally and figuratively, the former because GM officials chose to cancel the F-body platform that had supported both since 1967. Sheer numbers justified that decision as F-body sales fell off considerably during the '90s. Sure, a new Camaro is in the works as we speak. But whether or not it can stick around long is anyone's guess.

Mustang, meanwhile, continues rolling on, and it does so in much the same fashion as it has for 45 years now. But, if not for that fanatical following, the car that inspired the Camaro and Firebird might have experienced a radical rebirth 20 years back, an unfortunate transformation that in turn easily could've led to the untimely demise of Detroit's pony car progenitor.

As early as 1982, Ford planners had begun work on a future replacement for the third-generation Mustang's Fox-chassis platform, then only three years old. The initial project, labeled "SN-8," called for a frugal (yet sporty) front-wheel-drive compact priced a bit below the existing Mustang. To make the SN-8 idea a reality, Dearborn officials turned to their joint-venture partners (since 1979) from Japan—Mazda—a firm experienced in the art of fuel-efficient front-wheel drives. A new code name, ST16, appeared after this deal was done, and the companies from opposite

sides of the world had a working prototype rolling by 1985. Detroit's rumor mill took it from there, letting Mustang fans discover that something truly different would supplant their old Fox in 1988 or 1989.

"Hold your horses!" was the collective cry heard from Ford customers, who were soon bombing Dearborn with protest letters once news of the alliance project broke. Dealers also complained about the impending arrival of what press critics called a "Mazstang." *Mustang Monthly*'s Donald Farr was among the most critical. "The descendants of the '79 Mustang, namely the GTs, pulled the Mustang name out of the ditch that was dug by the Mustang II,"

he wrote. "And now, after the Mustang has clawed its way to the top of the pony car heap once again, Ford plans to turn it into a front-wheel-drive copy of a Japanese car. Un-American, I say."

The automaker didn't turn a deaf ear to the disapproving din. In August 1987, Ford officials announced that this new platform would debut with a new name: Probe. As for the venerable Fox-chassis Mustang, it would carry on through 1993, though with few upgrades due to the fact that no such plans had begun percolating until after the decision was made to run with the front-wheel-drive Probe. No problem: at least a repetitious horse was better than a dead one. In so many minds, moving the Mustang badge over to that Mazda platform would've been as good as shooting Old Paint right smack between the eyes.

No worries either for Ford product planners. Sharing most of its mechanicals with Mazda's own MX-6 sport coupe, the front-wheel-drive two-door Probe compact coupe debuted in the summer of 1988 (as a 1989 model) to reasonably positive responses. Also supplied by Mazda, its three-valve-per-cylinder 2.2-liter four-cylinder made 110 horsepower in standard trim. Three different trim levels—GL, LX, and GT—were offered, with prices beginning at $10,459 for the basic GL. The $13,593 GT featured a turbocharged four-cylinder rated at 145 horsepower.

First-year Probe production was 162,889—not bad, but still not what planners had hoped when they first envisioned this vehicle replacing the long-running Mustang. An optional V6 enhanced the attraction in 1990, and a makeover for 1993 came off quite pleasing. But sales still continued to disappoint the Dearborn crowd, with the count for the Probe's eight-year run reaching roughly 837,000. Cancelling the car was the only choice after only 16,800 were sold in 1997.

And to think that could've been the Mustang getting the axe.

was put into practice for the first time during SN95 development, and heightened efficiency was realized almost immediately. Only 35 months were needed to go from clay model to regular production, compared to four full years for previous programs. And the SN95 price tag was $700 million, down from the expected $1 billion typically required to ramp up previous new models.

Keeping Team Mustang working closely at the Allen Park site contributed greatly to those savings by economizing the project's time element. "A fundamental element of World Class Timing is to have the people who make the decisions housed together with the people who execute those decisions on a daily basis," explained Mike Zevalkink. According to Will Boddie, replacing traditional, far-flung "chimney-type" corporate channels with informal, close-knit "over-the-wall" communications clearly helped speed things up. "Someone could ask me a question at the coffee pot, and I could make a decision in 10 seconds that might have taken three weeks if it had to go through some formal chain of command," he said.

Job One rolled off the line in October 1993, two months ahead of schedule, thanks mostly to the WCT process. Coletti's early groundwork helped speed things along, too, as did Team Mustang's reliance on both existing powertrains and a revamped variation of the venerable Fox chassis. Little else carried over, however: reportedly 1,350 of the next new pony car's 1,850 components were making debuts when the 1994 Mustang went on sale on December 9, 1993.

But while so many nuts and bolts didn't roll over from 1993, many things that made the previous Mustang a Mustang did, beginning with that good ol' galloping horse in the grille. Telnack's three-element taillights and the familiar C-shaped bodyside scoops inspired additional reminiscing. "It was, it is," was the simple claim made by Ford advertisements for the 1994 Mustang. Promotional people touted the car's nostalgic tail even though those taillights ran horizontally instead of vertically like the original pony car's. Oh well. At least there was no mistaking that "dual-cockpit" layout inside, yet another touch that harked back to simpler days gone by. "By having a rich history, the Mustang provided us with dozens of styling accents from the past that we could draw on and enhance," said interior designer Emeline King.

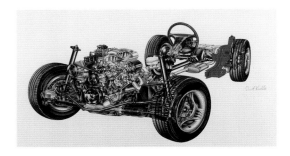

Basic suspension and steering layouts more or less rolled over from 1993, but truly new was a standard V6 engine for the base 1994 Mustang. Four-wheel disc brakes were also standard for both the V6 model and the GT 5.0-liter.

The Fox Mustang's proven 5.0-liter HO pushrod V8 remained in place for the fourth-generation GT. High Output in 1994 was 215 horsepower, up 10 horses from 1993. A Borg-Warner T-5 five-speed manual transmission was standard behind the HO; Ford's four-speed AOD automatic was optional.

"We brought back a lot of the Mustang heritage in a very contemporary way," added Bud Magaldi. "That seemed to be what people wanted us to do." "There's a latent passion that wells up in people when they see this car," said Mike Zevalkink. "It's a car for today, but it touches their past in a personal way. The wonderful changes that have been made in this automobile will, we feel, bring back this country's love affair with the Mustang."

Hiding beneath those memories was Ford's revised Fox-4 platform, an improved foundation that retained the previous Mustang's basic floor plan but was new and improved everywhere else. "This is not a carryover platform," claimed Boddie. "It's a more-developed, friendly car than its competitors. It's more refined." Much of that refinement involved increased unit-body stiffness. The new coupe measured 44 percent more torsionally rigid compared to its predecessor; its top-less counterpart was a whopping 80 percent stiffer. As for the third body style that was so popular during the Fox years, it was dropped because it simply couldn't tighten up enough. "It is very difficult, if not impossible, to build a torsionally stiff three-door hatchback," said Boddie.

In the 1994 convertible's case, that tighter, more aerodynamic body was as easy on the ears as the eyes. "You can cruise along at freeway speeds and hold a normal conversation with your passenger without raising your voice," explained Boddie. Slipping the car's one-piece convertible boot into place behind the rear seat also was a snap—that is if an owner chose to do so. "The convertible top is level with the deck," he continued. "The car looks good, even if the boot isn't put on."

Fox-4 chassis upgrades also included improved steering and handling characteristics made possible by revised suspension geometry up front and a standard anti-roll bar in back for base models, the latter installation representing a pony car first in non-GT applications. A wider track and slightly longer wheelbase also contributed to newfound road-holding abilities, a reality not missed by critics. "Where the old [GT] got by on its kick-butt, straight-line performance, the new car provides a much more entertaining, better rounded package," claimed *Road & Track*'s Jim Miller.

Last seen between pony car flanks in 1986, a V6 was standard for base models eight years later, and 1994's 3.8-liter six made 40 more horsepower than the 1993 LX's 105-horse 2.3-liter four-cylinder. The familiar 5.0-liter HO V8, now rated at 215 horsepower, carried over for the GT alone—the budget-conscious 5.0-liter base Mustang didn't return. Standard behind both the V6 and V8 was a Borg-Warner T-5 five-speed manual transmission; the familiar AOD-E four-speed electronic automatic transmission was again optional in both cases. Standard too for both models were power-assisted four-wheel disc brakes, a first for the breed.

As before, standard GT equipment also included a beefed suspension (variable-rate front coils and the Quadra-Shock setup in back) and a Traction-Lok rear axle. Among new GT features was an underhood brace that tied the shock towers to each other, as well as the cowl, to help preserve steering precision during hard cornering.

Optional for all 1994 Mustangs were anti-lock brakes (ABS), remote keyless entry, a CD player, and Ford's eight-speaker Mach 460 sound system, named for its 460 watts of peak power. Listed early on the options list was a removable hardtop for the convertible, a feature that failed to show up in the real world due to supply problems. This lift-off top did, however, reappear in 1995, but only for the SVT Cobra convertible.

Nothing notable changed for 1995, but a new model, the GTS, did appear in April that year. Like the Fox generation's LX 5.0-liter, the GTS offered GT performance at a lower price

Tagged the "Fox-4" platform in-house at Ford, the 1994 Mustang's foundation featured some 1993 Fox carryover components, done in white here. The red and yellow sections were new for the fourth-generation pony car.

While all topless Fox-chassis Mustangs were modified coupes, the 1994 convertible was engineered from the ground up to stand tall without a top, a practice not seen in Ford's pony car ranks since 1973.

OPPOSITE, BOTTOM: Nostalgic interior cues in 1994 included the embossed running horse steering wheel and "dual cockpit" layout. A tilt wheel and power driver's seat were standard.

QUICK THINKER: JOHN COLETTI

Mention Mustang in a crowd and, as expected, one other name soon will be heard: Iacocca. Mention Mustang Cobra amid a group of enlightened Ford performance enthusiasts and yet another moniker instantly comes to mind: Coletti. If any one person in Detroit truly can claim to have gasoline coursing through his or her veins, it's O. John Coletti, the former heart and soul of Ford's Special Vehicle Team and the performance-conscious engineer who led the charge to keep the Mustang a Mustang during the late '80s.

and there. With his B.S. in hand, he joined Ford in January 1972, working as a product design engineer in the General Products Division's ignition systems section, where he ended up overseeing the development of Autolite's gold-tip spark plug. At the same time he also teamed up with racing legend A.J. Foyt, then the main man behind Ford's Indy engine program.

Coletti moved on from there to regular-production engine development. But any real advancement at Ford had to wait until he obtained his MBA, that coming in 1986 via Michigan State University. Within a few years he was the Mustang's design manager, and in 1989 he was tasked with getting the SN95 program up and rolling.

Born in 1949 in Newark, New Jersey, John Coletti was destined to grow up into a gargantuan gearhead after moving to the Motor City three years later. He spent his wonder years in the suburb of Roseville a block or so away from Gratiot Avenue, where street racing was king back in the day. Detroit's legendary Woodward Avenue, according to Coletti, was mostly crowded with rich kids who tended to cruise on daddy's dime; Gratiot, on the other hand, belonged to the "blue collar" hot rodders, the guys who did all their own wrenching, not to mention funding.

Coletti got his first taste of organized drag racing during the summer of 1965, and then took to sanctioned competition himself three years later—running a Hemi-powered 1964 Plymouth. His weapon of choice back on Gratiot was an American Motors' AMX, a short-wheelbase two-seater capable of popping wheelies on demand thanks to its owner's already refined talents with a tool box.

Those talents, coupled with his all-American work ethic, took him to Detroit's Wayne State University, where he helped pay for an engineering degree with construction jobs and a hot rod engine built here

His original "Skunkworks" group kicked things off, and this group evolved into Team Mustang, formed the following year. As Team Mustang's business planning manager, he helped rush Dearborn's next new pony car to market in record time. His reward was a job he was born to do.

Coletti was made head of Ford's Special Vehicle Engineering one month after the 1994 Mustang went on sale in December 1993. SVE responsibilities included developing high-performance, high-profile "halo" machines then being marketed by the Special Vehicle Team, which was officially launched in February 1992 after undergoing development itself the year before. Reportedly Coletti resisted this assignment at first, basically because he wasn't all that impressed with SVT's earliest products. His superiors, however, wouldn't be

John Coletti became the main man at Ford's Special Vehicle Engineering department in 1993. His retirement was in the works about 10 years later when he was asked to help develop the exotic Ford GT (shown above), the 550-horsepower supercar that went into production in 2005.

denied; after two requests he was more or less directed to take the position, which appeared far more enticing after he was basically given free rein to build what he saw fit.

Under his direction, the SVT Cobra started taking on real muscle: 305 horsepower by 1996. A second limited-edition R-model Cobra had appeared the year before with a big 300-horse, 351-cube pushrod V8, this because Coletti had seen too many Camaros smoke the 1993 Cobra R on race tracks from coast to coast. Independent rear suspension appeared beneath the Cobra in 1999—the year the SVT F-150 Lightning pickup, originally marketed from 1993 to 1995, returned with a supercharged 5.4-liter single-overhead-cam (SOHC) V8 rated at 360 horse-power. Lightning output increased to 380 horsepower in 2001, and in August

2003 a stone-stock SVT F-150 Lightning became the "World's Fastest Production Pickup Truck," according to the *Guinness World Records* book, after doing 147.7 mph at the Ford Motor Company proving grounds in Romeo, Michigan.

Coletti's favorite SVT Cobra was the so-called "Terminator," the supreme Cobra developed, as he put it, "to terminate the war once and for all." General Motors' rival pony cars, Camaro and Firebird, were history by the time this sensational supercharged pony car arrived in 2003, but there was little doubt that Chevy and Pontiac people would've been left choking in dust had their horses remained in the

race another year. Powering the Terminator was a 4.6-liter DOHC supercharged V8 that made 390 horsepower—the most muscle a Mustang would flex until the 500-horse, SVT-tagged Ford Shelby GT500 appeared four years later.

Coletti was no longer SVT director by then, having officially retired on December 31, 2004. "John is an icon," said Phil Martens, Ford's group vice-president of product creation, soon afterward. "Inside and outside of the company, he is extremely highly regarded. You have to step back and say, quite frankly SVT is what it is today because of John."

Ford's iconic muscle man had intended on stepping down earlier but was asked to stick around a little longer by William Clay Ford to help shepherd the exotic Ford GT supercar—in his words the "icing on the cake"—into production for 2005. While working on the Ford GT program, Coletti also was personally involved with bringing Carroll Shelby back into the Ford fold, and the latest, greatest Ford Shelby GT500 has picked up where the original SVT pony car left off. No Cobras were built for 2005 or 2006, but those omissions were forgiven once the 2007 GT500 arrived to, at its price, blow away anything on four wheels—inside and out of pony car ranks.

As for the former SVT guru, he went back to work in January 2008 as the chief operating officer at EcoMotors, a startup company that hopes to someday market a 100-mpg engine capable of between 300 and 600 horsepower. Sound unbelievable? Don't bet on it, not with John Coletti at the controls.

John Coletti was always around during the 1990s when it came time to introduce Ford's latest hot rod to the press (above). Many younger Mustang fans worship him as much today as their elders still revere Carroll Shelby (left, in discussion with Coletti), the man who first put the spurs to the Mustang in 1965.

Ford officials promised an optional removable hardtop for the 1994 Mustang, but then changed their minds. This lift-off roof did finally appear the following year, but only for the 1995 SVT Cobra.

($1,200 lower) thanks to the deletion of some of the latter's standard items, most noticeably its foglamps and rear wing. Dropped as well were the GT's sports seats, leather-wrapped steering wheel, and illuminated vanity mirror inside. All other standard GT features—5.0-liter V8, 16-inch wheels, and sport suspension—carried over untouched. Available optional equipment for the GTS included all GT goodies—17-inch wheels, power group, etc.—save for the sport buckets and interior leather treatment, which couldn't be added at any cost, nor could the foglamps and rear spoiler, because they weren't offered as options for any 1995 model. Mention of the "GTS" name was found only on the car's window sticker; typical "GT" fender badges remained on each front fender.

Ford's "cheap GT" reappeared—without any GTS reference whatsoever, on paper or otherwise—for an encore and again was identified as the "248A" package. Setting a 1996 Mustang apart from its predecessor were new taillights with their three elements now arranged in vertical fashion, as they had been in 1964. The 1996 GT got new optional 17-inch five-spoke wheels, not to mention a new engine.

Although the popular 5.0-liter V8 was still highly revered in 1995, it nonetheless was considered a bit archaic by some once the SN95 era began. "For at least six years now, Mustang was a terrific engine in search of a better car," wrote *AutoWeek*'s John Clor in 1994. "Now it's a better car

The 1995 SVT Cobra R (front) followed in the tire tracks of Carroll Shelby's savage 1965 GT 350R (back), though the former was suited for both the race track and the street. A 300-horsepower 351-cubic-inch V8 was standard for the Cobra R.

A new standard engine—Ford's 4.6-liter modular V8—appeared for the Mustang GT in 1996. This single-overhead-cam (SOHC) small-block produced 215 horsepower.

in search of even more power." That search ended two years later after Ford's venerable pushrod small-block was superseded by the thoroughly modern 4.6-liter modular V8 with its single-overhead-cam (SOHC) cylinder heads.

According to Mustang vehicle line director Janine Bay, Ford's "mod motor" transformed the GT "from a good to a great car." "We've opened up the usable rpm range, providing a whole lot more fun and power through the entire rpm band," she continued. "What the 4.6-liter engines bring to customers is a new sense of performance and excitement," added John Hasse, supervisor of Mustang V8 engine systems. "Buyers of the 1996 Mustangs will feel the old excitement of the original mid-1960s pony cars, but they'll also appreciate the benefits of the mid-1990s technology."

Mod motor roots ran back to 1987, when engineers set out to create an adaptable engine family capable of easily morphing into various forms, sharing many parts along the way. Early varieties were of SOHC design, featuring aluminum cylinder heads and two valves per cylinder. Rated at 190 horsepower (210 with dual exhausts), the first of these appeared in 1991 for the Lincoln Town Car. Lincoln's Mark VIII then appeared two years later with an all-aluminum, dual-overhead-cam (DOHC), 32-valve, 4.6-liter V8 that produced a healthy 280 horsepower. That engine's use of four cams and four valves per cylinder represented Ford Motor Company regular-production firsts.

The 1996 GT's 4.6-liter SOHC V8 was rated the same (215 horses) as the HO V8 it replaced, but it still represented a marked improvement due to enhanced efficiency and its smoother, cleaner-running ways. Superior performance potential also was a plus, and Ford's Special Vehicle Team demonstrated much of that promise after adding DOHC heads, resulting in the 305-horse V8 that came standard beneath the 1996 Cobra's hood.

Stuffing the slightly taller SOHC V8 beneath the lid that formerly crowned Ford's old pushrod small-block meant a few modifications were in order for the 1996 GT. The subframe's main crossmember up front was reshaped and steering/suspension parts were lowered. Additional clearance was created by adding a compact brake booster that cleverly borrowed its hydraulic pressure from the power steering pump. Completing the job was a thicker front stabilizer bar, installed to compensate for the revised suspension geometry.

The base 3.8-liter V6 also was enhanced, beginning with a power boost to 150 horsepower. Other improvements included a stiffer, more structurally rigid cylinder block that reduced noise, vibration, and harshness (NVH); lightened valvetrain components; and a revised cam that helped create a smoother, quieter idle. Long-life platinum-tipped spark plugs appeared for all 1996 engines, V6 and V8, as did a durable stainless-steel exhaust system. Transmission choices also changed for 1996 as the T-5 manual was dropped in favor of a stronger, quieter T-45 five-speed stick. In place of the old AOD was the smoother, more efficient 4R70W electronic automatic.

Ford apparently temporarily exhausted its headline supply in 1996. No really big news was heard around the pony car camp the following year as only minor changes were made. Perhaps most notable was the passive antitheft system (PATS) that was now standard on all models, V6 and V8. New, too, was a mildly revised grille opening that allowed more outside air access to an improved cooling package for the GT.

Much the same could've been said in 1997, the year the GT's 4.6-liter V8 was pumped up to 225 horsepower to match the 5.0-liter's peak. Ditto in 1998. New options that year included a Convenience Group (floor mats, rear window defroster, cruise control, and a power driver's seat) and two "Sport" packages. The GT Sport Group included 17-inch wheels, an oil cooler, special striping for the hood and fenders, and a leather-wrapped shift knob. The V6 Sport Appearance Group included alloy rims, a rear spoiler, a leather-wrapped steering wheel, and lower body accent striping.

A twin-scooped hood was new for the SVT Cobra in 1996, and beneath that hood was the equally new 4.6-liter dual-overhead-cam (DOHC) V8. Cobras were available again that year in coupe (shown here) and convertible forms.

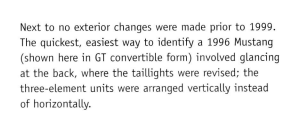

Next to no exterior changes were made prior to 1999. The quickest, easiest way to identify a 1996 Mustang (shown here in GT convertible form) involved glancing at the back, where the taillights were revised; the three-element units were arranged vertically instead of horizontally.

Precisely built by two-worker teams on a special line at Ford's Romeo engine plant, the 1996 Cobra's 4.6-liter DOHC V8 produced 305 horsepower.

Base price for the 1998 GT convertible was $23,970. Production was 17,714. More muscle (225 horsepower) became standard under the 1998 GT's hood.

ABOVE: Basically the only exterior change for 1997 appeared at the GT's nose, where the grille opening was revised slightly to allow more cooling air to reach an improved cooling system.

A 35th Anniversary package, priced at $2,695, was offered for GTs in 1999. A large hood scoop, black hood stripe, and the appropriate badge was included in this deal on the car's exterior.

OPPOSITE, TOP: The same basic interior layout seen in 1994 was still around in 1999. An extra inch of seat travel was added for the driver that year.

A commemorative 35th Anniversary model arrived in 1999, this after Ford officials had opted (in some minds coldly) to let the Mustang's 30th birthday go by unmarked in 1994. All 1999 Mustangs received 35th Anniversary fender badges and special "pony" seat embroidery, but that wasn't all. Available for GTs only was a truly special 35th Anniversary Limited Edition Package, priced at $2,695.

This option group (coded 54Y) added a raised hood scoop, large rear-quarter scoops, revised rocker moldings, and a unique rear spoiler. Brightly machined 17x8 five-spoke aluminum wheels with unique galloping pony center caps went on at the corners, a black tape appliqué adorned the hood, and a black honeycomb panel was inserted between the taillights. Inside was a Midnight Black GT leather interior with silver insert panels for the seats and doors, anniversary logo floormats, a silver instrument panel (also marked with 35th Anniversary script), and an aluminum shift knob for manual transmission models.

Also helping mark the Mustang's 35th year on the road was revitalized styling, a product of Jack Telnack's "New Edge" school of thought. Chiseled lines and sharp creases went prominently in place of the soft contours and compound curves that some critics had claimed made the 1994–1998 Mustangs look a little "Japanese" despite designers' attempts to steer clear of such impressions. Ford's New Edge pony car obviously didn't copy existing trends. It wasn't a cube, it certainly wasn't a dreaded "jellybean," yet it clearly was still a Mustang. "Our visual theme is based on the most stable geometric form—the pyramid," said chief designer Doug Gaffka. "We've also enhanced or revived some classic Mustang styling cues." Among these was the familiar chrome "corral" surrounding the traditional galloping horse now housed in a honeycomb grille.

Upgrades beneath that edgy skin included improved floorpan sealing, a revamped chassis (to further enhance ride, handling, and steering) and a widened rear track. Convertibles were

Enlarged three-inch diameter tailpipes were installed beneath the 1999 Mustang GT, still available as a coupe or a convertible.

reinforced to further inhibit inherent body shakes. New for 1999, too, was optional traction control, a Mustang first that required the additional installation of ABS, now standard for the GT. Standard GT muscle also was enhanced as the 4.6-liter SOHC V8 was fitted with straighter intake runners, lumpier cams, and bigger valves. Advertised output was now 260 horsepower. V6 output increased, too, to 190 horsepower.

"We've made improvements that are much more than skin-deep," said Janine Bay, now chief program engineer, in October 1998. "It all adds up to the fact that the 1999 Mustang really has a lot to offer. Its design is strong, contemporary, and true to Mustang's original concept. Performance improvements make the 1999 models very exciting and satisfying to drive. Make no mistake about it, everything we've done—and will continue to do—makes Mustang better and better, building on its heritage of free-spirited fun in a rear-wheel-drive, all-American sports car."

The only notable changes made to the 2000 Mustang were inside, where child seat tether anchors were installed behind the rear seat and a glow-in-the-dark decklid release was installed in the trunk.

That better pony car rolled over essentially unchanged into the next century. Released midyear, for the 2000 GT only, was the Spring Feature Package, a $995 option that added the scoops seen the year before on the 35th Anniversary Mustang. The scoop on the hood was treated to black decals sporting color-keyed "GT" lettering, and additional black lettering spelled out "MUSTANG" across the rear fascia. Completing the package were brightly machined 17x8 five-spoke wheels in place of the standard GT's 16-inch rims.

All 2001 GTs received those 35th anniversary scoops, as well as standard 17-inch wheels. Also new that year was a specific sub-model lineup that segregated the V6 and V8 lines into "Standard," "Deluxe," and "Premium" variations. Only the V6 coupe was offered in mundane Standard trim. All V6 convertibles and GTs (with or without tops) were equipped with either Deluxe or Premium equipment, with some of the items in these packages already included in the GT deal. Convertible applications of the Deluxe and Premium deals differed slightly, too, compared to their coupe counterparts.

First up was the Standard coupe, which featured the 3.8-liter V6, a five-speed stick, 15-inch painted wheels, four-wheel discs, air conditioning, dual front airbags, AM/FM stereo with CD player, and a fold-down rear seat. Next was the Deluxe package, which added cruise control, a six-way power driver's seat, floor mats, and a rear spoiler to the Standard stuff. At the top was the Premium collection consisting of the following extras: traction control and ABS, AM/FM radio with 6-disc CD player and Mach 460 sound system, a leather-wrapped steering wheel, and polished alloy wheels.

Those bright wheels measured 16 inches across in the V6 Premium's case. All GTs, Deluxe or Premium, automatically hit the ground rolling on 17-inch rims, as mentioned. And a topless Mustang V6 Premium, like GT Premium coupes and convertibles, also featured standard leather upholstery. Most of the items added as standard pieces at each rung of this pecking order were available at extra cost for the sub-models below.

Also introduced for 2001 was a special GT variant, the Bullitt model, inspired by the 1968 movie of the same name that starred Steve McQueen and his dark green Mustang fastback. Like McQueen's ride, the 2001 Mustang Bullitt GT was tweaked underneath, this time with stiffer springs and shocks, thicker anti-roll bars, and reinforced subframe connectors. Overall height was dropped by 0.75 inches and bigger brakes were added—this time with ABS and traction control to hopefully help avoid ditches like the one McQueen's stunt driver piled into near the end of *Bullitt's* famous chase scene.

Beneath the Mustang Bullitt GT's hood was a 265-horse 4.6-liter V8 enhanced with a specially tuned exhaust system. Mimicking McQueen's Mustang in 2001 were five-spoke wheels done in identical style to the American Racing mags seen in *Bullitt* 33 years earlier. Other special touches

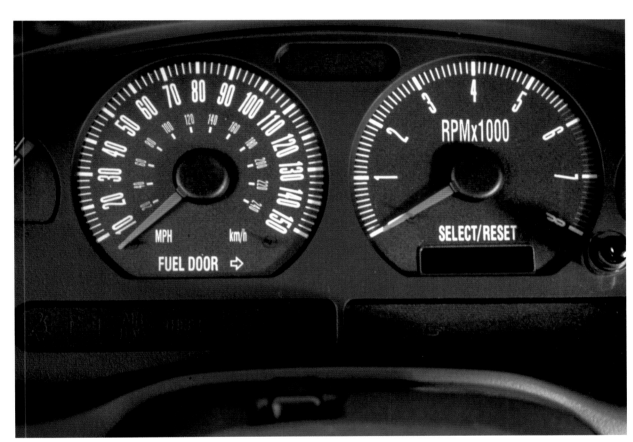

Commemorating the 1968 Warner Brothers' movie of the same name, the Mustang Bullitt GT appeared in 2001 with special door sills, five-spoke rims highly reminiscent of the mag wheels seen on the 1968 Mustang fastback that Steve McQueen drove in *Bullitt* 33 years before, special exterior identification, bucket seat upholstery and bright shifter ball, retro-style instrument faces, and bright foot pedals.

included red brake calipers, a competition-style brushed aluminum gas filler door, and "Bullitt" block letters on the tail. Retro-style instrumentation and upholstery, extra brightwork for the shifter and floor pedals, and exclusive doorsills further enhanced the image inside. Three exterior shades were offered: the appropriate Dark Highland Green, True Blue, and Black.

Ford's Standard/Deluxe/Premium order structure rolled over into 2002, as did the same basic pony car. A hip MP3/CD player became available for all models that year and standard 16-inch alloy wheels were introduced for base Mustangs. Notable was the limited offering of a V6 options group—available only in Florida and only with certain exterior colors—called the Regional Appearance Package. This option added a GT hood scoop, bright wheels, special door graphics, a leather-wrapped steering wheel, and a rear fascia adorned with "Mustang" black lettering. Brochures called this group the "Pony Package."

Deluxe and Premium base models could've been treated to a little GT feel with the addition of the Pony Package, available from coast to coast, in 2003. Various safety refinements also

appeared that year, as did a special package to help honor Ford Motor Company's 100th anniversary. Announced in December 2002, the Mustang Centennial Edition was one of five commemorative models (a Focus, Taurus, four-door Explorer, and F-series Super Duty Crew Cab pickup also appeared) done exclusively in black to honor the company's heritage. "Available in any color as long as it's black" had become the Model T's unofficial motto in 1914 after Henry Ford directed his workers to rely solely on black enamel paint due to its fast-drying characteristics, which in turn allowed his Highland Park plant to build more cars a day at a lower cost.

TOP: Though no standard-issue SVT Mustangs were built for 2000, a third Cobra R did appear, painted Performance Red with Dark Charcoal interiors. A big rear wing, huge 18- by 9.5-inch wheels, and aerodynamic front fascia were standard.

ABOVE: Beneath the 2000 Cobra R's bulging hood was an aluminum-head 5.4-liter DOHC V8 rated at 385 horsepower. The transmission was a Tremec T-56 six-speed manual.

Another time machine, the Mach 1, debuted in 2003 fitted with a nostalgic hood scoop modeled after the famed "Shaker" that appeared as a Mustang option in 1969.

A SPECIAL BREED

That Ford's SVO Mustang came and went so quickly and comparatively quietly during the mid-1980s wasn't exactly due to any perceived short-falls on the car's part. Even Ford officials were quick to admit later that making muscle, not marketing it, was the Special Vehicle Operation's strong suit. Offering world-class performance using the all-American pony car platform wasn't necessarily a bad idea, it simply should've been supported more surely from a business perspective. Such was the main goal of the Special Vehicle Team, founded in 1991.

"SVT's mission is to apply the best available resources, both from inside and outside Ford, to explore new ways of creating and marketing high-performance vehicles," read the group's original creed. "This cross-functional team is charged with delivering limited-edition, high-performance, niche-segment cars and trucks designed to delight serious drivers over a variety of road conditions and surfaces."

SVO had demonstrated that bolting such machines together was only a start. What set SVT apart was a refined promotional focus. The Special Vehicle Team didn't actually produce any niche-market cars and trucks; that job left was left up to another entity, Special Vehicle Engineering (SVE), which also opened for business in 1991. From the outset the SVT's main responsibilities involved familiarizing potential customers with these vehicles, making sure the products continued to improve, all to help keep a high-profile legacy running for more than a few years.

Furthermore, a tightly organized network of specially trained SVT dealers also was created to help keep these low-volume products from floundering in the marketplace like the SVO Mustang. A certified SVT dealer was tasked with guaranteeing that the customer remained satisfied, as well as interested, for year after thrilling year.

Robert Rewey and Neil Ressler were responsible for getting SVT rolling. Rewey was Ford's executive vice-president for sales and market-ing, Ressler was executive director of vehicle engineering, and both had a thing for high-performance vehicles. In the early '90s, Ressler asked engineer Janine Bay to warm up the existing Mustang using Ford's hottest hardware. Bay's hot-to-trot concept car got two thumbs up from Ford chairman Harold "Red" Polling and the race was on.

Ressler put together a development team modeled after Ford's European Special Vehicle Engineering group, an organization already well-versed in building limited-production specialty cars for overseas markets. This country's SVE was first managed in 1991 by Bay, then by Rod Mansfield, formerly the main man at SVE in Europe. John Coletti took over SVE reins in 1994 and remained the driving force behind SVT products until his retirement 10 years later.

Former BMW marketing man John Plant, who also worked with Michael Kranefuss during the SVO's earliest days, was made SVT manager in 1991. Plant's European background and his experience with the 1984–1986 SVO Mustang made him more or less the perfect person to oversee SVT operations. After all, it was the SVT's goal to produce another Mustang that, like the SVO rendition, offered a better-balanced, Euro-style brand of performance—a car that handled the pavement as well as roasted it. As Plant told *Automobile* in 1994, "SVT is not in the business to build hot rods. We build cars that feel exciting on real-world roads."

The Special Vehicle Team's first car, the Mustang-based SVT Cobra, debuted at the Chicago Auto Show in February 1992 along with its first truck, the SVT F-150 Lightning. Unlike the SVE-built Cobra, the Lightning was actually created by Ford Truck Operations, a group that had been working on its own high-performance products while the SVT/SVE tandem was forming. Once Ressler saw the Lightning, he just knew it had to team up with the Cobra in the SVT lineup. The two went on sale early in 1993.

SVT Lightning half-ton trucks were built from 1993 to 1995 and again from 1999 to 2004. The unique SVT touch also showed up on a special Contour model in 1998, as well as Ford's compact Focus begin-ning in 2002. The Cobra, meanwhile, wasted little time evolving into one of the best performance buys, not just in America, but on the entire planet. SVT Cobras were offering 305 horsepower by 1996, followed by a peak of 390 horses in 2003.

The supreme Cobras were the race-ready R-models built in limited numbers in 1993, 1995, and 2000. Each Cobra R was considerably hotter than the one before. The 1993 edition was basically a stripped-down, lightweight version of the original Cobra. Among other things, the 1995 Cobra R featured an exclusive 351-cubic-inch (5.8-liter) V8 that pro-duced 300 horsepower, 60 more than the standard Cobra's 5.0-liter small-block. And the 2000 R-model roll call included wild aerodynamic-conscious bodywork; huge wheels and tires; and an aluminum-head, dual-overhead-cam 5.4-liter V8 rated at 385 horsepower.

No "civilian-issue" Cobras were built for 2000, nor for 2002. But the SVT folks more than made up for those omissions in 2003 with their 10th anniversary model, powered by the so-called "Terminator" V8, a supercharged 4.6-liter DOHC V8 that made those aforemen-tioned 390 horses. The supercharged Terminator Cobra rolled out again in 2004, but the breed failed to reappear along with the new next-generation 2005 Mustang.

John Coletti's retirement at the end of 2004 also signaled the end of the line for Ford's Special Vehicle Team, at least in its origi-nal form. Existing basically in name alone, SVT sponsorship did return in 2007 for a new hot rod Mustang developed at Special Vehicle Team facilities and marketed by Ford Motor Company. The SVT-tagged Ford Shelby GT500 debuted that year with 500 horsepower, putting it in a domestic league with Dodge's Viper and Chevrolet's Z06 Corvette—at considerably less cost.

Offered only as a three-door hatchback in 1993, the second-edition SVT Cobra Mustang was available as a coupe (shown above) and a convertible.

Introduced as well at Highland Park that year was Ford's ground-breaking $5-a-day minimum wage, another Detroit milestone honored 89 years later. Beginning April 1, 2003, Ford offered a $5-a-day, 48-month "Centennial Lease." "Henry Ford helped create the American middle class when he introduced the $5 day age, and our effort to share this heritage with consumers has been a huge success," said Ford President Steve Lyons. "We've tapped an incredible reserve of goodwill for Ford and a deep well of Mustang excitement."

Like the four other Centennial models, the special-edition 2003 Mustang featured 100th anniversary badges (on the fenders and decklid) and Premium Verona-grain Imola leather seats done in two-tone parchment inside. Also part of the deal was a Centennial Gift Pack (including a watch, key chain, and black leather owner portfolio) and a copy of the book *The Ford Century*. Only GT premium coupes and convertibles could be ordered with this package.

Equally special was the 2003 Mach 1, a veritable time machine that began rolling off the Dearborn line in November 2002. Most nostalgic was the latest Mach 1's Shaker scoop, which, like its predecessor first seen in 1969, protruded right through the model's striped hood. "Let your mind go and it's the '60s all over the place," wrote *Hot Rod*'s Ro McGonegal about this memorable black breather.

Beneath the Shaker was a 2003 redo of the 2001 SVT Cobra's 32-valve V8 that simultaneously made the new Mach 1 even mightier than its 1969 big-block ancestor and the first non-SVT Mustang to offer DOHC V8 power. A *Popular Hot Rodding* road test of a 1969 Mach 1 Cobra Jet produced a 13.69-second quarter-mile pass. A *Mustang Monthly* test of a 2003 Mach 1 produced a mind-altering 12.97-second run. Advertised output in the latter's case was 305 horsepower.

A Tremec five-speed manual transmission was standard; a beefed-up 4R70W automatic transmission was optional. Additional mechanicals included power four-wheel Brembo discs, stainless-steel dual exhausts, and a Traction-Lok 8.8-inch differential with 3.55:1 gears. Present too was a lowered suspension that featured stiffer springs, Tokico struts, and exclusive aluminum "Heritage" wheels, 17x8 wheels shod in Goodyear Eagle ZR45 rubber. Blacked-out spoilers were added front and rear, as were retro rocker panel stripes. Standard interior treatments also brought back memories as the Mach 1 was fitted with a bright aluminum shifter ball and a "nostalgic instrument cluster," both carryover Bullitt Mustang features. All told, the Mach 1 was, in Ford's words, a "modern interpretation of an American icon."

All pony cars built for 2004, the last year for the SN95 era, wore another set of anniversary badges, these predictably marking the model's 40th birthday. Save for a slight power increase (to 193 horses) for the base V6, most everything else rolled over essentially unchanged from 2003. Both the SVT Cobra and Mach 1 returned, though both retired as 2004 production shut down.

Available in 2004 as well for all Mustangs, V6 and GT, was a special 40th Anniversary Package that added 17-inch five-spoke wheels painted exclusively in Arizona Beige Metallic

Retro-styled rocker stripes, badges, and wheels were standard for the 2003 Mach 1. Mach 1 production was 9,652 that year; another 7,182 followed in 2004.

Beneath the 2003 Mach 1's Shaker hood scoop was a 4.6-liter DOHC V8 with four valves per cylinder. Output was 305 horsepower.

All Mustangs built for 2004, whether V6 (shown here) or GT, were considered 40th Anniversary models and had special fender badges. The base V6 was boosted to 193 horsepower that year.

(with bright rims); additional Arizona Beige stripes on the hood, doors, and decklid; color-keyed foldaway mirrors; a Medium Parchment interior with matching floor mats wearing anniversary logos; and an anniversary plaque next to the shifter. Exclusive Crimson Red paint was mixed up for the 40th Anniversary Mustang, but two other choices, Oxford White and Black, were offered, too.

Two historic moments occurred before the SN95 story came to a close. On November 18, 2003, Ford's 300 millionth vehicle, a 2004 40th Anniversary Mustang GT convertible, rolled off the company's assembly line in Dearborn. Later, in May 2004, that line itself closed down after another 2004 GT convertible was driven off it. Scheduled for demolition soon afterward, Ford's aging Mustang plant had been home to some 6.7 million little horses dating back to 1964. Another 2 million or so were built in San Jose, California, and Metuchen, New Jersey, over the years. But Dearborn, Michigan, will always be remembered as the place where America's pony car was born.

GALLERY

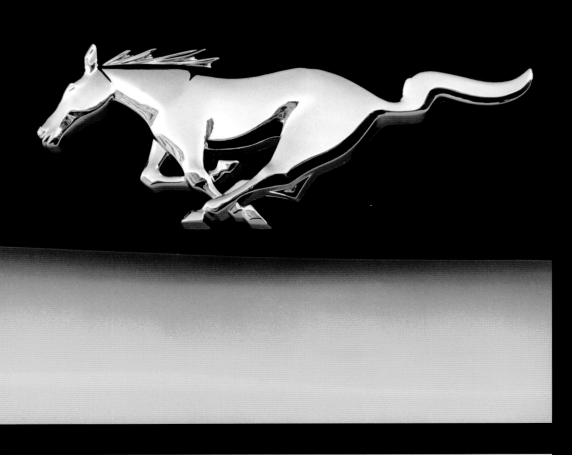

CHAPTER EIGHT

Dearborn's Latest, Greatest Mustang

Opened in 1918, Ford's venerable Dearborn assembly plant served first as a home to Eagle boats, fast, agile sub-chasers intended to defend America's shores against the dreaded Hun's undersea threat during World War I. Fordson tractors began rolling out its doors after peace broke out, as did the aging Model T's replacement, the Model A, later in 1928. Countless trucks, Mercurys, and other war machines (for a second World War) followed over the decades, then along came Dearborn's most historic product, Lee Iacocca's new Mustang, in 1964. Ford's very first pony car was driven off the Dearborn line on March 9 that year by Ford employee Oscar Horespian.

TIME MACHINE

Forty years later, Horespian, who had worked for Ford from 1942 to 1980, returned to Dearborn to ride another pony off that line. On May 10, 2004, he took a seat next to fellow Ford veteran (32 years) Fred Galicki as Galicki drove a red GT convertible beneath a banner announcing the "Final Stampede." This was the last Mustang built at the aging Dearborn facility—which was finally being torn down to make room for a new truck plant—and it also was the last of its kind. Waiting to build Ford's latest next-generation pony car, scheduled for release as a 2005 model, were workers at the 2-million-square-foot AutoAlliance International plant in Flat Rock, Michigan, home to Mazda products since 1988. Reportedly $644 million was spent on the AAI facility, located 15 miles from Dearborn, to allow the 2005 Mustang to be manufactured right alongside the Mazda 6.

PAGES 246–247: "Retro" was an understatement concerning the restyled 2005 Mustang. Keeping the running horse logo in the grille was a given.

Horse lovers first got a look at what awaited them for 2005 on January 5, 2003, as William Clay Ford Jr. invited journalists to take a look at the Mustang's near future, in prototype form, at Detroit's annual North American International Auto Show. "Something old, something new" was a fair description for the concept car seen that day, a way-cool machine that *AutoWeek* called the "Most Significant" vehicle displayed at that year's show. It screamed Mustang throughout thanks to various nostalgic touches, but its bold impressions by no means left witnesses lost in the past. Mechanicals definitely qualified as "cutting edge," with a super-charged, intercooled DOHC V8 (that pumped out as much as 400 horsepower) leading the way under the hood. Comparatively high-tech independent suspension held up the tail.

Shown off in coupe and convertible forms, the Mustang GT concept was created through a collaborative effort between Richard Hutting's Ford Design California facility and chief designer Larry Erickson's studio back east in Dearborn. And like the "prophetic" Mustang II showcar of 1963, Ford's latest, greatest concept 40 years later was based on regular-production developments then all but com-

pleted. While Erickson's group was taking care of all mainstream work on the 2005 Mustang, Hutting's team in Valencia, California, was off on a truly cre-ative vector, with the result of their efforts repre-senting just the tease Design Vice President J Mays was counting on. Unlike so many other concepts, which stand as nothing less than farfetched, the two Detroit autoshow-stoppers weren't intended to sim-ply be here today then roll off into the history books tomorrow. Not in the least. "The Mustang GT concepts are strong indications of the next-generation Mustang's design direction," announced one Ford press release.

Prophetic journalists then took things from there. "My suspicions are that the [Mustang] Concept is closer to production than you might think," wrote David Freiburger in *Hot Rod* maga-zine's March 2003 issue. "The buzz is that the general shape of the car is dead-on." Right on! Not one gawker was left wondering whatever happened to those concept cars when Bill Ford returned to the Detroit auto show in January 2004 with Mays' final product, which by the way was all but ready to go on sale later that fall.

Like Iacocca's original baby, the 2005 Mustang represented various different cars to vari-ous different drivers. Baby boomers, now well into their middle ages, could recognize various aspects of beloved past ponies, while today's hipsters weren't ashamed in the least to be caught behind the wheel. "Rest assured, we're not insisting on history at the expense of our future," stressed Mays in 2004. Techno crazies weren't overlooked either; they had more than enough toys to play with inside the 2005 Mustang. Especially playful was the new GT's power source, the Mustang's first to offer 300 horsepower in standard applications. This wild horse arguably represented the biggest bang for the buck ever heard around Detroit. "The new Mustang is pure American Muscle," added Mays.

"It's the most affordable 300-horsepower car made and the best rear-drive performance car under $20,000," bragged Phil Martens, group vice-president, North America Product Creation.

TOP: The GT-R interior was race-car spartan. Carbon fiber covered the dash and parts of the doors.

MIDDLE AND ABOVE: Ford's GT-R concept car debuted at the New York Auto Show in 2004. Huge 20-inch wheels and a competition-style rear wing (above) enhanced the image of what was basically a preview of the next-generation Mustang to come in 2005.

FRESH IDEAS: J MAYS

In August 1997 retiring design executive Jack Telnack sat down to dinner in Detroit with Ford Automotive Operations president Jac Nasser and a talented designer they'd flown in from the West Coast. At the time, 43-year-old J Mays (that's right, simply "J," no period) was working for SHR Perceptual Management in Newbury Park, California. He'd been serving as an outside consultant to Ford for a couple years, so upon hearing the invitation he figured it probably would be business as usual. But when Mays asked what he could do for the Dearborn gang this time, Telnack replied that he was hoping to turn the table. Mays then figured a job offer just might be in the offing, perhaps a vehicle center director's position or such, nothing he was particularly interested in. He was still preparing to respectfully turn down any and all proposals as dessert arrived that evening. Then Nasser spilled the beans: it was Telnack's top office that was open to him.

Born in Oklahoma in October 1954, Mays grew up about 45 miles south of Oklahoma City in Maysville, a small town named after a distant relative. His father owned a ranch and a go-cart track, with the latter business inspiring his son more than the former. Mays was sketching cars by age 5, but it was journalism that later became his focus at the University of Oklahoma. Not for long, however. Struggling in journalism school, he figured he couldn't do any worse at the Art Center College of Design in Pasadena, California, the same school where Telnack had gotten his start. Getting paid to sketch cars then became his goal.

A Ford-sponsored scholarship helped get him through the Art Center, but upon graduating in 1980, he went to work for Volkswagen subsidiary Audi AG in Ingolstadt, Germany, where he caught Jack Telnack's eye with his aerodynamic Audi 80 sedan, introduced at the 1983 Frankfurt Motor Show. Three years later, Mays moved on to BMW, but stayed in Munich only another year. Then it was back to Audi, where he was responsible for the sensational all-aluminum AVUS concept vehicle, unveiled in Tokyo in 1991, and Volkswagen's memorable Concept One, introduced at Detroit's North American International Auto Show in 1994. Concept One served as a precursor to VW's New Beetle, which debuted to rave reviews four years later. His short stay at SHR followed next before Telnack came calling in 1997.

To say J Mays was floored by his offer is like calling Mustang just a car. That Ford actually went looking outside its family to fill its top design post represented big enough news on its own; that their final choice was the relatively young Oklahoman left even him in shock. For starters, Nasser was asking him to take charge of about 1,000 designers working in studios spread all around the world. Up until then the most staffers he had directed were 200 or so at Audi. Nasser also knew Mays would have who knows how many bruised egos to deal with after passing over various veteran Ford people for the man who'd previously spent more than 10 years in Germany. But Telnack was confident they had the right man after fairly evaluating every suitable insider. The other candidates simply would have to get over it. As for Mays himself, he wasn't about to pass up the opportunity of a lifetime.

Following in Telnack's storied footsteps was, in Mays' mind, an expected honor. But he by no means let any excess awe get in the way of him making his own immediate imprint. Telnack's New Edge approach was just taking root at Ford when he retired, but Mays had his own "functional design language" in mind, a design approach that balanced off nostalgic cues with a thoroughly modern feel. Industry watchers were soon calling his idea "retrofuturism." Anyone wanting a translation here needed only one look at Volkswagen's 1998 New Beetle, which reminded more than one witness of the little Bug that first began buzzing about American roads nearly 50 years earlier.

Although Mays has more than once claimed he's never done a "retro car," evidence sure seems to point otherwise. At Ford, his

run of retro-actively fashioned concept cars included the Fairlane, the 427, and Forty Nine. First shown off in concept form in 2002, the Ford GT went into production in 2005 looking very much like the GT-40 racecar that won Le Mans in 1966. And who can forget the reborn Thunderbird two-seater, introduced as a concept vehicle in 1999 and then offered to the public three years later? More importantly, the latest-generation Mustang appeared for 2005 wearing a truly familiar face.

As much as Mays doesn't like the tag "Mr. Retro," he has always been willing to knock today's fad-conscious designers who feel that absolutely nothing old can ever be new again. In his humble opinion, heritage can play an important role in modern automotive design, and rightfully should when so much customer loyalty is at stake. "When you're designing a new Mustang, you're the steward of 40 years of automotive history," he said. "If you don't get it right, you've got 8 million Mustang fans to answer to. I think we got it right. By melding the true character of Mustang into a car with fully modern proportions, we ensured that even the uninitiated will instantly recognize these cars as Mustangs."

And many Mustang owners recognize J Mays as the man with a finger on their pulses.

J Mays stepped in to oversee Ford Motor Company's worldwide design efforts after Jack Telnack retired in 1997.

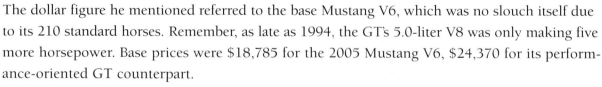

The dollar figure he mentioned referred to the base Mustang V6, which was no slouch itself due to its 210 standard horses. Remember, as late as 1994, the GT's 5.0-liter V8 was only making five more horsepower. Base prices were $18,785 for the 2005 Mustang V6, $24,370 for its perform-ance-oriented GT counterpart.

Balancing that whole retro thing with a thoroughly modern feel was the developmental goal from the get-go. Modernizing Ford's latest time machine was left up to chief nameplate engi-neer Hau Thai-Tang, who joined Ford in 1988. He worked with Ford Racing during the '90s then helped develop the 2000 Lincoln LS, *Motor Trend*'s "Car of the Year." In 2001 he helped herd that year's Mustang, SVT Cobra and Bullitt GT models into production. To get the 2005 Mustang up and running, Thai-Tang and his engineers relied on a foundation that qualified as new despite talk to the contrary.

Early reports predicted that platform would be a modified DEW98 design, which was used by the Lincoln LS and Jaguar S-Type. That idea, however, never did suit Thai-Tang. His design's MacPherson struts did mimic the Lincoln LS's front suspension, but that was about it as far as notable comparisons were concerned. Though the 2005 Mustang's structure, known internally around Ford as the S197 platform, did share about 30 percent of its makeup with other corporate vehicles, the resulting family ties were essentially unrecognizable. Contrary to the Lincoln LS (as well as the GT concepts), the S197 design did not feature independent rear suspension. Cost considerations came into play here as a solid axle is cheaper, and it's also more able to handle dragstrip-style launches, a virtue designers knew would remain just as important to many pony car customers in 2005 as it had been to their ancestors 40 years back.

"We talked to a lot of Mustang owners as we were developing this program," explained Thai-Tang. "They are a very passionate group, and a lot of them told us—very strongly—that the all-new Mustang had to have a solid rear axle."

"All-new" was all right. As you may recall, Ford's original Mustang was based on an existing platform belonging to the Falcon, introduced four years before. The 1974 Mustang II appeared

TOP LEFT: Nostalgic exterior touches abounded in 2005, including optional wheels fitted with simulated knock-off "spinners" reminiscent of the deluxe wheel-covers offered in 1964.

TOP RIGHT: The 2005 Mustang coupe's rear-quarter glass reminded many witnesses of the windows added to Carroll Shelby's GT 350 in 1966.

ABOVE: A simulated gas cap in back mimicked the fully functional forerunners seen on all Mustang tails prior to 1974.

with a three-year-old Pinto foundation and the purportedly new-for-1979 pony car was based on the Fox chassis, initially rolled out the year before beneath Ford's first Fairmont. The 2005 Mustang's substructure, on the other hand, clearly represented the breed's first truly new supporting cast, not to mention its best yet, even with that old-school live axle.

Compared to its SN95 forerunner, the 2005 chassis featured six extra inches of wheelbase, and that stretch, working in concert with an engine relocated rearward, translated into a better balanced machine. Weight distribution for the 2005 GT was 53 percent in front, 47 in back, compared to about 57/43 for its 2004 predecessor. The superior 2005 platform also was 31 percent stiffer in coupe form. According to Thai-Tang, the 2005 convertible was 100 percent more torsionally stiff compared to its 2004 forerunner. All this added strength meant various things: increased safety, decreased noise, vibration, and harshness (NVH), and improved handling, thanks to more precise suspension tuning.

Helping enhance safe operation further was a front structure specially designed to absorb head-on impacts and dissipate threatening forces before they even reach the reinforced "safety cage" passenger compartment.

The topless rendition of the new fifth-generation Mustang didn't appear until the spring of 2005.

"This all-new chassis design does everything better—accelerate, turn, stop—while isolating unwanted noise and making the most of the powerful new three-valve engine," said Product Creation group Vice-President Phil Martens about the 2005 Mustang. Those struts up front incorporated high-strength, lightweight coil springs and innovative "reverse-L" control arms on the bottom end that dampened road shocks better than A-arm or wishbone layouts. A beefed-up 8.8-inch axle brought up the rear and was held firmly in place by three control arms (one each below at the axle's opposite ends, one atop the differential housing) and a lightweight tubular Panhard rod, the latter piece added to inhibit unwanted lateral motions.

Steering chores were handled by an improved rack-and-pinion unit and brakes were four-wheel discs with vacuum-controlled power assist. A new four-channel antilock system was standard along with the GT's brakes, optional for base cars. Like ABS, traction control also was standard for the GT, optional for the V6.

The 2005 Mustang's 210-horse V6 was a 4.0-liter SOHC mill consisting of aluminum low-profile heads bolted atop a cast-iron cylinder block. Made completely of aluminum, the GT's 300-horse 4.6-liter SOHC modular V8 was based on a deep-skirt block that weighed 75 pounds less than the iron counterpart in Ford's conventional mod motor. And its three-valve Triton cylinder heads were similar to those seen previously on the 2004 F-150 pickup's 5.4-liter V8. Other notable high-tech additions included electronic throttle control for both engines, another first for Ford's pony car. The GT engine's variable camshaft timing (VCT) also made history as this fuel-saving, performance-conscious design had never before appeared in an American rear-wheel-drive V8 application.

Another groundbreaking feature, at least from a pony car perspective, was the 2005 Mustang's optional five-speed automatic transmission, a close-ratio 5R55S electronic unit used previously in

Both thoroughly modern and romantically nostalgic, the 2005 Mustang cockpit represented, in the words of chief designer Larry Erickson, a "$30,000 interior in a $20,000 car."

ABOVE: The 2005 interior's large dual instrument pods and bright air conditioning vents copied designs that debuted in 1967, the first year in-dash air conditioning was offered as a Mustang option.

the Thunderbird and Lincoln LS. The V6's standard transmission was a rugged Tremec T-5 five-speed manual with a 3.35:1 low gear. An even tougher Tremec 3650 five-speed, with a 3.38:1 low, was standard for the GT.

An industry first was the 2005 Mustang's optional interior illumination. The Interior Upgrade Package added an unprecedented color-configurable light system to the cockpit's nostalgic analog instrumentation. Using green, blue, and red diodes, this system could project a wide range of colors onto the instruments through "light piping." Those three colors could've been mixed into more than 125 different backgrounds, allowing a driver to, in Ford's words, "suit their personality, mood, outfit or whim." "During Mustang research clinics, we noticed that many of our customers already were customizing their interiors with different instrument panel features," explained chief Mustang electrical engineer Dean Nowicki. "The concept display was intended to offer choices, and we just decided we wanted all the colors."

From a much more practical perspective, the 2005 Mustang body offered a little extra space here and there, due mostly to that stretched wheelbase. The coupe's trunk capacity increased 13 percent to 12.3 cubic feet, and fold-down split rear seat backs enhanced cargo-carrying capabilities even further.

Drivers also found more freedom as head and shoulder room went up by a half inch and 1.1 inches, respectively. And those sculptured buckets in back gave passengers 1.1 inches more legroom and 1.2 inches more shoulder room.

"The tallest drivers in our customer base have not been fully happy with previous Mustangs," said package supervisor Keith Knudsen. "We've addressed that in this all-new car, while maintaining the 'cockpit feel' essential to a driver's car. But we wanted to improve comfort for passengers, too. The extra cabin space makes a world of difference on long drives."

That drive looked awfully familiar in 2006 as few changes awaited Mustang buyers that year. Air conditioning and a CD player remained standard on all models, as did a power fabric top with heated glass for convertibles. Standard wheels again measured 16 inches across for the base V6 model, 17 for the GT.

As in 2005, both the V6 and GT were offered in Deluxe and Premium forms for 2006. But this time the base Mustang group's scope was widened to include the more affordable Standard rendition. Meant to cut costs to the bone, the 2006 Standard package traded the Deluxe model's flashy alloy wheels for conventional 16-inch rims shod in conservative wheelcovers. Added into the Premium mix was Ford's Shaker 500 audio system, a six-way power driver's seat with power lumbar support, and chrome spinners for those 16-inch alloy rims. Wheel spinners were optional for the Deluxe cars.

New for 2006 was an optional Pony Package for the Mustang V6 Premium. Included in this deal were fog lamps, 17-inch painted wheels, rear spoiler, ABS brakes, and traction control. Various aluminum wheels were optional for the GT, including a bright aluminum "10-spoke" rim and a pair of big 18-inch five-spokers. V6 buyers also could've added the Exterior Sports Appearance Package, which included lower body logo stripes and a rear deck spoiler.

A new model appeared for 2006 but was not initially for sale to the public. Early that year Shelby Automobiles, Inc., which became a Ford partner three years before, announced it would be creating its own time machine, this one reminding veteran Mustang fans of the days 40 years before when anyone could've stepped into a Hertz rental car office and driven away in a GT 350 Mustang. In 1966 it was Shelby American's GT 350H models that Hertz rented out. In 2006 it was Shelby Automobiles' GT-H.

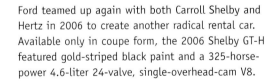

Hertz launched its "Fun Collection," a group of "leisure" rental vehicles ranging from comfortable sport-utilities to sexy convertibles in January 2006. Adding a reborn Shelby Mustang into this mix was a no-brainer; hence a limited collection of about 500 GT-H rental cars became available at select major airports that spring. "Like the original Hertz cars, the Ford Shelby GT-H will be fun to drive," said Carroll Shelby himself in April. "We started with a terrific Mustang and modified it with some Ford go-fast parts and gave it a distinct look for Shelby-style driving. Whoever gets the opportunity to rent one of these unique cars will get an experience of a lifetime."

As in most cases in 1966, that distinct look in 2006 was supplied by a gold-striped black finish, a Hertz tradition dating back to the 1920s. Hertz Edition emblems went on the fenders and were complemented by gold rocker stripes that incorporated "Shelby GT-H" lettering. Hertz Shelby GT-H sill plates and a numbered dash plaque, signed by Carroll Shelby, went inside. Additional customizations included a special Shelby Performance hood (with tie-down pins), a brushed aluminum grille, a unique front fascia, a set of nostalgic body side scoops, and a winged spoiler out back.

Beneath that striped hood were various Ford Racing Performance Parts components that boosted output to an estimated 325 horsepower. Present was an FR1 Power Pack, which included a cold air kit (with larger 90mm throttle body), "performance calibration," and a cat-back exhaust

Ford teamed up again with both Carroll Shelby and Hertz in 2006 to create another radical rental car. Available only in coupe form, the 2006 Shelby GT-H featured gold-striped black paint and a 325-horsepower 4.6-liter 24-valve, single-overhead-cam V8.

OPPOSITE, BOTTOM: No noticeable changes were made for the 2006 Mustang, shown here in GT convertible form. Seventeen-inch wheels were again standard for the GT.

system with tuned mufflers that, according to Ford, emitted a "throaty sound that will make this car unmistakably a Shelby Mustang." The FR3 Handling Pack was added, too. This package included lowering springs, special sway bars, a strut tower brace, and tuned dampers. Bringing up the rear was a Ford Racing differential containing 3.55:1 gears.

"Any Mustang that traces its roots to a Shelby GT 350H has to boast increased perform-ance and handling over the factory stock configuration," said Ford North American Marketing, Sales and Service group Vice President Cisco Codina. "Ford Racing's involvement with niche performance Mustang builds like this Hertz project is a natural for us as well as for Hertz and Shelby."

Also like the 1966 GT 350H, the GT-H run used only automatic transmissions to hopefully keep a lid on customers' excitement. After all, this rental car could, according to *Car and Driver*, trip the lights at the quarter-mile's far end in 13.9 seconds. Zero to 60 mph required only 5.3 seconds, making rental returns a snap.

All GT-H rentals were sent to auction once their jobs at Hertz were done. Collectors also eventually got the chance to bid for a similarly equipped GT-H convertible, introduced at the New York International Auto Show in April 2007. The first of these was sent to a Barrett-Jackson auction to help benefit the Carroll Shelby Children's Foundation and the Juvenile Diabetes Research Fund. It went for $250,000.

Back in regular-production ranks, the Deluxe and Premium packages carried over into 2007 but the low-cost Standard didn't. Optional heated front seats became available for all models except the new Ford Shelby GT500, which also was joined that year by the less brutal Shelby GT. Another memorable model, the GT California Special, first seen in 1968, was dusted off as well in 2007.

Available for Mustang GTs only, the new California Special package featured high-profile body side stripes and rear-quarter side scoops that reminded Mustangers of similar touches seen on Ford's 1968 forerunner. Also part of the deal were 18-inch polished aluminum wheels, unique front and rear fascias, and bright exhaust tips.

New for 2006 was the optional Pony Package, which dressed up a Mustang V6 Premium to look a little like a GT. Among other things, fog lamps, a rear spoiler, and 17-inch wheels were included in the Pony Package.

No Cobra Mustangs appeared in 2005 or 2006, and then along came the Ford Shelby GT500 in 2007. Beneath its striped hood, the GT500 featured a 5.4-liter DOHC V8 rated at 500 horsepower.

HORSE LOVERS

Like Mustangs themselves, organizations for Mustang enthusiasts are plentiful to say the least, with seemingly every generation and variation honored. But if you want to go right to the horse's mouth, if you want to belong where it really counts, you're talking the Mustang Club of America (www.mustang.org), now headquartered in Pensacola, Florida. Originally founded in Atlanta 30 years back, the MCA today claims more than 11,000 members belonging to about 170 regional groups located here in the United States and abroad. No member's favorite pony is overlooked. While factory correct restorations remain the MCA membership's main focus, modified machines and racers are welcome as well, as are Shelbys, SVT Cobras, and the various "tuner" types like Saleen, Roush, Steeda, and McLaren.

And to think it all started so humbly in March 1976 after four horse lovers—Stan Jones, George White, Garry Goddard, and Tom Taylor—met outside of Atlanta in north Georgia's gorgeous Stone Mountain Park to discuss the possibilities of forming a national club devoted to their pride and joys. An advertisement in the *Atlanta Journal-Constitution* then inspired 10 more enthusiasts to show for an organizational gathering a week or so later. More than 100 appeared for a meeting in May, and membership had risen to more than 250 by the time the fledgling Mustang Club of America held its very first Grand National Meet, again at Stone Mountain Park, in August 1976. More than 100 Mustangs from 20 states were officially entered for the MCA's inaugural national show.

MCA membership initially was limited to owners of Mustangs built from 1964 to 1973, leaving the Mustang II guys out in the cold. This rule remained in place until 1986, when organization officials asked its members if all years should be welcomed. The answer was a resounding "no" by nearly a 2 to 1 margin, but the board of directors approved a new open-door policy anyway—an unpopular decision then, a wise move as far as the club's future was concerned. Its present diversity clearly helps explain why the MCA has been around so long and remains so healthy while other Mustang groups have come and gone in the meantime.

"Whether you have restored your Mustang to showroom standards or have a modified/resto-mod performance

pony, whether your favorite drives are down the quarter-mile or to the neighborhood cruise night, MCA is for you," said president Bill Johnson in 2008 while inviting new members to walk right in. A year's worth of membership costs only $40, a rather humble markup from the $10 required back in 1976.

Included along with an annual membership is a subscription to the monthly *Mustang Times* magazine, which helps keep tabs on the many events staged by the more than 170 regions during the year. Crowning things each show season are four National MCA meets and one Grand National extravaganza. In the past the group has also worked in concert with Ford officials to host the Mustang's 30th, 35th, and 40th anniversary parties. And as these pages are being printed, work is progressing on a 45th birthday celebration, scheduled for April 16–19, 2009, at Barber Motorsports Park in Leeds, Alabama, just outside of Birmingham.

What does the Mustang Club of America have in mind for the Mustang's big 50th? Join up and stay tuned.

Still another blast from the past, the GT California Special appeared in 2007 to remind Mustangers of the Shelby-style cars marketed by Southern California Ford dealers in 1968.

Various GT500 touches came directly from Shelby's original Mustangs, including the coiled snake in the grille (above) and on the faux gas cap in back (below). Blue stripes on a white finish (right) were the only real choice for buyers truly interested in going back in time to 1965.

Inside were Dark Charcoal leather-trimmed seats with Dove or Parchment inserts, and special floor mats. The GT Appearance Package, a new option for 2007, also could've been paired with the California Special treatment. A bold hood scoop, bright exhaust tips, and an engine cover featuring Ford's traditional running horse logo were included in that Appearance Package.

The Shelby GT was announced in August 2006 (as a 2007 model) for pony car buyers who didn't want to go auctioning. "We have been overwhelmed at the number of people who want to buy a version of the Shelby GT-H," explained Carroll Shelby. "The Shelby GT will deliver the power and balanced handling of the Shelby GT-H, but with more performance potential, especially due to the available manual transmission."

Yes, the new Shelby GT could've been equipped with the five-speed automatic or a Hurst-shifted five-speed manual. Save for wheels and tires, most other GT-H features rolled over: the 2006 Hertz Shelby used 17-inch Bullitt-style five-spokes, while the 2007 Shelby GT relied on 18-inch five-spokes. Ford also officially certified the latter machine's FRPP-enhanced 4.6-liter V8 at 319 horsepower in 2007. Atop that engine was a standard Mustang hood wearing a riveted-on scoop, and no rear wing appeared in back. Sold only in coupe form, the Shelby GT was available in white or black with silver metallic stripes.

The outrageous Ford Shelby GT500 appeared in 2007 wearing another badge familiar to pony car performance fans: "SVT." Although no Cobra Mustangs were built in 2005 and 2006, at least the legacy was revived, if in name alone, by simply the mightiest Mustang ever built. First seen in concept car form in March 2005 at the New York Auto Show, the SVT-tagged Ford Shelby GT500 was, unlike the original GT500s of 1967–1970, true to its name. Standard beneath its striped hood was a whopping 500 horsepower, far and away the most muscle ever bolted between Mustang flanks.

Making all those horses was a 5.4-liter DOHC V8 topped by an intercooled Eaton supercharger that supplied 8.5 psi of boost. Bolted up behind was a Tremec T-56 six-speed manual transmission. Brakes were 14-inch vented Brembo discs with four-piston calipers up front, 11.8-inch vented discs with two-piston calipers in back. Wheels were enormous 18x9.5 10-spokers wrapped in P255/45R18 rubber up front, huge P285/40ZR18 tires in back.

The GT500's white striping was pure Shelby, as were its various coiled snake logos, dating back to long before SVT Cobras began hitting the streets in 1993. A ducktail rear spoiler and a special front fascia fitted with gaping intakes also reminded many witnesses of Shelbys of old. As for SVT identification, those three letters appeared on the wheels, doorsills, and tachometer, as well as on the traditionally autographed V8 beneath that bulging, vented hood. Originally introduced for 2007 in coupe form only, the GT500 was quickly joined by a convertible model wearing only the second cloth top in Mustang history—the first had appeared atop the 2003 SVT Cobra.

The Shelby plot thickened further in 2008 after a topless GT debuted along with the even more muscular GT500KR, last seen midyear in 1968. "The Mustang convertible is the number one selling convertible in the U.S.," said Ford Division Car Marketing Manager Robert Parker in June 2007. "[And] since the Mustang program never stands still, we wanted to continue offering consumers what they want, and they told us it was a Ford Mustang Shelby GT convertible."

"The birth of the Ford Shelby GT was so well received last year, especially by young enthusiasts, that we brought the car back for the 2008 model year," added Shelby Automobiles President Amy Boylan. "The enormous response to the Shelby GT-H convertible [also] convinced us to offer

The Shelby GT returned for 2008, available as a coupe and a convertible. Only one color combination was offered to the public—Vista Blue with Metallic Silver stripes—but Carroll Shelby created a handful of yellow examples just for fun.

Output for the base Mustang's SOHC V6 remained at 210 horsepower in 2008, the same as in 2005 and 2006. Note the fog lamps in the grille, meaning this 2008 model was equipped with the optional Pony Package.

a drop top Shelby GT. And we had so many requests for blue that we decided to make it our signature color in 2008." Mechanicals beneath that blue skin more or less mirrored those seen in 2007.

Introduced in the spring of 2008 at the New York International Auto Show, Shelby's GT500KR raised the output bar even further to an estimated 540 horsepower. "The return of the Shelby GT500KR further established Mustang as the true king of the pony car segment," said Parker proudly in March 2008. "With the unveiling of the new KR we are staying true to the promise we made our loyal Mustang fans to continue Mustang's prowess by bringing new, exciting and more powerful Mustangs to market."

Another new pony car, Ford's second edition Mustang Bullitt, also appeared for 2008, again wearing trademark Highland Green paint but with 315 standard horses this time. High Intensity Discharge (HID) headlights also were new that year, as were 18-inch wheels for V6 models and a limited-edition "Warriors in Pink" package created to help raise funds for a great cause, the Susan G. Komen for the Cure fight against breast cancer. Offered for V6 Premium

Ford fired off a second Mustang Bullitt in 2008. Again painted in Highland Green (black was optional), the second-edition Bullitt model also carried special exterior identification (top) and relied on Ford Racing parts (above) to make 315 horsepower—15 more ponies than the standard GT V8.

LEFT: Like Steve McQueen's 1968 movie car, the 2008 Mustang Bullitt was stripped of its running horse grille logo.

Like the 2001 Mustang Bullitt GT, the 2008 rendition rolled on retro-styled five-spoke wheels that mimicked the mags bolted on at the corners of Steve McQueen's 1968 fastback.

Ford launched its "Warriors in Pink" campaign in 2006 to help battle breast cancer. First came sales of special Warriors in Pink apparel, with all net proceeds going to the Susan G. Komen for the Cure Foundation. The "Warriors in Pink" edition Mustang followed in 2008 to help deliver additional funds to the foundation.

coupes and convertibles, the latter option included pink rocker stripes, a unique grille with a chrome bezel and foglamps, a leather-wrapped aluminum-spoke steering wheel (with contrasting pink stitching), special fender badges, Charcoal leather seats, and Charcoal floor mats also done in pink stitching. Portions of Warriors in Pink Mustang sales were slated to go to the Susan G. Komen for the Cure Foundation.

A truly exciting expansive glass roof panel option appeared for both V6 and GT coupes in 2009. "Mustang is an icon in our product lineup, and we are committed to keeping Mustang news fresh every year," said Derrick Kuzak, Ford's group vice-president of Global Product Development. "As the automotive landscape becomes increasingly competitive, features such as a panoramic glass roof will help differentiate our products from the competition." Or at least it will as long as you've got the $1,995 asking price.

That transparent top apparently will roll over for the restyled 2010 Mustang, which you should be familiar with by the time you read these words. Scheduled for release in March 2009, Ford's latest new pony car will retain the breed's existing foundation, but, according to chief nameplate engineer Paul Randall, all sheet metal except for the roof panel will be new. "The goal for 2010 was to move the Mustang out of its recent retro past and into the future, still using the platform that debuted in 2004," explained *AutoWeek* senior editor Bob Gritzinger late in 2008.

Reportedly the 210-horsepower V6 will remain constant as well, but the GT's V8 will get a boost up to 315 horsepower. Wheel sizes, too, apparently will increase: 17- and 18-inchers will be available for the V6, 18- and 19-inchers for the GT. Most other features will be familiar to Mustang drivers who remained madly in love with Ford's 45-year-old pony car in 2009.

Still crazy after all these years? You betcha.

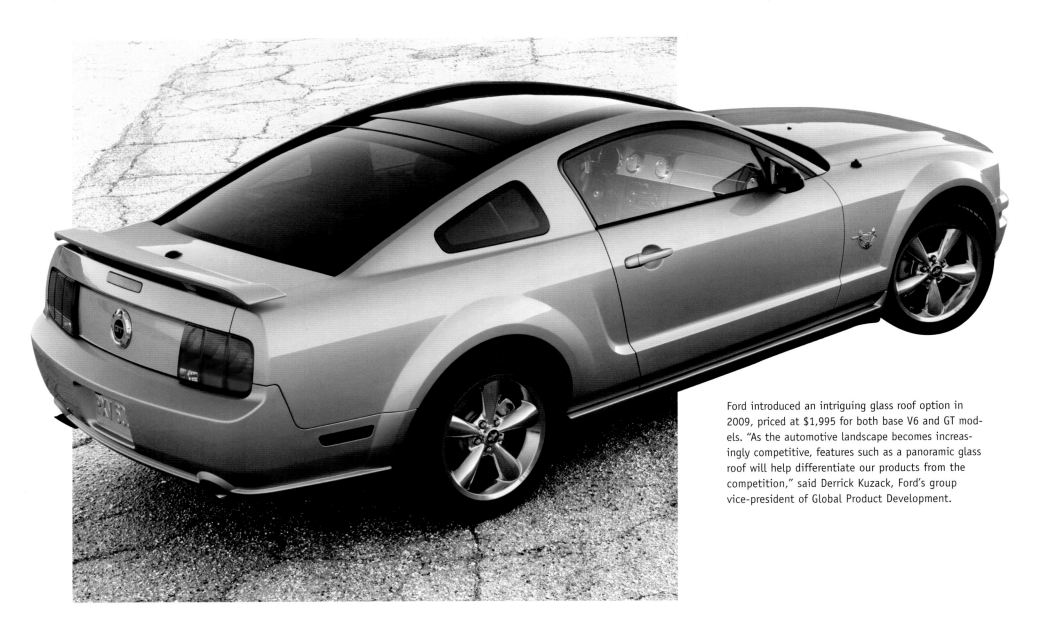

Ford introduced an intriguing glass roof option in 2009, priced at $1,995 for both base V6 and GT models. "As the automotive landscape becomes increasingly competitive, features such as a panoramic glass roof will help differentiate our products from the competition," said Derrick Kuzack, Ford's group vice-president of Global Product Development.

OPPOSITE, TOP: Mustang buyers in 2009 found the GT interior very familiar. No notable changes were made.

OPPOSITE, BOTTOM: Though it looks familiar, too, the 2010 Mustang features restyled sheet metal. According to chief engineer Paul Randall, all panels, save for the roof, are new.

LEFT: A 2009 Warriors in Pink Mustang shows the pink striping included as part of this option. Pink stitching also appeared inside.

1960 Lee Iacocca is promoted to Ford Division general manager in November, replacing Robert McNamara, who moves up to Ford Motor Company president.

1961 Initial sketch work on Mustang prototypes begins in earnest at Gene Bordinat's styling studio.

1962 Carroll Shelby begins building Ford-powered Cobras in Southern California using 260-cubic-inch Windsor V8s, soon replaced by 289 Windsor small-blocks.

1963 The Mustang II show car debuts at Watkins Glen, New York, a year after Ford introduced its Mustang I mid-engined roadster there.

1964 Ford Mustang rocks the automotive world, debuting in April at the New York World's Fair.

1965 Carroll Shelby introduces his Shelby GT 350 Mustang, the car that instantly becomes a Sports Car Club of America racing champion.

1964-1/2

1971

1977

1966 Ford's 1 millionth Mustang rolls off the Dearborn assembly line at 11:02 a.m. on Wednesday, February 23, 1966, with Lee Iacocca on hand for the festivities.

1967 A redesigned Mustang appears with an enlarged engine compartment able to house the breed's first optional big-block V8.

1968 Former General Motors' executive Semon E. "Bunkie" Knudsen is hired by Henry Ford II as Ford Motor Company president.

1969 Henry Ford II fires Bunkie Knudsen in September after repeated warnings about his aggressive behavior.

1970 Lee Iacocca becomes Ford Motor Company president in December.

1971 The Mustang Boss 351 appears for this year only, picking right up where the Boss 302, built from 1969 to 1970, left off.

1972 Annual Mustang production (125,405) falls for the sixth straight year.

1973 An energy crisis results after Organization of Petroleum Exporting Countries (OPEC) cuts back oil deliveries to the West in protest of U.S. support of Israel.

1974 The smaller, lighter, more affordable Mustang II debuts and wins *Motor Trend*'s "Car of the Year" honors.

1975 Mustang II sales fall by half after initial excitement subsides.

1976 Cobra II conversion, performed by Jim Wangers' Motortown shop, becomes available for Mustang II.

ABOVE, LEFT TO RIGHT: 1964-1/2 convertible, 1971 Mach 1, 1977 Cobra II.

OPPOSITE, LEFT TO RIGHT: 1979 Indy 500 Pace Car replica, 1983 convertible, 1995 SVT Cobra R.

1977 Mustang II production drops to 153,000 before surging slightly for 1978.

1978 Henry Ford II fires Lee Iacocca less than a month after Ford celebrates its 75th anniversary in June; Iacocca then heads for Chrysler.

1979 Ford's redesigned Fox-chassis Mustang paces the 63rd running of the Indianapolis 500 in May.

1980 Jack Telnack rises to the top of Ford's styling department and Donald Petersen becomes corporation president in March.

1981 The rather garish Cobra package appears for its last year.

1982 The Mustang GT returns after a 13-year hiatus with a 157-horsepower 5.0-liter High Output V8 as standard equipment.

1983 A convertible Mustang, last seen in 1973, returns.

1984 Both the turbocharged SVO Mustang and the 20th Anniversary edition are introduced.

1985 The midyear SVO Mustang debuts with 205 horsepower, a peak for its turbocharged four-cylinder engine.

1979

1983

1995

1986 Ford's electronic fuel-injected (EFI) High Output V8 debuts for Mustang GT as carburetors are eliminated.

1987 Henry Ford II dies of pneumonia at age 70 on September 29.

1988 Ford's new Probe, once planned as the latest next-generation Mustang, goes on sale in March 1988 as a 1989 model.

1989 Ford's 6 millionth Mustang is built.

1990 Ford offers a special-edition Emerald Green LX convertible to mark the Mustang's 25th birthday, even though the car was born in 1964, not 1965.

1991 New 16-inch five-spoke wheels help this year's GT set itself apart from its all-but-identical 1987–1990 forerunners.

1992 This year's GT convertible becomes the first Mustang base-priced above $20,000.

1993 The Special Vehicle Team begins marketing its Cobra and F-150 Lightning pickup.

1994 An SVT Cobra convertible becomes the third Mustang to pace the Indianapolis 500.

1995 The Special Vehicle Team rolls out its second Cobra R, this one powered by a 300-horsepower 351-cubic-inch V8.

1996 The GT's venerable 5.0-liter V8 is replaced by the 215-horsepower 4.6-liter modular V8 with single-overhead cams; a 305-horse dual-overhead-cam 4.6 "mod motor" appears for the SVT Cobra.

CHRONOLOGY

1997 Racer Tommy Kendall wins a record 11 races in a row in his Mustang on the way to the 1997 Sports Car Club of America Trans-Am championship.

1998 Output for the GT's 4.6-liter single-overhead-cam V8 goes up to 225 horsepower.

1999 William Clay Ford Jr. is elected Ford chairman of the board.

2000 No standard-issue Cobras are built, but SVT does release a third Cobra R, powered by a 385-horsepower 5.4-liter dual-overhead-cam V8 with aluminum heads.

2001 A nostalgic Bullitt Mustang debuts to remind horse lovers of the mag-wheel-wearing model Steve McQueen drove in the 1968 Hollywood hit *Bullitt*.

2002 General Motors cancels its F-body platform, home to Chevrolet's Camaro and Pontiac's Firebird since 1967, leaving Mustang alone in the pony car field.

2003 Ford Motor Company celebrates its 100th anniversary on June 16.

1998

2006

2010

2004 Ford's Dearborn assembly line rolls out its last Mustang, a red GT convertible, on May 10.

2005 Production of Ford's latest all-new Mustang moves from Dearborn to the Auto Alliance International (AAI) assembly plant in Flat Rock, Michigan.

2006 Hertz begins renting Shelby GT-Hs again 40 years after it first offered this deal.

2007 A Mustang GT California Special makes an encore appearance, as does a Ford Shelby GT500.

2008 A Dodge Challenger returns to give the Mustang a run for its money in Detroit's pony car race.

LEFT TO RIGHT: 1998 GT convertible, 2006 Shelby GT-H, 2010 GT convertible.

2009 The next great redesigned Mustang is scheduled for release as a 2010 model.

PHOTOGRAPHY CREDITS

© Rich Chenet: 8–9, 12–13, 80–81, 272T, 272ML, 272BL, 273.

Courtesy of Ford Motor Company: 2–3, 4–5, 6–7, 10–11, 14–15, 16–17, 18–19, 22M, 22R, 23, 36–37, 39 (both), 43 (both), 46B, 49B, 50–51 (all), 58BL, 66B, 71T, 72B, 73 (both), 75M, 75B, 90–91, 94T, 96T, 98B, 99M, 100B, 110–111, 121T, 122TR, 128BL, 128BR, 129T, 133B, 134T, 134B, 140–141, 150–151, 154T, 155, 156B, 157 (both), 158–159 (all), 160–161, 162–163, 164–165 (all), 166–167, 168–169 (both), 170–171, 174–175, 176–177, 178–179 (all), 180, 181T, 181M, 182T, 182B, 183 (all), 184B, 185B, 186 (all), 187M, 187B, 188TR, 188BL, 188BR, 189T, 190–191 (all), 192–193, 194–195, 196–197, 198–199, 200–201 (both), 202–203, 204–205, 206–207, 210B, 211, 212B, 213B, 216B, 217 (all), 218–219 (all), 220–221 (all), 222 (all), 224B, 226–227 (all), 228–229, 230–231, 236–237, 238–239, 240–241, 242–243 (both), 246–247, 248 (all), 250 (all), 251B, 252 (both), 254T, 256T, 258–259 (all), 260 (both), 261T, 262–263, 264–265, 266–267, 268–269, 272–273BM, 274–275, 276–277, 278–279, 282R, 283M, 284L.

© Ron Kimball Stock/kimballstock.com: 20, 22L, 46T, 49T, 49M, 52–53, 56–57, 60–61, 66T, 67T, 69T, 69BR, 72T, 75T, 76BL, 78–79, 82–83, 84–85, 86–87, 88–89, 95TL, 96B, 98TL, 100TR, 102–103, 104–105, 106–107, 108–109, 112–113, 114–115, 119B, 125B, 127, 131B, 133T, 135T, 136–137, 142–143, 144–145, 148–149, 208–209, 232–233 (both), 234–235, 244–245, 251T, 253, 254B, 256M, 256BL, 256BR, 257 (both), 261B, 270–271, 280–281, 283L, 284M, 284R.

© Mike Mueller: 28, 29T, 35B, 42T, 44–45 (all), 48–49, 54–55, 58–59 (all but bottom left), 62–63, 64–65, 67B, 70 (all), 71M, 71B, 74L, 74R, 76–77, 76BR, 95M, 116–117, 118 (both), 119T, 120 (all except bottom), 121M, 122B, 123, 125T, 135B, 138–139, 146–147 (all), 172–173, 188TL, 216M, 223, 224T, 224M, 225, 282L, 283R.

Courtesy of Mike Mueller: 21, 24–25, 26–27 (all), 29M, 29B, 30–31 (all), 32–33 (all), 34 (all), 35T, 38, 40–41 (all), 42B, 47, 68, 69BL, 74T, 75B, 77T, 92 (both), 93, 94 (bottom three images), 95TR, 95B, 96M, 98TR (all four images), 99T, 99B, 100TL, 101 (both), 120B, 121B, 122TL, 124 (all), 126, 128T, 129B, 130 (both), 131T, 132 (all), 134M, 152–153 (all), 154B, 156T, 181B, 182M, 184T, 185T, 187T, 189B, 210T, 212T, 212M, 213T, 214–215 (all), 216T, 249.

Courtesy of Rocky Mountain Mustang Roundup, www.rmmr.org: 255 (both).

INDEX

Page numbers in *italics* refer to photographs.